Chicken Soup
for the Soul®

Teens Talk Middle School

Chicken Soup for the Soul:
Teens Talk Middle School; 101 Stories of Life, Love, and Learning for Younger Teens
by Jack Canfield, Mark Victor Hansen, Madeline Clapps, Valerie Howlett
Published by Chicken Soup for the Soul Publishing, LLC   www.chickensoup.com

The publisher gratefully acknowledges the many publishers and individuals who
granted Chicken Soup for the Soul permission to reprint the cited material.

Front cover photo courtesy of PunchStock/Blend Images. Front cover illustration courtesy
of iStockPhoto.com/graphixel. Back cover photo courtesy of Jupiter Images/Photos.com.
Interior illustrations courtesty of iStockPhoto.com/graphixel, and /Ceneri.

Cover and Interior Design & Layout by Pneuma Books, LLC
For more info on Pneuma Books, visit www.pneumabooks.com

Distributed to the booktrade by Simon & Schuster. SAN: 200-2442

Publisher's Cataloging-in-Publication Data
(Prepared by The Donohue Group)

Chicken soup for the soul : teens talk middle school : 101 stories of life,
  love, and learning for younger teens / [compiled by] Jack Canfield ... [et al.].

  p. ; cm.

  ISBN-13: 978-1-935096-26-9
  ISBN-10: 1-935096-26-5

1. Middle school students--Literary collections. 2. Middle schools--Literary
collections. 3. Teenagers--Literary collections. 4. Teenagers' writings. 5. Teenagers-
-Conduct of life--Anecdotes. 6. Middle schools--Anecdotes. I. Canfield, Jack, 1944-
II. Title. III. Title: Teens talk middle school

PN6071.Y68 C453 2008
810.8/02/09283   2008935975

PRINTED IN THE UNITED STATES OF AMERICA
on acid∞free paper
16 15 14 13 12 10 09 08   01 02 03 04 05 06 07 08

Chicken Soup for the Soul.
Teens Talk Middle School

101 Stories of Life,
Love, and Learning for Younger Teens

Jack Canfield
Mark Victor Hansen
Madeline Clapps
Valerie Howlett

Chicken Soup for the Soul Publishing, LLC
Cos Cob, CT

Chicken Soup for the Soul

Contents

❸
~Embarrassing Moments~

❹
~Bully Payback~

❺
~Finding Your Passion~

6

~In Like, In Love, and Just Not Into You~

7

~Being Happy with Yourself~

8

~Tough Times~

9

~That's My Family~

10

~The People Who Are There For Us~

⓫

~Doing What's Right~

Chicken Soup for the Soul

Foreword

The first day. The first kiss. The first time you got ditched by a friend because you weren't cool enough. The first time you were given real responsibilities. The first moment you realized you were growing up, changing, and becoming who you really are. These are the things that middle school is all about, and trust us — we know middle school.

We've been reading your stories and living through your best moments, as well as your worst nightmares. We've been cringing right alongside you as you totally made a fool of yourself trying to impress girls, or discovered that the people you thought were your best friends had left you out in the cold. But we've also been smiling as you've gone through those exciting, adrenaline-filled moments. Like that time your crush asked you to slow dance and you practically died of happiness — we were rooting for you. Or the time you found an activity that made you feel like you were finally pretty awesome at something. We were right there, giving you a standing ovation.

Middle school wasn't too long ago for us, and it's still fresh in our minds. It can be a painfully awkward time in your life, but the lessons you learn are invaluable to the growing-up process. That's why we're glad we could give you this — *Chicken Soup for the Soul: Teens Talk Middle School*. Think of it like a guidebook. Kids just like you are describing the rocky journey, pointing out some of the best and worst points, but then allowing you to make your way and experience them on your own.

Thanks to you, we've gotten to relive a lot of this stuff. We sat in our office, giggling about our first crush or the stupid things we wore when we were trying to fit in. We couldn't believe what we did to be popular, but we were also proud of ourselves for the times we stood up for what we believed in. And when you look back, that's what you'll do too. You'll feel proud that you trudged through middle school and got out relatively unscathed. One day, when your braces are off and your hair stops doing that weird frizzy thing you can't seem to get under control, you'll laugh too. Because middle school is, above all, funny. And don't worry—we already think you're pretty cool.

~Madeline and Valerie

Teens Talk Middle School

Introduction

Introduction

Letter to a Younger Self

She generally gave herself very good advice,
(though she very seldom followed it).
~Lewis Carroll,
Alice's Adventures in Wonderland

Ten years after I was thirteen, one of my old teachers mailed me a letter I had written to my twenty-three-year-old self in middle school. The letter was full of silly things like who I had a crush on (much too big of a secret to reveal here) and how much I totally hated my brothers. After I read the letter, I wished I could write back to myself at thirteen. If I could, I would have these thirteen things to say:

1. Your Beanie Babies will end up in a box in your closet. (Except for the elephant. You seem to really like the elephant.) They are not a financial investment; I'm sorry.

2. Similarly, don't get too attached to your electronic toys. They will be confiscated by a teacher who doesn't understand that you can't go a day without technology.

3. I know this whole changing schools thing is tough and you're leaving your friends behind, but life has some amazing surprises in store for you when it comes to friendship. One of your friends from your old school will be your best friend ten years from now, and it's definitely not the one you expect.

4. When everyone's giving you grief because you're holed up in your room writing stories, don't pay attention. It will work out pretty well for you. I know you're only doing it because sometimes your characters are the only ones you can count on to always be there when you need them. But that's perfectly okay.

5. Both your brothers will cease to be so annoying after you all make it through puberty alive.

6. You aren't going to marry your crush (or even date him), but that doesn't mean you have to stop crushing.

7. This divorce thing isn't going to get easier for a really long time, and I'm sorry about that. I wish I could be there with you, but unfortunately it doesn't work like that. You're going to go through a lot of this stuff feeling completely alone. You have to keep believing that it will get better. It's going to get a little worse, and then, little by little, it's going to get a lot better. You'll all figure out how to be a family again.

8. It's okay that you're hurting. It doesn't mean that you aren't strong enough. It doesn't mean that you aren't there for your family. It just means that you're hurt, and that's okay. You deserve to feel hurt. Your family just broke and splintered—it's when you pretend that you're fine that it will hurt the worst and you will feel the most alone.

9. You know how you're 99% positive that you know everything

there is to know about the world? You're wrong. (Now you only know 97%.)

10. Everyone's going to tell you that the blue mascara is stupid, and when you're my age you'll laugh with your best friend about how unfashionable you were. But secretly, I love that you wore blue mascara. I like that you aren't afraid of color.

11. Just clean up your room already. It's going to drive Mom nuts for like, ten years.

12. You've got a lot of incredible adventures coming your way. You're going to climb up a snow-covered mountain, walk through a rainforest, and tiptoe carefully on an active volcano crater. You're going to fall in and out of love and have crushes and kisses. You're going to get through almost ten more years of school and when it's over, you're going to miss it (shocking, I know). You'll go to Paris, Florence, Scotland, London, and countless more beautiful, wondrous places, and you'll meet more friends than you can count. Ten years from now, you'll have a life that you're in love with.

13. The whole thing with middle school is that you really are in the middle right now. You're in the middle of your parents' divorce. You're the middle child. You're in between childhood and tentative adulthood. You are right in the thick of pain, and heartbreak, and disappointment, but it was happier in the past and you will be so happy in the future. So hold on tight. There are some more obstacles in your way, some more difficulties ahead. It sounds unfair, I know, but from where I'm looking, the hardest stuff you go through makes the good stuff even better.

You are so much stronger, and more loved, than you could ever understand right now. So just trust me. You'll get through.

~AC Gaughen

Chapter 1

Teens Talk Middle School

True Friends
and New Friends

Best friends are like diamonds, precious and rare.
False friends are like leaves, found everywhere.

~Anonymous

I'm Not Thirteen Yet

*A true friend reaches for your hand
and touches your heart.*
~Author Unknown

Sixth grade was a tough year. Some days, walking the halls was like trudging through peanut butter—nearly impossible. I had entered the world of teenagers, and I wasn't even one of them yet. Lynette Gardner had always been my best friend, until February, when she turned thirteen. I wouldn't be thirteen until August.

Lynette started bringing new thirteen-year-old friends to our lunch table. Then Lynette and these new girls began holding thirteen-year-old clubs after school. Obviously they were far more mature with the word "teen" attached to their age. It wouldn't be long before there was tape down the middle of the cafeteria, dividing it in two. If you weren't thirteen, you dared not enter the thirteen-year-old side. If you tried, the lip-gloss army would hurl you back.

Gradually, Lynette stopped inviting me over after school. One day, on my way into the girls' bathroom, I overheard Lynette and Shelley Abrams discussing their after-school plans at Dale's Ice Cream.

"This afternoon is going to be so much fun," said Lynette. "It's going to be you, me, and the rest of the 'Fab Thirteens.' Just remember, no twelve-year-olds."

I heard a toilet flush and scurried into an empty stall. Their giggles felt like needles. I heard the sinks running and knew they were tossing their locks in the mirror. This couldn't be happening. But I was quickly getting the picture that it was.

With spring turning to summer, the rift between the twelve- and thirteen-year-olds grew worse. What if by September, when I was finally thirteen, they had fourteen-year-old clubs?

One day, I came home from school and Mom gave me the news that she had signed me up for summer camp.

"Oh, like a day camp?" I said.

"No, Honey, I signed you up for two weeks at Camp Shenandoah."

My backpack fell to the ground. I stood there with my mouth open. Two weeks stuck at some bug-infested camp where I didn't know anyone? What was she trying to do to me? Make my life worse?

"I talked to Margaret's mom," she said. "Margaret will be there at the same time as you. Maybe you can be bunkmates."

I could have shaken her. Margaret Bowman was a thirteen-year-old who wore bras and was a bona fide member of the "Fab Thirteens." My mom knew nothing. Margaret wasn't going to be my friend.

Three weeks later, I reluctantly boarded the bus with all the other Shenandoah-bound kids. Just before I stepped on, Margaret's mother and mine asked to take a picture of the two of us. I wanted to throw up, but smiled graciously as the camera flashed and our moms grinned.

Two hours later, as the buses pulled in to Camp Shenandoah, I saw crowds of counselors jumping up and down, singing and cheering—all for us. I was immediately a bit less nervous.

As the first day turned into the third, I still missed home. I made friends, but not with Margaret. I chose the bed farthest from where she slept. I figured I could avoid her for two weeks, no problem.

However, one evening, Margaret and I wound up on the same team during a color war. We didn't talk, but when our team won, she gave me a huge high five. I was taken aback. Shouldn't she be rubbing her thirteen-year-old glory in my face?

After the game, we had an ice cream party in the dining hall to celebrate our victory. I sprinkled my last spoonful of chocolate sprinkles and walked toward a table.

"Hey Jamie," a voice called, "come sit here."

I swore it sounded like Margaret. It turned out it was Margaret, and she wanted me to sit next to her.

"Ok... thanks," I said and took a seat, probably with a confused look on my face.

"I love the way you arrange your toppings, in perfect order from ice cream to fudge and chocolate sprinkles. You're a great sundae builder," said Margaret. "Look at mine. I can't even keep it together."

We both laughed as I looked at Margaret's sundae, which slightly resembled a Leaning Tower of Pisa that someone got sick on.

From that day on, Margaret and I curiously became great friends. Sometimes I forgot about her being in the teenage club back at school, but I also wondered what would happen to our friendship in September.

During the last few days at camp, we had a soccer tournament against the boys. I played forward and Margaret was on defense. We started on the field in the glitter T-shirts we made the night before. I was never an athlete, but I had a newfound confidence lately, and I think camp and Margaret had a lot to do with it.

It was mid-game and I felt energized. I saw the ball making its way toward me and went in for it. Richard Neeland had the ball. I ran up and kicked it through his legs. A surge of adrenaline ran through me. I could hear all of my teammates screaming my name in excitement. But before I knew it, I was flat on my face, grass in my eyes and up my nose. Richard had tripped me.

Right away, Margaret was kneeling next to me. "Are you okay? Are you okay?" she asked. "Richard, you big jerk, what were you thinking? This is my best friend, and if you want to mess with someone, don't pick her. Oh — and you stink at soccer!"

At this point, I was lying on my back, and my head shot up when I heard the words "best friend." I squinted and saw Margaret standing above me. She extended her hand. She was ready to help me up. She grinned. From then on, I knew who my best friend was.

She didn't care what age I was, and never would. To this day, we both have the framed picture of us at the bus stop that first day of camp.

~Amy Bernstein

Moving into Friendship

Strangers are just friends waiting to happen.
~Rod McKuen

My world was in a constant state of change and I was having trouble keeping up. Life with Mom, Dad, and my sister, Linda, had always been comfortably predictable. My grades were good, and Linda and I got along fairly well. We played together and fought together, the way sisters do. As the older one, I was used to being told to set an example, which wasn't too difficult, since Linda was only two years younger, and she usually wanted to do anything I did, anyway. Life was pretty good.

Then the changes started coming.

First, Mom sat us down, a very serious look on her face. She said she had something very important to tell us. Soon, we were going to have a new little sister or brother. "A baby?" I thought. Instead of being the older of two girls, I would now be the oldest of three. Well, okay, this sounded like it wouldn't be too bad. After all, I already had experience in the big sister department. The baby was born that June, and I was thrilled that it was a girl—I didn't know anything about little boys. During the following year, I settled into the role of being big sis to my new baby sister.

Then came another family meeting with some additional news that would change my world even further. We were moving. Our new home would be across the Verrazano-Narrows Bridge, in another borough of New York City. We were leaving the only home I had ever known. Even worse, it would occur right before the beginning of sixth grade. Not only would I not be able to graduate elementary school with my friends, but I would have to start middle school with a class full of kids who had known each other, and bonded, since kindergarten. Where would that leave me?

I spent the summer adjusting to a new neighborhood, literally being the new kid on the block. Making friends didn't come easily to me, and it didn't help being the eldest child of immigrant parents. I was different, and different is the last thing any middle schooler wants to be. The fear of starting a new school hung over me like a black cloud, tainting each summer day.

The first day of school arrived way too quickly. I entered my new classroom trying very hard not to appear as scared as I felt, but it wasn't easy. Twenty-eight faces turned to look up at me as I followed the Assistant Principal into the room. They all looked so cool, and some of the girls even wore make-up. How would I ever fit in? I was out of touch in every way possible. I wasn't allowed to wear make-up or nail polish. I wore leotards instead of stockings, and much of my wardrobe was handmade, sewn by my mother and grandmother.

Mr. Bernstein welcomed me to the class and introduced me to the other students. He directed me to an empty desk in the back of the room, next to another girl. Her name was Janet and she was assigned to be my buddy for the day. I slowly walked across the room while twenty-eight pairs of eyes stared at me as I took my seat.

There wasn't time for conversation before Mr. Bernstein began to rapidly detail the requirements for our class. I wrote as fast as possible, stealing occasional peeks at my seatmate. What was she like? Was she part of the in crowd? Did she resent being saddled with the new girl? I would find out the answers soon enough, during lunch period.

We walked to the cafeteria, sat together, and opened our lunch bags. Between bites of our sandwiches, we began to ask each other questions. Her responses were not at all what I expected. Sisters? We both had two, although I was the oldest and she was the youngest. Home? It turned out that we lived about a fifteen-minute walk apart.

Upbringing? Her parents were as strict as mine: no make-up, nail polish, or stockings, and she also suffered similar early curfews and bedtimes.

The smiles on both our faces broadened with each new exchange. On this first day in a new school, I still didn't know if the in crowd would accept me. I did know, however, beyond a shadow of a doubt, that it was going to be a good year after all.

It has now been over thirty-five years. A lot has happened in both of our lives: graduations, college, marriages, divorce, and children. I've since moved more than one thousand miles away. But the friendship that began that first day of middle school is still going strong.

~Ava Pennington

4

A Friend

What is a friend?
A single soul dwelling in two bodies.
~Aristotle

A friend doesn't have to be handsome or pretty,
We don't choose our friends just because they are witty.
My friends are not perfect and others may be
Smarter or sweeter or nicer to me.
Sometimes we fight
But that's quite all right
If we're mad in the morning
We make up before night.
Because a friend, is a friend, is a friend.

Why are we friends? Don't ask us why.
We can't explain it, we don't even try.
Friends are not perfect, they have plenty of flaws,
but that doesn't seem to matter at all.
Because a friend, is a friend, is a friend.

So,
Whoever we are,
Whatever we may be,
We're friends cause I'm me,
We're friends cause she's she.

Whoever, whatever they may be
Friends are as close as family.
Because a friend, is a friend, is a friend,
'Till the end.

Inspired by my friends Ashley and Kiana.

~StarAsia Smith

5

The Makeover

Kindness is more than deeds.
It is an attitude, an expression, a look, a touch.
It is anything that lifts another person.
~C. Neil Strait

Middle school was a difficult time for me. Home was an emotional roller coaster: My parents were getting a divorce and I never knew what to expect when I came home from school. My father was an alcoholic and I never knew if he'd be drinking. Or would my parents be fighting? Plus, I was going through a really awkward stage. I felt ugly and kids teased me every day, which only fed my insecurities. I was one of the "smart" kids, and that only incited more teasing.

When I found out that kids were calling me "Professor" behind my back, I started purposely making mistakes on tests so I wouldn't always get the highest grade. That didn't make me feel better. I didn't think things could get much worse, but somehow they did.

The friends I'd had for many years claimed I'd changed and wouldn't hang out with me anymore. I didn't think that I was acting differently but maybe I had changed. It doesn't matter, they weren't there for me when I needed them the most, so I faced everything alone.

Then a funny thing happened. One of the "cool" kids started inviting me to hang out. Her name was Dina, and she invited me to parties and over to her house. The teasing from some kids didn't stop, but it slowed enough to make life tolerable again. Although I still didn't talk about my problems, at least I wasn't alone anymore. Dina's parents were divorced too, and she may have seen that I needed a friend. Or maybe she just thought I was nice. Either way, when kids teased me about being smart or ugly, she told me they were crazy. I never completely fit in with her group of friends—I thought they were a little boring—but I was happy to have a place to go.

Middle school graduation was approaching and I couldn't wait. I knew there was a chance that high school might be as horrible as middle school, but maybe it would be great. It was a clean slate and it would get me away from all the bad memories of middle school.

Unexpectedly, the day we were taking graduation pictures turned out to be a life-changing moment for me. I came to school like I always did, with my long hair pulled back in clips away from my face. My too-big glasses were framing my eyes like giant magnifying glasses, and I was definitely not wearing make-up, although many of the girls were. Make-up was forbidden at my house until I reached high school, and I didn't think much of it—that was who I was. That was who I thought I would always be.

I was getting ready for the photographer when Dina grabbed me.

"What are you doing?" she asked.

"Going to get my picture taken," I replied, matter-of-factly.

She laughed and said, "Not like that, you're not!" dragging me into the girl's bathroom. Dina and her friends pulled out some supplies and started giving me a makeover. They changed my hair, they put make-up on me, and they took away my oversized glasses.

I couldn't see how I looked, (I couldn't actually see much of anything), but they said I looked great and I was just hoping it wasn't all a big joke. I let them lead me to where I had to stand for the pictures, hoping the photographer would tell me if I looked like a clown or something. The flash went off and Dina gave me back my glasses. I can't remember if I thanked her. Even though she had always been nice to me, the way my old friends had turned on me made me wonder if Dina would do the same.

When I got home from school that day, my mother was pretty upset about the make-up. She yelled at me for a while and told me that I didn't look like myself. She said some pretty harsh stuff, but I didn't care. I took it as a big compliment. I didn't want to look like my old self. I didn't want to be my old self.

A few weeks later, the pictures came back from the photographer. They actually did look great, and I looked like a new, happier person. I was surprised to see that I looked pretty and felt glad that I could now look back on middle school with one really good memory.

I will always be grateful to Dina for what she did for me. She saved me back then. She helped to bring me out of my shell and to lay a foundation that I would later use to build the woman that I would become someday.

Dina and I went to different high schools and would talk on occasion. High school turned out to be great. I made wonderful friends and had a great time. By the time we got to college, Dina and I had lost touch. I heard from friends that she was doing well and was happy, which made me happy too.

I write this because I never did get to thank Dina for all she did for me. During college, Dina was killed in a plane crash. She was on her way home from working as a volunteer in Africa as part of her medical studies. She did a lot in her short time here, and she made a difference in my life. I'm glad I had a chance to know her and be her friend.

~Lena James Edwards

Three Dimensions: My Unexpected Best Friend

*A friend who is far away is sometimes much nearer
than one who is at hand.*
~Kahlil Gibran

I sat on the plane and wondered if I would end up hating her. That same part of me also wondered if I should have gone at all. What if I was stuck for three days wearing a false smile and pretending I found her halfway tolerable? Or what if, instead, I was the one who ended up on the receiving end of the false smiles, being regarded with minimum tolerability? What if we found each other so unbearable we would never speak again? There were so many things that could go wrong.

First of all, she was Jewish. And she lived in an entirely different part of the country: Alabama. I had never been to a Bat Mitzvah before, nor had I ever visited any of the southern states, except for Disney World, which hardly counts. I had no clue what "opening the ark" entailed. And I had never been very graceful—what if I tripped and knocked something over in the middle of the service?

Then there was also the fact that I had never met her.

In person, at least. In theory, I knew her better than anyone. We had been writing back and forth as pen pals for two or three years, and we shared so many similar interests, primarily horse-back riding and writing. Most importantly, we could tell each other everything and vent all of our problems without fear that we would be judged. I assumed I would never meet her, so there was never any reason to hold back any thoughts that seemed insane or dreams that seemed improbable. After exchanging messages daily for those three years, she invited me to her Bat Mitzvah, which was three months away.

Somehow, although I'm not exactly sure how, I convinced my parents to take me to a different city and spend three days with a family they had never met.

After arriving in Alabama, we checked in at the hotel where most of Emily's family was staying. When we got in the elevator, I wondered if I was standing next to Emily's sister or cousin. But I had no way of knowing.

We had agreed to meet at a nearby restaurant. Unfamiliar with the city, my parents and I arrived at the wrong restaurant — one with the right name but an incorrect location. I remember walking in with reluctant excitement. I was so thrilled that I was going to meet her, but I was also kind of scared, too. When I realized we were at the wrong place, however, I was really disappointed, because I had never really doubted that Emily would be exactly the kind of person I thought she was.

When we finally arrived at the correct restaurant, I was able to spot Emily immediately in her trademark rain boots. I recall my dad making some comment about a rooster to break the ice, because at first it was kind of like: *Whoa. You are a real three-dimensional person.* To me, she was always the person who replied to my letters and spoke to me through the magic device called a telephone. Somehow, I don't think it sunk in that she was going to be here in all her three-dimensional glory. And then my thoughts slowly changed. It became, instead, *Oh my God! You're here! Yay! I've wanted to meet you forever!*

That weekend, I went horseback riding with Emily, stayed at her house, and attended her Bat Mitzvah ceremony, where I was honored to open the ark (without tripping), as well as attend her amazing party.

In other words, one of the most important events in my life was a Bat Mitzvah. It wasn't my own, but the Bat Mitzvah of a girl I had met over the Internet who lived halfway across the country. When people ask me how I know Emily, I just smile. Some people don't understand how I could possibly have gone to visit a girl I had never met in person. But in many ways, I know her better than the friends I see every day. We still keep in touch, and I hope that we continue to do so forever. She's one of the few friends I can imagine calling when I am a little old lady living in a nursing home (or in my own house, with a walker, if I'm too stubborn).

I almost said no to her pen pal request when I was ten years old. At the time, I was very busy, and I wasn't sure if I had time to write to another pen pal. If I had said no, I never would have met my creative, intuitive, smart, and funny best friend, Emily. But I said yes. And I can only say I'm glad that I did.

~Julia McDaniel

Meeting Julia

The language of friendship is not words but meanings.
~Henry David Thoreau

I was around ten years old when my pen pal craze started. I had always loved meeting new friends — I would try new activities to meet people and talk to people my age I saw in stores or other places. However, when I was ten, I wanted to make friends from other states. I thought it would be fun to communicate with people all over the country and learn new things about other places. I also thought writing letters might help with my writing, which was one of my favorite hobbies.

I told everyone I knew that I wanted a pen pal, but no one knew of any way that I could meet one. Then, one day, I found an online pen pal site where people could create a profile and find other pen pals who had similar interests. One girl was named Julia. She was ten years old and liked horseback riding, writing, and animals. She lived in Ohio. She sounded a lot like me, and I wanted to be pen pals with her.

That night I asked my parents if I could join the pen pal club. They told me I could as long as I didn't give out any personal information and didn't get my hopes up about meeting a pen pal in real life. I agreed, but I secretly thought I could get them to change their minds about the meeting.

The next day, as soon as I got online, I wrote Julia a letter describing myself and asking her if she wanted to be my pen pal. She wrote back saying that she would love to.

Julia and I talked about everything. I told her about novels I was writing, and she told me about her various publications. We told each other about horses we rode and good books we read. One time, Julia told me about a project she was working on about passing a law against horse slaughter in the U.S. She told me about the fashions and events in Ohio and I told her what was happening in Alabama.

Later, when we were twelve, we were both going through difficult times. I was bullied at school, causing me to have low self-esteem. Also, Julia took three sixth grade classes and three seventh grade classes. She had trouble fitting in with friends since she was caught between two grades. We stuck by each other through these times and gave each other support.

My writing skills also improved because of Julia. Not only did we write letters back and forth, but we wrote stories together. In June we signed up for Script Frenzy, a program in which writers all over the world write a twenty-thousand-word script in a month. We chose to write the script together. We didn't finish our script, but we laughed a lot and became even better friends because of it.

My Bat Mitzvah was coming up on September 29th. A lot of camp friends and out-of-town family would be coming to it, and I wanted Julia to come too. My parents told me that I would never be able to meet a pen pal in real life, but Julia and I had been writing for almost three years and knew each other pretty well, so I decided to ask my parents if I could invite her to my Bat Mitzvah.

My parents said they would consider inviting Julia, but they wanted to talk to her parents first. They exchanged e-mails with her parents and eventually talked to them on the phone. After they had gotten to know each other well, my parents agreed to send Julia an invitation. Two weeks later, she RSVPed, and her answer was yes. Julia would be coming to visit me from September 28th to September 30th.

The Friday before my Bat Mitzvah, September 28th, I talked nonstop about Julia at school. I had only seen a few pictures of her, and they were from a year or so ago, so I wondered what she would look like. I wondered how she would act in person and if things would be the same between us in person as they were online and on the phone. I also became nervous about making a good first impression for her.

After school, Julia and I met at a restaurant. She looked a lot different than I had expected, but she was the same talkative, creative, fun person I had always known her to be. We talked a lot, laughed a lot, and after meeting, we went horseback riding together. It was one of the best days of my life.

At dinner that night, all of my family and out of town relatives ate with us. Julia enjoyed meeting my grandparents, aunts, uncles, and cousins. Most of my family thought that we talked and laughed together as if we were life-long friends, and they were surprised when they found out that we had met just hours ago!

Saturday morning was the service. Julia got to participate in the ceremony by opening the ark, and it was fun to see her on the bema with me. We also had a blast at the Kiddush luncheon and the party. She had to leave Sunday, and I told her I would miss her a lot. We hugged each other goodbye and promised to keep in touch.

Now it is mid-March, and we have kept our promise. In November, we both wrote fifty-thousand-word novels for a program called NaNoWriMo (National Novel Writing Month) and edited each other's novels. We write e-mails to each other almost every day and call each other every weekend. This summer, I plan to go to Ohio to visit Julia.

Julia is nice, smart, creative, funny, and such a great person. I am so happy that I got to meet her and know her. We'll always be best friends.

~Emily Cutler

Jenna's Story

A friend hears the song in my heart
and sings it to me
when my memory fails.
~Anonymous

As a teenager, nothing really matters to you except your plans for the weekend, your latest crush, or what you're wearing to school tomorrow. That's how I was until the summer I met someone I will remember forever.

My family goes to Orlando every July for a weeklong vacation. We were nearing the end of our vacation when I saw some kids playing tag in the pool. I wasn't doing anything, so I asked if I could play tag with them. The boy I asked, Brandon, said okay.

I started playing, and while I was running around I almost ran into a little girl named Jenna, who was Brandon's sister. Even though there was an eight year difference between us, something connected, and we were instant friends. I spent the rest of the day with Jenna and her family, just talking and getting to know them. It was Jenna's last day at the resort, so I was disappointed to say goodbye. But her mom promised we would stay in touch.

We stayed in touch with Jenna's family for the next six months, and in the middle of November my mom got an e-mail from Jenna's mom saying that Jenna had suffered a a brain tumor. They were scheduled to remove the tumor on December 10th, three days after my birthday. When my mom informed me of this, I couldn't help but cry. I couldn't imagine bright, bouncy Jenna in a hospital. On my birthday, during a pre-surgery phone conversation with Jenna, she asked if she could come eat birthday cake with me. I promised that I would eat cake with her on her birthday—which falls on Valentine's Day.

Operation day rolled around and everything went smoothly. However, Jenna didn't wake up until two days later. While the whole tumor was removed, there were still some issues. Jenna developed Cerebellar Mutism, which means that she had very limited motor skills, so she couldn't speak or swallow. There was also some swelling on the brain because of trauma. She also caught some infections, but they were nothing out of the ordinary. Luckily though, the tumor was not cancerous, so there was no chemotherapy or radiation.

Because Jenna couldn't swallow, she had to have a feeding tube through her nose. That was very aggravating to her and affected her attitude towards her physical therapists. Luckily, in early January, she passed a swallowing test and was allowed to stop using the feeding tube. Because of not being able to swallow since her surgery, Jenna had to spend extra time in the hospital. She came home on January 25th, after about two months in the hospital.

Once she came home, Jenna learned how to walk and talk much better with a lot of support and pushing along. She was home for about three weeks when my mom and I fulfilled my birthday promise. I went to Jenna's house and spent her sixth birthday with her, going to the park, watching TV, playing with dolls, eating cake, and—best of all—opening presents! It was nice to spend time with my little friend again.

Now, six months after her surgery, Jenna is as healthy as any normal six-year-old. She is still learning to talk better, but you can understand what she says. She can swim, walk, run, play games, and she's still my best six-year-old friend. Our families are close, and we're looking forward to our summer reunion in Orlando. Going through Jenna's ordeal made me realize that not everything is about what you're doing with your friends. I know that your elders are supposed to be the ones with the most wisdom, but Jenna has taught me a lesson that I'll never forget.

~Kelsey Johnson

I Really Do Care

Friends show their love in times of trouble,
not in happiness.
~Euripides

Mary had always been my close friend. She was part of our inseparable clique of four. At the beginning of middle school, there was nothing that could touch us four. We were incredibly tight. Then, as the year went on, Mary got a boyfriend. She started to spend more and more time with him, and less and less time with us. Soon, she was acting different, being mean and dramatic. She would wave us off and walk away if we approached her. She was saying and doing things that weren't... well, Mary.

We were still always there for her, but she never seemed to be there for us. After a while, our friendship began to drift away. A few months later, we were total enemies, always glaring at each other, never talking anymore. We were no longer friends and I told myself there would never be another moment when I felt compassion or sympathy for her. Never.

Then came that Friday in May when I proved myself wrong.

It was a very foggy Friday, near the end of sixth grade. Tarra sat next to me in art class and we were talking as usual. Conversation soon turned to Mary.

"I feel sorry for Mary," she said in a half whisper.

"Why?" I asked in a tone that implied, "Why would you feel

sorry for her? That's exactly what she wants—she's just looking for attention."

Tarra's eyes filled with worry as she answered my question. "Because she tried to kill herself last night," she whimpered. I probably looked as if I had just been zapped by lightning. I stood frozen, my face full of shock, trying to speak but unable. It was like a horrible nightmare where you know you need to run but you can't feel your legs. Flashbacks of all the good times I had with Mary rushed through my mind as I tried to breathe without hyperventilating.

"W-w-what?" I managed to stutter, still trying to stay quiet because Mary was nearby.

"I know," Tarra sighed, disapprovingly, shaking her head.

I finally sat down, slowly, and put the paper I had been folding back down on the table. Then I stopped myself. Why do I even care? We're not even friends anymore! But then I pushed that thought away. I knew that this was bigger than friends. This was about someone's life and I wasn't about to let some small argument get in the way. I squeezed all the details of the incident out of Tarra. It was horrible to hear, and I almost wished I hadn't asked. She said Mary had cut herself all over. Her wrists were scarred and she had a long cut down her left cheek. Apparently, she had used a kitchen knife.

I couldn't believe what I was hearing. I glanced over at Mary—at her gorgeous hazel eyes, stunning red hair. Yet she wore a huge gray sweatshirt and sat slumped over the table, sketching with a pencil and never looking up. What I was hearing about Mary wasn't the usual Mary news. Normally, information about Mary had something to do with her refusing to dance with her boyfriend, or getting into a fight with her mom. This was news I never thought I would have to hear—at least, not in middle school. And then it hit me, hard. I felt compassion and love for her even though I never thought I would. I felt sad and helpless. Was her life really so bad that it had resulted in this?

The biggest question flashing through my head was "Why?" She was beautiful, had great grades, tons of friends, and a loving boyfriend. Why would she try to kill herself?

I wasn't the only one wondering why. There were rumors about guns and harassment and I didn't know what to believe. Everyone I heard whispered things to me and told me not to tell anyone. But I had to. When you know that your friend is in that much pain, even if she is your "ex-friend," it bubbles up inside you. All the secrets and lies crush you under their weight. So I told her group of friends. I was worried that one day I would come into school and instead of finding her in her usual seat, I would hear the news that she had tried again... and succeeded. I would think to myself, "You could have saved a life, but no. You were too afraid of what your friends would think of you for telling." I shuddered at the thought, and I told my mom.

Mary has been getting help ever since the incident. Rumors were cleared up and things started to settle down. I still don't understand why she tried to kill herself. I probably never will. I thought I knew Mary, but I had never really looked deep enough into her to understand who she really was. We continue to make small talk on the way to classes, but I don't think our friendship will ever be the same. Still we are building it together, block by block.

On the last day of school, we were signing yearbooks. I came to Mary's yearbook and paused. This is what I wrote:

Mary,

I miss having you as a friend, and I want you to know that I am still always here for you. And I really do care.

Love,
Jos

~Josy Hicks Jablons

Diana and the Purple Diamond Gang

Life's not about fitting in;
it's about standing out.
~Anonymous

Diana was intelligent, and talented, and kind,
And yet, she felt inadequate, in her self-despairing mind.
She volunteered, wrote stories, played the violin, and sang,
But she yearned with all her heart to join the Purple Diamond Gang.

For, the Diamonds were selective, and accepted very few,
And to earn a bid for membership was difficult to do.
But Diana ached so badly for the girls to take her in,
That she would do almost anything, so approval she would win.

So, with all the girls' opinions, she pretended to agree.
And she wasted all her money on a spendthrift shopping spree
To purchase Diamond clothing, of purple violet blue,
And although she thought she liked these things,
    she wasn't being true
To herself, for in reality, she favoured clothes of red,
And she hated Britney Spears, she liked her Jewel CD instead.

But Diana's likes and dislikes, the Diamonds didn't know,
So Diana thought being phony was the only way to go.
For, if she acted differently, they'd think that she was weird,
And therefore, would not accept her, or so Diana feared.
So, when the Diamonds asked of her, her favourite book and song,
And TV show and movie, she feared she'd answer wrong
If she told the Diamond girls the truth,
        that she liked to groove to Jewel,
For she thought that non-conformity was against
        the Diamonds' rules.

But when Diana left the room, to go and wash her hands,
The leader of the Diamonds said, "I do not understand,
Why Diana acts so strangely in our presence. She's too shy
To tell us what she truly thinks, I really wonder why.
For, I really like Diana, she's a sweet and funny girl,
But she hides her personality, to fit into our world.
Why does she feel she has to? I can't say that I know,
But until she learns to be herself, Diana has to go."

The other girls agreed with her, but they were very sad
To deny Diana membership, for potential, they knew she had.
But when the disappointing news, the Diamonds had to tell,
Diana was heartbroken, but a bit relieved as well.
She went back to her apartment, donned her favourite shirt of red,
Synched some Jewel into her iPod, slipped her earphones
        on her head,
And revelled in being herself once more, with no doubts
        or misgivings,
For always pleasing others is a crummy way of living!

So Diana started acting real, and the Diamonds stayed her friends,
And so, with a simple moral, our tale today must end;
If you live your life dishonestly, no one will ever know,
How wonderful you really are, if you never let it show.

So, cast away the cloaks and masks, and let your soul shine through,
And despite what other people think, to thine own self, be true.

~Emily Adams

A Fallen Friend Gets Back Up

A friend encourages your dreams and offers advice—
but when you don't follow it,
they still respect and love you.
~Doris Wild Helmering

It wasn't too long ago—reality is beginning to sink in—but a part of me is still in doubt of the change. Autumn is coming again and the leaves in our old school are already turning crimson and orange. I remember last autumn, when we were the best of friends and worst of enemies. We fought over having the highest average in class, the Art Award, the English Award, and everything we could possibly compete for. Back in those days, we discussed our future, our dreams, and our goals. You were always full of them, while I was always confused about what I wanted to do with life. I was only in eighth grade, after all. But you seemed to be wiser than your age.

"I'm going to go to Harvard to study law when I grow up, just like my cousin. I'm even starting to study for the SATs," you'd tell me all the time during recess. Then I'd laugh, telling you that we hadn't even reached high school yet. But then, you were always thinking one step ahead of all of us. While most of us only cared about going to the hottest party of the year or dating the cutest boy in the grade, you only cared about your future plans and grades. I remember how you always were with grades—you wouldn't even be happy with a ninety-nine percent. Whenever you didn't get a perfect mark on an assignment, you would go up to the teacher (and drag me along for support), to ask what you had done wrong.

That's how you used to be. It's strange how a person can change so quickly.

It started off with you meeting some new friends from another class, and they invited you to a party—one of the cool parties. I was bummed because you got invited and I didn't. Now that I look back at it, I couldn't be more grateful that I wasn't invited, because that party was where it all started.

The day after that party, you started experimenting with alcohol. It started with only a few sips per day, then a couple of gulps, and then an entire bottle at once. You were only thirteen back then, and I thought you were joking when you told me how you got drunk. You said vodka and rum made you feel like you were floating. I simply thought you were trying to strike up an interesting conversation on a boring day. One day, you said I should to come over to your house and try drinking because I would like it, and that it made everything so much clearer. I agreed because rebellion sounded fun. I never did, though. My lost conscience came back to me at the last minute.

A couple of days later, I saw you going over to your popular friend's place for lunch. That day, you came back extremely late and the teacher made you stay after school to explain yourself. You lied and he let you off with a warning. It didn't matter what lie you ended up telling the teacher—what mattered to me was how you were slurring your speech that day and how your breath smelled of alcohol. I even had to support you while you walked because you were so dizzy afterwards.

It was then that I realized you weren't joking. It was serious. Your old intelligent self faded quickly, and the only thing you cared about was booze and popularity. On the outside, you pretended to be happy so you could keep up the new popular image. But after a while, everything starts to show—especially to me. The deep cuts on your wrists, hidden by heavy bracelets—cuts that only I noticed—told the entire story.

More and more your mind became clouded. Later, you even fell victim to eating disorders because you felt "fat" next to your popular friends. When I followed you into the bathroom, I saw you puking your guts out. You would do anything just to keep up with them. And after starving yourself, you decided to start wearing revealing clothing.

A long time ago, I told you that I wanted to be one of those cool, popular girls in our school. And then you told me, "Popularity isn't anything—just because something looks cools doesn't mean it actually is. Once you grow up, people won't hire you based on how many people you have dated or all the popular friends you had."

It's strange how the advice you gave me then was the same advice I tried to give you, but you refused to take it. "Who cares about grades anymore these days? Get a life," you told me when I tried to tell you what you were becoming. Your grades dropped and our friendship dwindled.

Seeing what those people were doing to you, I started to oppose everything about them. I even threatened that if you ever got drunk again, I would tell your parents and our teacher. You became angry with me. You said that all I ever wanted was to get you in trouble and that I'm no fun to hang around with. Then, you started to skip class and said that I ratted you out whenever you got caught. You even spread rumours about me—hurtful and untrue things. And after a while, I became angry as well. Angry at what you had become, angry at how I couldn't stop you, angry at how you treated me, angry at everything that made you this way. Unsurprisingly, we ended the year on bad terms.

Later that summer, I heard that you wouldn't be coming to the same high school as me. Your parents wanted you to get away from those people, after they found out what happened when you were caught skipping. I was happy for you, but a little sad at the same time. At my high school orientation, you gave me my birthday present and a card with a smile. I guess being away from those people did make you feel better after all. Either way, I accepted it with a simple "Thank you," because I didn't really know what to say.

"Thanks for being such a great friend to me," you wrote in the card.

I read that line over and over again. The meaning in that simple sentence overwhelmed me and I called you. We talked for a while, and for once, you sounded like my old friend again. Your voice sounded so much happier and livelier than when I had last heard you talk — as if you are actually content again. Even though you won't be in the same school as me from now on, at least everything is starting to go right again for you. That's the best thing that can happen. I hope that in your new school you will be able to find yourself again and reach the goals that you had once set for yourself.

The trees in our old school are turning crimson and orange again, and I hope that this autumn will be a beautifully sweet one for you, with new friends and a new start.

~Carol Wong

Teens Talk Middle School

Mean Girls... and Boys

Calling somebody else fat won't make you skinnier.
Calling someone stupid doesn't make you any smarter...
All you can do in life is try to solve the problem in front of you.

~Cady Heron, Mean Girls

The Gift of Lost Friendship

You have enemies?
Good. That means you've stood up for something,
sometime in your life.
~Winston Churchill

W hen most people look back on middle school they remember their teachers and their best friends. But what I remember most is one person who isn't even my friend anymore. Lots of people will give you the gift of friendship, but this person gave me an even bigger gift. She gave me the gift of no longer being my friend. I know that sounds strange, but let me explain.

My heart was pounding as I climbed onto the school bus on the first day of middle school. I adjusted my backpack as I looked for a place to sit. My eyes landed on two girls sitting next to each other. They smiled at me and patted the seat adjacent to theirs.

"Hey!" the blond said. "My name is Heather. What's yours?"

"Rachel..." I stammered. Normally I'm not shy, but I barely knew anyone and was anxious to make new friends.

"Nice to meet you," said the brunette. "My name's Jessica."

I sat down on the hot vinyl seat and faced the girls. I looked at my Converse All Stars and frowned. Why hadn't I worn more stylish shoes?

"Do you live around here?" I asked.

"Over there," said Heather, pointing left.

"I just moved here from across town," explained Jessica.

It turned out we had first period together and we became friends. We ate lunch together, hung out at the park and had *Smallville* marathons in Jessica's room on weekends. We became the three musketeers. But our friendship wasn't without its faults.

Jessica made Heather and me laugh. She was very fashionable and we'd go to her for make-up and clothing advice. But she had an "I'm-the-boss" personality that demanded attention. She always had to be in charge.

One time, the three of us went to the mall. Being the preppy one, I wanted to go to Abercrombie & Fitch.

"Abercrombie, are you kidding?" Jessica said, rolling her eyes. "I'm not setting foot in there. We're going to Rave."

Not wanting to argue, I followed her into Rave, my eyes lingering on the door to Abercrombie.

"This skirt would look great on you," Jessica exclaimed. "Try it on!"

"I don't like it that much..." I said.

Jessica gave me a death glare so I made my way to the dressing rooms.

I ended up buying the skirt. I spent fifty dollars on a skirt that I didn't even like, just to make Jessica happy.

Throughout sixth grade, this was how it was. If Jessica went somewhere, Heather and I went there too. We had little fights, but nothing major. That summer was filled with sprinklers, lemonade, midnight trips to the pool and afternoon tanning in the backyard. But when seventh grade started, things were different.

Heather and I became Jessica's sidekicks. If Jessica wanted to go ice skating, Heather and I were obligated to come. If we were busy with other plans, it didn't matter. We had to come or she would say we "didn't care about our friendship." If Jessica was mad at me, Heather always took Jessica's side. When she was mad at Heather I did the same thing for fear of being yelled at by Jessica. Even though most fights were just minor misunderstandings, they usually ended with Heather or me apologizing and praying for Jessica's forgiveness. Then we'd mumble to each other about how ridiculous the latest fight was.

As time went on, I found I was behaving as a pretend version of myself just to please Jessica and to keep her from being mad at me. She complained I was different when I was around other people, when in truth I was being myself. I was always afraid she'd get mad at me for saying something that I wouldn't normally think twice about.

I was obligated to take Jessica's side even when I didn't agree. For instance, one time she got in a fight with a girl named Leslie and she expected me to be mad at Leslie too. When I told her I had no reason to be mad and that Leslie was my friend, Jessica didn't speak to me for three days.

Then, summer came around. Jessica invited Heather and me to go to Cape Cod with her. I decided to go to Florida with another friend instead, and Jessica got angry. When I came home, Jessica was gone. I went to camp and didn't hear from her.

One hot day, my phone rang and the caller ID glowed "Jessica." If I answered, I'd be yelled at. If I didn't, Jessica would get even madder. I flipped open the phone.

"Hey... How are you?" I asked.

"Fine," Jessica replied curtly.

"Is something wrong?" I questioned, biting my lip.

"Why do my other friends call and you don't?!" she demanded.

My heart raced. I remained silent for fear I'd say something wrong. Finally, I took a breath, "I'm sorry.... I've been at camp and in Florida. If you wanted to talk so badly, why didn't you call me?"

"You don't care enough to call me!" Jessica exclaimed. "I can't be your friend anymore if you don't care."

I needed to tell her the truth. I took a breath and whispered, "Jessica, I'm afraid of you. You're fun to be with, but you're intimidating. I never know when you're going to get mad at me." My voice shook. "It's hard to have a friend who's always angry—there, I said it. I'm sorry if it hurts your feelings. I want to work things out but I thought you should know how I feel."

The line went dead. She'd hung up on me. Heather had a similar falling out with her within weeks.

I sometimes wonder what life would be like if I hadn't told the truth. But telling the truth is never a mistake, and that's what Jessica taught me. Without knowing it, Jessica showed me that real friends listen to what you say and care how you feel. Real friends are there for you through the toughest times—they don't cause them. Real friends respect who you are and encourage you to be yourself, rather than asking you to be who they want you to be just to please them. Lots of people will give you the gift of friendship, but once in a while someone will give you the gift of lost friendship.

~Rachel Joyce

When I Was Twelve

A man cannot free himself from the past more easily
than he can from his own body.
~André Maurois

I was twelve years old and in the seventh grade. The school itself was a modest light brown building with no distinguishing features except for the awkward sculpture protruding from the front. The sculpture looked like a heap of twisted metal—nothing special.

Every day I would wander the sterile white halls lined with brownish-yellow lockers, wondering where I fit in. Even at the age of twelve, cliques had begun to form. There were the wealthy girls who dressed in Abercrombie & Fitch and carried Prada bags. There were the Jocks, who played sports on weekends and considered themselves too good to associate with non-Jocks. The different cliques usually never mixed. In a school of predominantly white students, I didn't fit in anywhere. I was one of about four Asian students, so I ended up hanging out with the other minorities and the people who were considered "losers." With them, I felt a small sense of belonging.

During almost every lunch period, I would play a card game called Magic: The Gathering with my friends. I first learned it back in the fifth grade. When all of the students were herded out to the schoolyard for recess, my four friends and I sat at the off-white, garbage-littered lunch table, each with our own deck of about sixty cards. We would take turns drawing a card from the top of our decks and "attacking" with it. One by one, my other friends usually lost until only I and one other Chinese kid, Evan, remained. Evan was short and chubby and always wore grey sweaters and beige khaki pants. He was the kid who would come over to you during lunch and ask for your Tater Tots. No matter how many times we played, I was never able to beat him.

Evan was a good student and he knew it. He would also make sure that you knew it. He constantly talked about high school-level classes he was taking and would always be the first to answer a question with a long-winded response. Even when we played cards, he was the best and he knew it. When he beat us, he did so with a smug look on his face. Then he'd always explain the flaws in our decks like a professor lecturing his students. It was like he knew everything and we knew nothing. But it didn't matter because he was my friend — or so I thought.

I was too naïve, too trusting, and too open. I set myself up for disappointment. Because I considered Evan to be one of my closest friends, I often followed him around and talked to him about everything: video games, homework, baseball, anything that came to mind. I felt that since we were both Chinese, we could somehow relate to each other.

One afternoon, I was walking with Evan down the science wing on the second floor. I was my usual talkative self — I rambled on with no end in sight and Evan walked silently in front of me. As we turned a corner right outside the plant-growing room, Evan turned to me and said the ten words that I can still hear clearly in my head today. "Why are you talking to me? I'm not your friend." Those were the exact words he said to me that day. I stood there dumbfounded. It was as if I had just been told that one of my relatives had died. I was completely devastated. He kept walking and never looked back. I ran off to my next class with tears welling in my eyes.

We rarely spoke to each other after that. I escaped into a shell, like a turtle, to hide from the world. For the rest of my time in middle school, I didn't allow myself to get close to anyone. I pushed away most of my other friends for fear of being hurt again. I avoided unnecessary conversations. The rest of my middle school days went by in a blur.

It wasn't until high school that I was able to poke my head out of my shell and begin trusting people again. But even today, I am still cautious in choosing who I open up to. It takes me a very long time to warm up to someone.

I was twelve then. I was too trusting and I took what Evan said personally. Maybe he was having a bad day or maybe I was talking too much. In my view, the circumstances are a moot point. What he said to me that day changed the course of my life. But if it were not for that incident, I wouldn't have had to make new friends in high school and I wouldn't have met the people who are my best friends today.

I understand that, in middle school, we were all young. We were all trying to find our place in life. I have been able to forgive all the people who bullied me, but for some reason I can't seem to forgive Evan. Those words that day hurt me more than anything any other school bully said or did. I want to believe that one day I will be mature enough to forgive Evan too. But right now I am not mature. I am still that twelve-year-old boy running down the hall with tears welling in his eyes.

~Kevin Chu

It Was Over

Labels are for filing. Labels are for clothing.
Labels are not for people.
~Martina Navratilova

iddle School. For three long, hard years those two words meant only one thing to me: torture. It all started during my first week of school when I started taking the bus. My family was too poor to afford a car at the time, so that was my only way to get there without having to walk two and a half miles. As soon as I got onto the bus, things were different. The kids were acting like jerks!

Halfway to school, the kids had already started picking on the special needs kids who had been mainstreamed that year. They had already made fun of their looks and their weight when I couldn't take it anymore. I looked at David, the leader of the bullies, and said, "Hey! Shut up! How would you feel if someone did that to you?"

At that moment, I felt like I was on top of the world. The kids who were being picked on looked at me as if I were their hero. Even the bus driver stopped the bus to look at me. I thought that I had stopped the teasing when suddenly David looked at me with a mean smirk. "I don't know," he said, "How does it feel, FATTY?" That was when I became the center of their torment.

Every day when I got on the bus, I had to deal with them. I had gum stuck in my hair, food thrown at me, and I was called the cruelest and most disgusting names. Sometimes, the bullies would even take my backpack from me and throw it outside. They would watch me run after it from the windows. As a result of all the bullying, my grades suffered terribly. I went from having all As and Bs, to having Ds and Fs. I was miserable. All I wanted to do was go back to elementary school where I felt safe and happy.

When my mom finally bought a car, and was able to drive me to school, I thought that things were going to get better. I was wrong. I had become the bullies' little pet. They made fun of me every day in the hallway. They would wait for me to do something that they could tease me for. I had practically no friends because nobody wanted to hang out with the butt of everyone's teasing. I was all alone. I felt as if I were holding the weight of the world on my shoulders.

During this lonely period, I started writing. I would write horror novels and sequels and prequels to books that I had read. It was my only form of escape. One day, in Language Arts class, our assignment was to write a dragon slayer novel. Just when I was about done writing my story, the kid who sat next to me grabbed it and started to read it. I half expected him to tear it up when he looked at me and said, "Hey, this is pretty good! My name is Ricky. You're Jennifer, right?"

When Ricky said those words, he made me one of the happiest people in the room. That day, I felt like I was walking on sunshine. I had lunch with him and his friends that day. We talked about our favorite horror movies, books, and the math teacher that all of the sixth graders thought was evil. We also talked about the bullies. We all bonded together over how hurt we were by them. Somehow, we all understood each other. We could joke around and be ourselves and not try to fit in.

After a whole long year of torment, I felt wanted. I was no longer being teased. It was finally over.

~Jennifer Perkin

15

It Was The Year

Memories may be beautiful and yet
What's too painful to remember we simply choose to forget
So it's the laughter we will remember
Whenever we remember the way we were.
~Barbra Streisand, "The Way We Were"

It was the year of changes
And the year of telling lies.
It was the year of friendships
And the year that friendships died.

It was the year that opened with
A hopeful, promising start.
We'd never thought that, through it all
We'd slowly drift apart.

In those past years, we'd always think
That it was all cliche:
In every single TV show
Old friends would fade away.

We held each other near and dear
We were ourselves, we said.
We laughed and cheered and played and smiled

And lived the life we led.

And then came seventh grade, of course
Went through the start together
Then you met her, and then I thought
Old friends don't last forever.

You had new clothes, you had new shoes
You had a whole new crew.
You always said to be yourself
But what happened to you?

You had new friends, you had new phones
You laughed and never cried.
I sat there, thinking, as you talked
And I just stared and sighed.

I guess I was just uncool then
But that didn't excuse
The way you looked at me that day:
You said I had no clue.

So then the ignorance began
And you moved on, I guessed
The new friends came, replaced the old
And they became your best.

You kept on saying, through and through
That I was still your friend
But still, I kept on thinking that
Our friendship met its end.

The days dragged by, so slow and sad
I felt like I was there
Because I needed just one friend

And not because you cared.

I wanted to believe that, still
We were great friends at heart
Reality convinced me that
We'd grown too far apart.

So you'll hang out with your group, then
And I'll hang out with mine
But I won't cut our bonds for good
I won't forget those times.

We were great friends for three long years
I guess that was enough
To prove to me you needed change
But change is just too much.

I'll still remember times at school
We used to run and play.
We used to dream about our lives
And laugh our lives away.

I guess all that is over now:
You've got your friends, not me.
For now, I guess that I'm alone
With all my memories.

~Ariel Chu

Bellybutton Betrayal

Trust can take years to build,
but only a second to break.
~Unknown

"You want to see something cool?" China asked.

"Sure, I guess so." We were in China's room after school. I hadn't been to her house very often, but I liked hanging out. She had her own horse, which was awesome, and her parents didn't bother us too much. Her mom worked late, and her stepdad didn't pay a lot of attention.

We'd been lying around, talking and listening to music, and then—boom—she showed me her bellybutton. When I looked close, I could see it had been pierced, even though she didn't have a ring or anything in it at that point.

"Wow, cool." I wanted to get my bellybutton pierced more than anything, but my mom kept telling me I had to wait till I was older. Since I was only in eighth grade, she said it would be a very long time until I could do it.

I did have my ears pierced, but whoop-de-doo. Suddenly, that didn't seem like much of a thrill.

"I did it myself," China said, "and my mom doesn't even know. If you want to try it, I'll show you how."

I guess I was pretty dumb back then, because I didn't really stop and think too much about it. I wanted more piercings, and if I didn't need Mom to sign for me, so much the better. "Cool. Sure," I said. "How do you do it?"

"Hang on." China ran downstairs and grabbed some ice cubes, a lighter, and a couple of safety pins. She dumped all that and went into the bathroom to wash off her belly. When she came back in, she put the ice on her bellybutton to make it numb, and then used the lighter to heat up the safety pin. I guess she thought it would kill the germs or something.

Next thing I knew, she had stuck the pin right through her bellybutton skin.

"OK," she said. "Your turn."

I hardly hesitated. After all, I'd had my ears pierced at the mall, and I knew what that was all about. How bad could it be? Well, it hurt. But when I looked down at my newly-pierced bellybutton, I thought, "All riiiight!"

China told me to leave the pin in for a couple weeks, and then I could put in an earring. I went home with my shirt covering the evidence. I felt a bit sneaky—but cool.

I waited about a week, but then my piercing began to hurt. I'd had an infection in my earlobe the last time I'd gotten a piercing, so I knew exactly what that felt like—and this was it. My bellybutton was red and swollen and really, really sore. I took out the safety pin and just kept putting peroxide on the hole, hoping for the best. Finally, to my relief, it cleared up without my having to tell my mom what I'd done. I put away the safety pin and didn't stick it back in. I just wanted to put it all behind me.

Summer vacation soon came, and everything was okay for a while. But one day, I got a letter in the mail. It was from China. There I was in the yard, in my shorts and flip-flops, reading this thing. And it said that China had been to the doctor, who had found her piercing. It turned out that China had a blood disease and was supposed to be very careful with needles and anything involving her blood. The doctor flipped out when he saw her piercing—and so did her mom.

She said her mom demanded to know why she did it. China told her I had dared her—that I'd paid her twenty dollars to do it!

Apparently it didn't matter that I didn't even have twenty bucks to my name. China said she was no longer allowed to hang out with me or talk to me on the phone or computer. She said we could still send letters over the summer.

My heart started pounding like it would explode — I was furious. How dare she blame me? I was so mad, I ripped up her letter into little pieces. Then I stormed inside and told my mom everything.

Mom was speechless. She wanted to see my bellybutton and wanted to hear everything that had happened, from the beginning. She thanked me for confessing, but still grounded me for a month. She told me I knew how wrong what I did was, and the only reason I wasn't punished even worse was because I had confessed to her — and I was already suffering the consequences, all on my own.

Our school district had just built a new building. One evening a couple of weeks later, Mom and I went there for orientation. The gym was so packed, we ended up standing for a while. Next thing I knew, China was standing across the room. I saw her walk in with her mom and felt my temper start to boil over.

She kept trying to catch my eye and wave at me. I ignored her, but she didn't seem to take the hint. After the administrators talked awhile, they told us we had to break into small groups for a building tour. I ended up with some of my classmates, a couple of friends, and some kids from band. China split off with another group, and I just tried to concentrate on the tour.

We walked through classrooms, labs, the library, the cafeteria, the big, new fitness center, and the fine arts wing. I started to relax again, and kind of enjoyed myself. The tour ended with the administration office. I was one of the last to walk into the room from the hall.

Suddenly, I heard someone yell my name. I looked back, and there with another group was China, acting like we were still best friends forever. "Hey, hey," she said, "our parents aren't here, so we can talk."

I turned to her and lost it. "How can you stand in front of me, talking like we're buddies, when you made up a lie about me like that? How can you live with yourself?" By now, a crowd had gathered. I was right in China's face, and two of my friends had to hold me back. Luckily, the tour leaders moved in. They had seen China leave her group and approach me, so they told her to go away. They pulled our group into the office and shut the door in China's face.

My experience with China taught me to be wary of following someone else without really considering the consequences. After the do-it-yourself piercing, I asked myself why I did it. It was stupid and I should have just waited and done it the right way, later on, if I had wanted it so much. Instead, I risked infection and getting into trouble. Coming from a small school like mine and going into a new, bigger school with a lot of different people, I made a bunch of bad judgment calls. But the important thing is that I learned from them. Now, I only befriend people who really show they are worthy of my friendship. And I think twice before I get involved in any other people's bright ideas.

~Rosario Rivera

True Friend

I cannot give you the formula for success,
but I can give you the formula for failure,
which is: Try to please everybody.
~Herbert B. Swope

Springtime had never been so cold. In spite of the warmth of the sun, I could not protect myself from the icy blast of hatred that rushed at me relentlessly during spring of eighth grade.

A few months prior, I had been enrolled in Wagner Junior High School after a year-long stay in California. The year had been filled with trouble and reached a boiling point when a gang-related incident involving my best friend's brother kept me out of school for two weeks because of threats of retaliation. My mother and sister decided that my staying in California would be detrimental, so I returned to New York to live with my sister.

With a grade point average that was bordering D and two suspensions already on my record, my sister had a hard time convincing the administration that I was really a bright student. As a result, I was placed in the second lowest eighth grade class, a class which consisted mostly of kids with behavioral issues. It didn't take long before I hooked up with a girl named Sophia. She was an intimidating girl whose mouth was ten times bigger than her borderline-anorexic body. To this day I do not understand why, but there was no mistaking that she was the boss of that class. Eventually, she also became the boss of me.

If Sophia said jump, I jumped. If I liked someone and she didn't, I instantly adopted her disdain so as to stay on her good side. So desperate was my need to belong, I was willing to do almost anything.

In spite of one failing grade in gym, a result of my adamant refusal to wear an ugly one-piece gym suit that had shorts and looked like a parachute with elasticized legs, my first report card was perfect. Mr. Kasper, one of the gym teachers, became my strongest advocate in a fight to get me placed in a better class, and by mid second quarter, he had won.

In my new environment, I began to flourish. I continued making good grades and my behavior began to improve. I even began wearing that hideous gym suit. I met other students who shared my love of the arts, something I had suppressed but not forgotten. I joined the Drama Club and began participating in other extracurricular activities.

Despite being in my new classroom, I attempted to maintain my ties with Sophia and the gang. It was difficult to say the least. Accusations of me being a phony and a traitor began to fly regularly. They had no problem expressing their utter contempt for me. Crank phone calls to my home became a normal occurrence. In spite of the mistreatment, I wouldn't let go. Sophia's world and my new life were on a collision course, and I did not have control of the steering wheel. A crash was inevitable; it was just a question of when.

In the Drama Club, I met a boy who I genuinely liked. He was funny. He was talented. He loved music. He was identical to me, the true me, with two exceptions: he was a boy... and he was white.

Time passed and we decided to try and take our relationship to another level. We never actually became boyfriend and girlfriend, but we came awfully close. One day after school, we went to a friend's house to hang out. It was there that we shared our first kiss. The very next day, in spite of it being springtime, the season had changed back to winter.

Upon entering the school, I was greeted with stares of hostility by the majority of the black students. People who normally spoke said nothing. I went through most of the day experiencing this excruciatingly painful and well-orchestrated silent treatment, not knowing what the cause was.

At 3 P.M., I exited the school and came face to face with Sophia and about twenty-five other students. Their stares were cold. A few snickered, but no one said a word. Sophia stepped forward from the crowd and handed me a sheet of paper folded neatly into a perfect square. This letter held the answer.

In it, I was called every kind of name you can imagine, names too horrible to repeat. The venom spewed off the page as if it were molten lava erupting from a volcano. One line made my heart stop and my stomach churn violently: *Now you think you're better than us. What's wrong, you too good to go with blacks, so you had to get you somebody white?*

The tears burned like fire and ice. They formed, but wouldn't fall. I spent the remainder of the day in a stupor and prayed for an awakening, which I knew would never come, from this nightmare.

The following days brought no relief. The silent treatment was in full effect. No one who I knew would speak to me, and my pain intensified. When it became evident that this cruel and unusual punishment would not be ending anytime soon, I resorted to taking a 20-minute crosstown bus ride home and back just to experience a few minutes of peace during my brutal school day.

After finally becoming accustomed to my new reality, the unimaginable happened. I first noticed her on the crosstown bus. She was beautiful and unusually tall. I vaguely remembered seeing her before, but wasn't sure where or when.

We both got off the bus at the same stop and I wondered if she went to my school. We began to walk in the same direction, and I surmised that she did. That's when it happened. That's when I heard the most beautiful sound I had heard in a long time. She said, "Hello."

That one word caused the icicles to thaw. That one word was the balm that I needed to heal my wounds. She told me her name, Brynne, and I told her mine. We talked. It seemed like she was oblivious to my dilemma and the fact that none of my friends were speaking to me. I didn't know how or why, and I really didn't care. She was taking the time to talk to me, and I was so grateful.

I didn't go home for lunch that day or ever again. Brynne welcomed me into her circle of friends and her family—a place where I could be me without fear or intimidation. Thirty years later, we are still friends.

Eventually, Sophia decided to speak and to let her crew speak to me again. I must admit I was relieved, but her presence in my life no longer held the significance that it once did. At the coldest point in my life, a true friend appeared, and to this day, she remains.

~Nancy Gilliam

Becoming a Mean Girl

*Popularity is the easiest thing in the world to gain
and it is the hardest thing to hold.*
~Will Rogers

When I first stepped into the linoleum halls of Boulan Park Middle School, I felt on top of the world. In fifth grade I was the (self-proclaimed) most popular girl and sixth grade was shaping up to be the same way. Boys paid attention to me and wanted to "date" me and girls wanted my curled hair and cool Abercrombie & Fitch clothing. (Who else had the initials "AF" written all over their clothes?)

But something changed in seventh grade. I was one of the youngest in my class, so while the other girls were coming out of puberty with big boobs and straight teeth, I was entering awkward pre-pubescence with braces, acne, and a flat chest.

Nonetheless, I was still confident in my place in the middle school social world. In fact, I was one of those unusually rare kids who always thought I was the most beautiful, smart, and popular girl, even when I wasn't. I would sit at the cool kids' lunch table and pretend not to notice that my reserved seat was always taken and my invite to parties was never directly from the host.

One day after school one of the mysterious, up and coming popular girls, Jenny, and I, were hanging out in her basement. We were checking our e-mail and came across a survey chain letter that rated the girls and boys in our middle school. There were nearly thirty categories for discussion: best hair, most popular, best-looking, etc. My name was mentioned only once. Jenny's name was mentioned a few more times than mine, but we were still a little appalled at how our "competition" was mentioned in categories we felt we deserved.

"How did Laura, of all people, get best eyes? Ewww!" we gossiped and giggled to one another.

That's when Jenny had a brilliant idea on how to pass the next few hours before dinner. "Let's make up our own survey," she said.

"Okay," I agreed excitedly, my eyes widening with excitement.

But Jenny had a trick up her sleeve. "Instead of best of, let's do the worst of," she said innocently.

We both paused for a second, looked at each other, and started grinning from ear to ear. It was one of those grins with matching devilish eyes that were sparkling at doing something a bit naughty, and therefore so exciting.

Jenny and I began plugging away. We copied and pasted the super long survey into a new e-mail. The "best eyes" category became "worst eyes." The "best-looking girl" became the "worst-looking girl." We added some original negative categories to capture the girls we really disliked, emphasizing their acne, annoying voices, or what we saw as "tag-along" attitudes.

The really popular girls we didn't hit as hard as the girls we thought didn't deserve to be on the fringes of the popular crowd. The irony of the fact that we WERE those second-tier girls never occurred to us. Jenny was on her way in and I was on my out and both of us were desperate to impose our self-worth on our peers. Pointing out the flaws of others made us feel great about ourselves and very, very powerful.

An hour later, we finished the malicious survey and before we could evaluate the consequences, the e-mail was sent to all our friends, all the popular kids in seventh grade.

The catch? The e-mail was sent from my e-mail address with no ownership on Jenny's part.

I went home for dinner excited about the e-mail. There's something seductive about gossiping and laughing at other people. I felt I was back on top of my game. I felt this e-mail would bring me closer to the popular girls, a sort of "insider's only" gossip.

An hour or two later I got a call from my lifelong neighbor and best friend.

"Andrea, did you write that e-mail?" she asked, gasping. I knew immediately from the tone of her voice that I had done something very wrong.

"Uh, yeah, why?" I hesitantly asked.

"It's sooooo mean," she said slowly.

"Really?" I asked perplexed. "I thought it was funny." Truthfully, the thought never occurred to me that this survey would be taken as anything but a hilarious inside joke for the popular clique.

"Everybody's calling me asking if you actually wrote it," she said to me.

"Really?" I asked again, feeling my cheeks flush with embarrassment. Everybody? All the popular kids? Did they hate me?

I had to defend myself. "It wasn't just me, it was Jenny's idea."

My best friend knew better than to take the excuse. She hung up the phone and I knew I had made a big mistake.

School wasn't the same after that day. Jenny became the most popular girl in school and I spent the next year trying desperately to re-establish broken relationships and cling to a social circle I had only myself to blame for betraying. My phone eventually stopped ringing and I spent countless weekends watching TGIF by myself. If I did go to a party, it was because I had called a million people beforehand. No one seemed mad at me when I showed up; they just simply ignored me. The invisibility crushed me. I felt so ashamed and misunderstood.

Jenny's manipulative ways were eventually uncovered and she fell off the social radar as well, but my social status never recovered.

In high school, the isolation continued and I had to make the choice: be angry with everyone or learn to make myself happy without friends.

I chose the latter.

I found my calling at fourteen when I traveled to Australia and was recognized as the beautiful and kind person I was deep inside. I spent the rest of high school traveling around the United States and the world making incredibly unique, life-long friends (and boyfriends!). I became independent and confident. My "invisibility" became appealing "mystery" and I won back a lot of my friends I had lost in middle school. But I was never to be part of a group again.

After graduation, I moved to New York, my home, and have never returned.

Looking back I am still ashamed at my e-mail but am so proud that it made me a stronger, wiser, and nicer person. I learned important lessons at an early age. First, respect the power of the Internet in unleashing the negative. Second, popularity does not give you the right to be mean. And third, no one is untouchable.

In middle school, I sealed my fate as a mean girl, and even in the movies the mean girl never comes out on top. In real life, you fall much faster than you ever thought possible.

~Andrea Feczko

The Curiosity of Popularity

Fame is a vapor,
popularity an accident,
and riches take wings.
Only one thing endures and that is character.
~Horace Greeley

It was the end of August, two thousand and six.
When something did happen, something had clicked.
We walked in the door that second day of school,
And suddenly knew who was normal and cool.
On the top of the ladder were all those who played sports,
Or were wealthy and went shopping to buy things of all sorts.
They were good-looking, clean, but not always nice,
They play football, lacrosse, or hockey on ice.
And then, way back at the bottom of the ladder,
Were the people who were smarter, clumsier, or fatter.
They played on computers, or played violin,
They didn't have cell phones on which you can dial in.
We're all in one school, but our fates have been sealed.
When we entered sixth grade, two worlds were revealed.

Four elementary schools, molded into one,
Some schools were different, people had more fun.
Some of the boys, you know what they'd shout:
"Hey! Me and Lisa? Guess what, we're going out!"
They'd walk, holding hands, and they thought they were supreme,
As they went to the movies, or out for ice cream.
While the rest of the kids, from the other side of town,
Walked around with no hand, on their face was a frown.
Something that last year that seemed totally absurd,
Now, if someone didn't do it, they became a nerd.
Most of the adults said, "No, it's not time yet."
But most kids gave in. They wanted a "someone," you bet.
We guessed that real "dating" would soon come about,
But for then, people were still just "going out."

The popular people had such a weird way,
As they roamed the hallways, looking for prey.
You could be at your locker, just keeping to yourself,
Getting your books and binders off your locker shelf.
And then, they would spot you, and walk right up,
And say things like, "Oh, hey, you. What 'sup?"
What are you supposed to say? "The ceiling, I guess."
That only creates several seconds of awkwardness.
You just kind of leave after you collect your pens,
And the popular kids go back out with their friends.
Sometimes the Populars do it as a joke,
To see your reaction, to see if you choke.
Maybe you give it a shot, to be nice and sincere,
But you realize, soon after, you'd rather disappear.

Then there's something you notice about your new school,
That Populars spend time on the field or in the pool.
They play their baseball, basketball, water polo, and lacrosse.
They have swimming, back and forth in the pool, they cross.
They play football, where they can get dirty in the mud,

And soccer, where they'd kick the ball as much as they could.
But then, those less popular people play things as well,
They seem to find things and still manage to excel.
They play violin, really working their right arm.
They play chess and menacingly find an opponent to disarm.
While they play real sports too,
The ones popular kids do,
They might not be as good,
At these sports as they "should."

Middle school — sixth grade — is way different, that's for sure.
The day you walk in school, everyone is suddenly "mature."
While most of the times that you have will be good,
You've got homework, friends, and things in your neighborhood.
But school is a part of living, and it's a part of life.
You've got to go through it, all the fun and the strife.
And now I will say this, with all sincerity,
Do your best to survive the perils of popularity.

~Hale McSharry

20

Dirty Little Fingers

Holding resentment is like eating poison
and waiting for the other person to keel over.
~Unknown

His name was Jeremy and everybody in the sixth grade class thought he was hilarious. That is, of course, except for our teacher. It was apparent that he had a true behavioral problem, but we were in a pre-Ritalin time period and it was still acceptable to punish children who had attention and hyperactivity issues.

Jeremy was a constant disruption to our class and he had been since the fourth grade. He called our teacher funny names, blurted out inappropriate comments, and threw objects across the room. Early on, he was reprimanded and sent out of the classroom. But that only enabled him to cause more of a ruckus by pressing his mouth against the window like a blowfish and writing bad words in the condensation of the glass.

Our teacher then tried other forms of punishment, such as placing him in a corner and tying him to his desk with a jump rope. Somehow, he always managed to make a scene and the punishment was usually more disruptive than the initial act.

Still, Jeremy was outrageously funny and his behavior was a welcomed distraction for the sixth grade class. It was much more enjoyable watching him spit paper at the ceiling or draw stick figures on his desk with a permanent marker than learning how to divide fractions. He completely exhausted our teacher but we were so thankful for him.

One of Jeremy's favorite hobbies was picking on people. He made fun of the overweight children, the boy who got braces, and the girl who was just beginning to develop. He picked on anything and anyone he could, and each time he did, his audience roared. He was a real comedian.

It was a Tuesday in March, and Jeremy had arrived at school in typical form. His outbursts were frequent and his comments were more lewd than ever before. And as usual, his fans were thoroughly entertained. We were about to go to art class when Jeremy turned around in his seat, pointed his dirty finger at me and shouted, "Look y'all! Melissa's picking her nose!"

Of course I wasn't. But try telling that to twenty-five hysterical twelve-year-olds. Red in their faces, they all stared, laughed, and pointed at me, even the ones I thought were my friends. I cried.

Jeremy said I was picking my nose so it had to be true. I even started questioning myself. Was I picking my nose and I didn't realize it? Maybe I had scratched my nose from an angle and made it appear that I was picking. I didn't know what had happened. But I did know that I felt humiliated, upset, and very, very alone.

The next day was nearly as tragic. At snack time, Jeremy announced, "What do you have for snack today, Melissa? Is it a Boogerfinger Bar?" I held back the tears and ate my granola bar while my classmates laughed at me. And for three more days, I endured ridicule from Jeremy and his twenty-four devotees.

Then, just as the teasing had begun, it suddenly stopped. Jeremy was easily bored and he had found another target. A new girl, Diane, entered our class and she had very curly hair. "You're a spaghetti head!" he laughed. "You've got oodles of noodles on your scalp!" Everyone roared, except for me. I didn't think Jeremy was funny anymore.

Jeremy left our school the following year and did not return until we were well into high school. He was very different from how I remembered him, perhaps more mature, or maybe just medicated. He was calm, well-mannered, and not at all funny.

After graduation, I heard he was earning a living by driving trucks across the country. I pictured him pointing his dirty finger and laughing at the other drivers. Sixth grade was long ago; but I couldn't help but remember him that way.

I somehow survived the traumas of my sixth grade year and have even forgiven Jeremy for the way he teased me. I haven't forgotten; I have forgiven.

Two years ago, I saw Jeremy. I had just moved back to my hometown and had accepted a position as a sixth grade teacher at my former school. I saw Jeremy after class one day making ice cream sundaes at his sister's restaurant. I recognized him when I watched him jokingly point his finger at a customer. It still looked a little dirty to me.

But when he walked to my car, he was so excited to see me that he gave me an enormous hug. I ordered a Butterfinger sundae and he brought it to my window. We caught up on the past ten years of our lives and reminisced about our middle school days. When I got ready to leave, Jeremy said, "It was so good to see you Melissa! I wish you the best in everything."

"You too," I replied. And I meant it.

~Melissa Face

21

Closure

*You can out-distance that which is running after you,
but not what is running inside you.*
~Rwandan Proverb

I was an athlete in my youth, a competitive figure skater with an unyielding desire to win. Gym class was my place to show off and I did so with absolute abandon. The only obstacle to my domination was a tall, good-looking boy with long legs and unusual muscular strength for his age. I will call him David Young. He was equally proud of his athletic abilities, and our rivalry played out every day after lunch. That he was a boy and I a girl fueled this competitive fire. So did the fact that I was white and he was black. Though we were not aware of this at twelve years old, our rivalry perfectly mirrored the racial tensions of the time in our community.

In the spring, we began our testing for the Presidential Physical Fitness Awards, a standardized Federal program. The final event, the six hundred yard run, carried the most weight and was my best event because of the stamina that my conditioning afforded me. I had made it into the top percentile ranking three years in a row, and in the seventh grade, I fully expected to enjoy similar success.

What none of us realized was the importance of these awards for our gym teachers. Their performance was linked to ours, and they came up with a brilliant plan to ensure results. On a hot spring day, the six hundred yard run was assembled. The class was placed in rows and given numbers to wear on their backs. They set the timers and pulled the trigger, and everyone started to run. Everyone except David and me.

When the class finished, they were sent to the bleachers. The teachers then guided me and David to the track, side by side—just the two of us at the starting block. I could feel my heart pounding in my chest. This was, for both of us, the final showdown. And everyone was watching.

The trigger was pulled and we were off. I don't remember the number of laps, only the sight of David a few feet ahead of me for all of them. My legs were numb, my breath heavy as we turned the final corner. Then something inside me burst open and I felt the speed gather at my feet. The other kids were cheering wildly, some for David, others for me. But it didn't matter. I had to win. The few feet turned to inches and soon there was nothing in front of me but the finish line. I crossed it with David just at my heels.

It was, overall, a great success. David and I had our best scores, boosting the class average that would be reported to the Federal Government. Our school and the gym teachers would be recognized for the job well done. As for me, I had earned another patch with the navy stitching and bald eagle emblem. But the thrill of the victory was laced with guilt when I saw the humiliation take hold of my opponent.

We both avoided the crowd, walking ahead to the locker room doors around the side of the school. When we turned the corner, I felt the pull on my arm, then the hard pavement against my back. David had thrown me to the ground and was on top of me, his face anguished, his fists pounding into my gut. I didn't react. It was over in a few seconds. David ran to the boys' locker room and I got up off the ground, stunned but not hurt. I didn't cry—at least, I don't remember crying. What I do remember is that I took a shower and got on with my day. I never told a soul. The following year I moved to Colorado to train with a new coach. I never saw David again.

Twenty years later, the memory of that day lay buried beneath everything that had happened since: rocky teen years, first loves, college, and adulthood. I now had my own children, a house, a husband,

and a new fledgling career as a writer. Still, as I would discover, the scars were there waiting to be healed.

I was at the kitchen counter writing when the doorbell rang. The cable guy had come to fix our reception and I let him in. He asked to go upstairs and I told him I had a baby sleeping and he would have to be quiet. He politely agreed, wiped his feet carefully and proceeded to the master bedroom where the problem had been. I went back to my work.

Later, I was in the middle of reading a chapter when he appeared from the front hall. With clipboard in hand, he apologized for interrupting me, then explained how he had fixed the problem. Distracted by my work, I took the clipboard without looking at his face. I signed on the line and handed it back to him, this time meeting his eyes and saying thank you. I expected him to pack it away and then allow me to walk him to the door. But instead he just stood there, staring at the name I had written.

"Is this your married name?" he asked, and I was a bit surprised. I told him it was.

"Did you grow up around here?" he asked again. His face was serious, and I began to study it to see what connection he was trying to make.

"Yes," I said. Then I told him the name of the town.

He took a breath and looked down before speaking again. Then he said the words that I will never forget.

"I'm David Young."

There was a long pause as we looked at each other, each of us feeling the memory work its way out of the past and into my kitchen.

"You live here?" he asked, though the answer was apparent.

"Yes," I said.

"And you have children?"

"Yes. Two," I answered again.

He seemed relieved, and I knew exactly the calculations he was making. No, he hadn't hurt me. My mind and body were intact. I asked him about himself, and he told me of his brief stint in the military, and how he now dedicated his life to athletics. He ran several sports teams for underprivileged children and kept himself in peak condition. And we both knew he was doing more than catching me up. He was trying to explain.

We didn't speak of the incident that had obviously lived inside both of us all these years. Instead, we gave each other clues with our words and the genuine kindness with which they were spoken. Through this benign social interaction, he rendered his apology, and I let him know that I understood the many influences that had been upon us that day in the seventh grade. The conversation came to an awkward end, and I walked him to the door, closing it after him.

I thought about David for many days, struck by the power that young adulthood can have throughout our lives. From the moment my cable box broke, to the timing of my call to have it fixed that placed him on the schedule and brought him to my door, there were forces at work that I will never understand. What I do know is that we were both given an incredible gift that day—the gift of closure.

~Wendy Walker

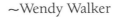

Teens Talk Middle School

Embarrassing Moments

The rate at which a person can mature is directly proportional to the embarrassment he can tolerate.

~Douglas Engelbart

22

Brace Yourself

Man is the only animal that blushes.
Or needs to.
~Mark Twain

His name was Dusty. His blond hair always looked wind-tossed. His blue eyes reminded me of the color of the ocean, and his smile could melt solid ice. He was a year older than I was, and like many of the girls in my class, I had a crush on him. Not just a he's-so-cute infatuation. More of a weak-kneed-kiss-my-pillow-and-pretend-it's-him kind of crush.

He'd walk into the lunchroom and all the girls would sigh in unison. But it was useless. Word was he was involved with someone at another school. There had actually been Dusty-and-girlfriend sightings.

Not that I had a chance anyway. I was double cursed—glasses on my face and braces on my teeth. My mousy, thin brown hair and a failing sense of fashion didn't make me any more appealing. I was smart and funny, but that didn't make me Homecoming Queen material.

One day, I was walking down the school hall behind Dusty and some of the other A-listers. Too bad A-list didn't have anything to do with grades. The way things were, I was more of a C+.

Some papers fell from Dusty's notebook, but he didn't notice. I picked them up. They looked like his homework. I stared at the pages for a moment, admiring his handwriting.

It was my lucky day. I'd return the papers and actually get to talk to him. I resisted the urge to sprint over. I didn't want the others to hear me. He went to his locker and I followed, hoping to impress him with my wit, but feeling a little like a stalker.

"Dusty," I squeaked. He turned around. Breathe. Smile. Now talk. "You dropped this. It looks like it might be important."

He reached for the paper and his hand brushed mine. I was in love!

"Hey!" He lifted his head and looked straight at me with those robin's-egg-blue eyes and smiled. "Thanks for finding it. Sorry, but I don't know your name."

I quivered from my legs, through my stomach and it came out in my words. "It's Carole, with an 'e.'"

"Nice to meet you, Carole with an 'e.'"

I smiled broadly. Unfortunately, so broadly that the two rubber bands holding my braces in alignment popped out of my mouth and bounced off Dusty's flinching face.

I stood there horrified. As the wet, disgusting things rolled around on the floor, I wanted a volcano to explode and cover me with ashes. I so wanted to die. To make things worse, I was sure a piece of my lunch, a ham sandwich, was stuck on one of the bands. My throat went into a huge spasm.

Before I could apologize, another guy hollered out to Dusty. When he turned his head toward the voice, I hunched over, like maybe he wouldn't notice me sneaking away as quietly as I could. I always hated those braces. Now they were the source of my biggest shame.

I didn't tell anyone about this catastrophe, not even my longtime best friend, Jennifer. I carried the embarrassment with me all day, fighting back tears each time I thought about what had happened. I didn't even raise my hand in class, as I usually did. When school was over, I hurried home by myself and curled up on my bed, believing I would never be able to show my face in school again.

I was sure by the next day Dusty would have told everyone about how I shot rubber bands with my mouth. To my surprise and complete relief, the following day no one teased me about the incident. The school day went by agonizingly slow, but was finally over.

Jennifer and I were walking home together that day. I was still a geek, but because she was nice, and pretty, she was easing into the popular crowd. We were almost out of the parking lot when she called to three guys to walk with us. One of them was Dusty. As they joined us, my palms started sweating and I was sort of dizzy. Any minute I knew someone would snap a rubber band and Dusty would dodge it, making it all into a big joke.

Jennifer, always polite, introduced the boys to me. Dusty was last. He stopped her and looked straight at me. "I know you."

I knew I'd have to leave town.

He smiled. "You're Carole with an 'e.'"

I went limp with relief. I couldn't believe he didn't tell anyone.

I didn't die from embarrassment, and over time Dusty and I became good friends. He never told anyone about the rubber band incident, which goes to show Dusty was as gorgeous inside as outside. Still, it took a long time before I could look at any rubber band without wincing.

~Carole Fowkes

23

The Sand Castle Summer

Humiliation —
the harder you try, the dumber you look.
~Larry Kersten

That summer was hot. Even the spring had been hotter than usual, causing the last month of seventh grade to seem like a year. Maybe it was just the changes my young body was going through that made it seem hotter. I hadn't remembered perspiring like this before.

When Brad called to invite me to go to South Haven with his family, I must have looked desperate to Mom as I asked her if I could go. "What time will you be back?" she asked. This was always to be established before any further deliberation on such a request.

"Before dark," I replied. "Brad's dad hates to drive at night."

"I suppose it'd be okay," she said, "but be careful. You know I hate lakes."

"Yeah, I know. I promise to be careful. Do you know where my new swimsuit is? Is it clean?" I asked hopefully. I knew that my mother would not let me wear the suit unless it had been washed, even though the trunks had only been worn in our small pool. Growing up in a large and poor family had made her a fanatic about clean clothes.

"Wear your old one. It's clean."

"But my old one is too tight!" I complained. "Remember...?"

"If you want to go with Brad, you'll wear the old one. You're not going out in public with a dirty bathing suit. Now, are you going, or not?" she asked.

I knew I had no choice. I really wanted—no—had to go! Maybe I could just suck in my gut when I saw girls looking at me. Girls. That magical name for those magical creatures. Lovely, beautiful girls. At thirteen, my preoccupation with girls had turned into obsession. I loved girls. I adored the way they looked and smelled and walked and talked and I wondered if they even felt different. I couldn't wait until I got a date. The only girl I had ever kissed was Jeannie, the girl next door, and I wasn't going to pass this opportunity up. Yes. I could wear that suit!

The ride to South Haven was long, hot and quiet. Brad's mom didn't approve of "that disgusting racket that they try to pass off as music," as she classified anything we liked. Brad's dad had a "hearing problem," (as in "I don't wanna hear a buncha noise from you kids or I'll turn right around and head for home, you hear?"), so the only sounds to be heard were road noises and squeaks from the bad suspension. Brad, his brother Brian, his sister Barbie, and I sat sweaty and motionless in our appointed seats, wearing our cloaks of boredom, windows fixed tight to their frames.

When we finally arrived at South Haven, it was late morning. Whispering, I said to Brad, "Maybe my suit will fit me now. I think I lost ten pounds of sweat."

The sun had promised another July scorcher. South Beach was already crowded with nearly a full day's complement of swimmers, sunbathers and gawkers. And there seemed to be a million fresh-faced sixteen-year-old girls; the object of every thirteen-year-old boy's fantasies.

As we approached the water, I noticed a hundred sand castles dotting the beach, waiting for the waves to wash over them and destroy all of the dreams that went into making them.

Finally, after we found a spot to put down our stuff, it was time to swim. "Let's go! Last one in is a monkey-butt!" we cried, running down to the water.

The first jolt from the cold water brought shockwaves to the nerves, causing involuntary spasms. Barbie, standing on the edge of the water, noticed our reaction and shouted, "Dorks!" As I looked back to reply, I noticed the three most beautiful bikini-clad girls I had ever seen stretching out a blanket by the swing set. Their radio was playing a Beach Boys song.

"Brad!" I shouted. "Brad!"

"What?" he answered excitedly.

"Look! Up by the swings! Do you see what I see? Wanna go play on the swings for awhile?" I asked, even as I headed toward the swings. "Go get Brian!"

Taking a wide turn around the girls, so as not to seem too obvious, I came to a swing. Putting on my best "I'm-not-looking-at-you" face, I searched the young ladies with furtive glances, hoping and praying that somehow one of the girls would notice me.

"Hey, Don. Watch this!" Brian was swinging furiously, going higher and higher. As the swing made a forward arc, he jumped. "Geronimo!!!" He landed with an audible thud on the hot sand, and flew forward, landing on his face.

Brad and I started laughing. Brian got up. He was caked with sand and his whole body shook with great heaving fits of giggling. Then it was Brad's turn. He maneuvered the swing into a violent pendulum, exiting in a graceful arc. He landed on both feet, nearly crushing a grandmother who had been making her way to the swing with her granddaughter. Again, we all erupted into fits of laughter.

Seeing a chance to impress the loves of my life with my skills, daring, and athletic prowess, I hatched a plot to enable me to strike up a conversation with them. I would jump from the swing and land next to them! This would require swinging at an angle, but I could do it! Starting on an angular path, I began to gain momentum. Higher and higher I flew. The swing began to lose its line and I knew I would veer off course. I had to jump now or abort the plan!

Away I flew, and not very gracefully. I felt a sensation like a punch in the stomach a split second after my release. I was flying headlong toward the objects of my desire. Landing on my left shoulder, I did a bizarre somersault, which resulted in rolling right next to the blanket on which the girls were so well-displayed. It was at this moment that I realized that something else was wrong—my swim suit was still hanging from one side of the wildly thrashing swing! It had somehow become entangled in one of the 'S' hooks used to hold the swing onto the chains! And I was lying next to the three girls, hurt and naked! Yes! Naked!

"Please help me!" I shouted to no one and everyone. The girls just looked at me with wide eyes. One got up and began to run toward the policeman sitting at a picnic table. "Brad, get me a towel! Please!!" And Brad and Brian and Barbie and the remaining two girls and everybody in the whole world was laughing at me, as I tried to cover myself. "Brad! Brian! Someone help me!" I screamed. Days passed before Brad brought me a towel.

Wrapping myself in the towel as I ran toward the car, I felt a flush of embarrassment and humiliation. The ringing sound of derisive laughter followed me to the car. The throbbing in my shoulder was intense, but the terrible reality of the moment was far more painful.

And so my summer search for teenage love ended. Like castles of sand, youthful dreams sometimes also perish against the tide.

~Donald Verkow

Coasting on the Thunder Bolt

If you are never scared, embarrassed or hurt,
it means you never take chances.
~Julia Soul

"Whatever you do, absolutely do not ride the roller coaster!"

Like a screeching broken record, my mother's words repeated in my head as I stood in line with the rest of the seventh graders waiting to climb aboard the death defying "Thunder Bolt" on our class picnic.

My best friend, Marybeth, was a roller coaster fanatic. No roller coaster on earth was too high, too long, too fast or too berserk for Marybeth. She lived for the sole purpose of feeling her stomach take a flying leap to the back of her throat by way of one roller coaster after another.

Staunch as Marine recruits, Marybeth and I inched toward that rickety wooden death trap. To the naked eye, "brave" was my middle name. The naked nose however, is nobody's fool. As anyone with a lick of sense will tell you, socks sopping with unchecked terror, tucked into a pair of sneakers purchased from the bargain bin, create an unfortunate, unpleasant, undeniable stink bomb. Marybeth stood downwind and turned her face in the other direction even when she was talking to me.

Once on the platform, the ride operator pried the damp and shriveled ticket from my hand. His bulging stomach jiggled while a brass happy face belt buckle played peek-a-boo from underneath his overflowing belly. Even the buckle sneered at me as I stepped over the threshold of defying my mother. Having surrendered our tickets, Marybeth grabbed my cold clammy hand, and dragged me to our seat while my stinky sneakers squished clear across the platform. Frank, the ticket taker, pulled the safety rail toward us and locked it into place. Then Frank gave his partner the go ahead to start the ride.

Marybeth and I sat in the second car. Our teacher, Miss Murphy, in an unprecedented display of courage, braved the front seat. In a moment, the car lurched forward and stopped abruptly, prompting me to gnash my teeth and clench the guardrail with a knuckle-whitening grip. We started chugging forward again; then all of a sudden we jerked to the right and I slammed into Marybeth. "Isn't this fun?" she shrieked.

"Oh, yes. It's a blast!" The words were hardly out of my mouth when Mount Everest loomed in front of me and I felt our car hook into the climb. Miss Murphy looked back at us and asked, "Are you girls going to scream when we go over the top?"

Marybeth threw her head back and squealed, "Sure we are!!!" I threw my head back and gasped for air.

Chug. Chug. Chug. We teetered at the top for only a second — then whoosh! Over we went going Lord knows how fast. Our coaster car formed a ninety-degree angle with the earth and I found myself promising God everything from my firstborn child to my first paycheck in return for getting me through this alive.

Faster and faster we raced, while I imagined Mom's disgruntled face leaning over my bruised and battered body as I lay unconscious in the emergency room:

I told her not to ride the roller coaster, Doctor.
Did she listen? No!
I told you Annie.
Didn't I say you were going to break your neck?

Just then, something huge and hairy landed on my face and thunder bolted me straight from my hallucination into total darkness. I shook my head but it refused to let go.

At the same time, my classmates roared out of control while the sound coming from Miss Murphy in the front car sounded more like whimpering and sniffling. We careened up and down the track making wild turns, but the enormous fur ball on my face never budged.

By now, Miss Murphy's whimpering had grown into full-blown sobs, and the roar of the crowd fell to a hush. In fact, about the only thing I could hear was Miss Murphy downright bawling.

What if... what if the fur ball actually killed me and, because I had denied my mother, the wrath of God now descended upon me? Is this what hell is like? Surely God had a better sense of humor than that! Maybe so, since at last we were back on flat track and as the pull of the brake slowed us down, the furry "critter" slid slowly down my face.

Panic subsided until I got a look at Miss Murphy who now looked as if she was getting ready to rob a liquor store. A stocking cap contraption was pulled way down over her head, and the only sound that pierced the air was Miss Murphy's wailing. In disbelief, I bowed my head and there in my lap sat Miss Murphy's wig perched upon my knees like some kind of obtuse afghan. No wonder she was hysterical.

As we slowed down, Miss Murphy reached back, grabbed the wig, and slammed it on her head, cocked to the side like an ill-fitting French beret. By now, the nylon stocking head holder thing had shimmied down her forehead like a bathing cap, sandwiched between her head and the hairy French beret. When the car came to a complete stop, she jumped out faster than a... thunder bolt, and tore down the steps to the ladies' room. Marybeth and I felt sorry for Miss Murphy. Unfortunately, all the sympathy we could muster did not quell our collective compulsion to laugh like crazy over Egg-Head Murphy and the "beast" that ate my face.

Once home, Mom asked if I'd had a good time, and of course I answered "yes," not mentioning the entire fiasco.

I survived unscathed so it seems, but the mantle of guilt lingers on. Since that day, I haven't ridden a roller coaster—or worn a wig. For that matter, I don't think Miss Murphy has either. In fact, the whole experience leaves me wondering whether or not Miss Murphy herself defied her mother that day too.

~Annmarie B. Tait

The Love Letter

I bet people can actually die of embarrassment.
I bet it's been medically proven.
~Angela, My So-Called Life

'd had a crush on Michelle for three years, dating back to sixth grade. Whether it was due to her adorable black curls, sky-blue eyes, or preternaturally developing chest, I cannot say (though I could guess). Even though Michelle continued to show a remarkable ambivalence towards me, my secret crush continued. Every time we spoke, my mind froze to the point where I couldn't conjure an original thought and therefore just repeated whatever she said.

"Hey Harris."

"Hey Michelle."

"Whatcha doing?"

"Nothing, whatchoo doing?"

"Nothing."

"Yeah, same here. Nothing at all."

Pause.

"See ya later Harris."

"Okay, see ya later Michelle."

Eventually, I decided that enough was enough. It was time to step up to the plate and be a man. So I did. Sort of.

Since I remained far too shy to talk to her, I did the next best thing—I wrote her a letter. In it, I told her how much I liked her, how much I talked about her when I wasn't at school, and how much I wanted to go out with her. Though my plan seemed to make sense at the time, if I could do it all over again, I'd probably do two things differently. One, I wouldn't have written it in the third person, and two, I wouldn't have signed my brother's name.

My idea was to have my brother "write" a letter to Michelle, explaining the aforementioned details, but also explaining how shy I was, and how if she felt likewise towards me, she should ask me out. What could go wrong?

"Hey Harris," Michelle greeted me in the school hallway, the day after I dropped the note in her desk when she was away.

"Hey Michelle."

"I got a note from your brother yesterday."

"Really?" I asked, scrunching up my face. Why was she telling me? It specifically stated not to tell me that he wrote the note.

"It was real interesting," she smugly stated.

"Why would Rich write you a letter?"

"He supposedly wrote it to tell me that you liked me." Supposedly? I had a sinking feeling.

"He what?!? I'm gonna kill him!"

"You don't have to."

"Oh, no? Why not?" Hmmm, I thought, maybe she does like me. Maybe she's going to tell me so right now. Maybe this'll be the beginning of a great story to tell our grandkids someday.

"Cause I asked him about it."

"You," I stammered, "you asked him about it?"

"Yeah. He didn't know anything about it. So I showed it to him."

"You, um, you showed it to him?"

"Yeah, he said you wrote it."

"Me? I wrote it?"

"That's what he said."

And then we stood there. She, eyeing me, waiting for some sort of explanation. And me, my mind going... blank. Completely, absolutely, unequivocally blank. I stared at the note, trying to make it burst into flames. No luck.

"Well?" she finally asked, leaning in.

After a few more excruciatingly long seconds, I gave her the only answer I could.

"He's lying."

Taken aback a bit, she asked, "Why would he lie?"

"I don't know, you'd have to ask him."

"But I did ask him. He said you wrote it."

"And I'm saying he's lying."

"But... well, I guess it doesn't really matter anyway," Michelle countered. She crumbled up the letter and continued, "Just don't leave any more notes in my locker, okay?"

"I'll be sure to tell him."

"Whatever," she said, starting to walk away from me.

As I turned to walk to the school bus, I felt numb. I couldn't believe that my ingenious plot had backfired. Love had blinded me to the possibility that she might attempt to contact the author to seek more details, or to explain her non-interest.

I knew that from that moment on, every class I had with Michelle was going to be a chore. I'd have to avoid eye contact at all costs, worried that I'd catch her friends pointing and laughing at me, as she read passages from my love letter with a cartoon-like voice. I guess it could be worse, I thought. After all, I was only in three classes with her. It could've been six. Though still numb, I began to feel a little better.

Then I stopped in my tracks and felt sick again. I broke out in a cold sweat as a knot the size of a baseball took residence in my throat. I may only have had three classes with Michelle, but I lived with my brother.

~Harris Bloom

The Guarantee

You will find that you survive humiliation
And that's an experience of incalculable value.
~T.S. Eliot

Nervously walking through the lunchroom,
I glance side to side for my middle school crush.
Spotting him quickly, my eyes move to zoom,
My frightened cheeks fidget and I start to blush.

I walk past the table of this cute boy,
Turning my head in the faintest of ways.
My feet slightly quicken as if to destroy,
My limited journey through this school maze.

My right foot slides backwards,
The left foot unstable,
My sandal flies toward,
My crush's lunch table.

Lying on the ground, unable to move,
I look up at the boys, who are laughing at me.
Pull myself up, reach into the groove,
Go under the table, I'm shocked to see.

The sandal is next to my crush's blue sneaker.
I quickly grab it and then run away.
My life couldn't possibly seem any bleaker.
Not a good start for my very first day.

I sit by my locker, frozen in grief,
With tears rolling down, I wish they would stop.
A girl walks by and I see with relief,
A long train of tissue stuck to her flip-flop.

I'm not the only one with a shoe mishap.
At least I'm not the only one who had to be
The only student caught in this embarrassing trap.
It happens to all, it's a guarantee.

~Anna Kendall

Spelling Bee Blues

My spelling is Wobbly.
It's good spelling but it Wobbles,
and the letters get in the wrong places.
~A.A. Milne

A s a kid, the words "spelling bee" churned a considerable amount of acid in my stomach. In fact, my history of spelling bee fiascoes grew so notorious, Daniel Webster turned in his grave every time I stood up and headed for the contestant line.

Most of the time, striking me out of the competition didn't take long at all. I rarely made it past the second round. Yet with all that free time it never occurred to me even once to bone up for the next match. Watching others spell words with ease, confidence, and above all else, correctness, consumed me. Worse than that, the teacher had a dome-shaped bell on her desk that she slapped with the palm of her hand to ring out the triumph of every classmate who spelled a word perfectly. The clang of that thing pierced my heart straight through. Oh, how I ached for the skill necessary to set that bell dinging for me.

One classic spelling bee disaster occurred in the sixth grade and involved a word most fourth graders can breeze through — cheese. I simply refused to believe that any one-syllable word contained three e's and practically right next to each other. How absurd! So there I stood, visualizing the challenge word, knees knocking, and fingers nervously twirling through the curls in my pigtails.

"Cheese" I said, stepping forward. "C-h-e-a..."

I figured the ripple of snickers spreading through the class meant things weren't going so well. Still, I forged ahead like an Olympic figure skater skidding across the ice, flat on my face headed straight for the judges.

"s-e, cheese."

"I'm sorry. That's not correct Annmarie. Please sit down."

The thin veil of sympathy on Miss Divine's face did little to disguise her disgust. Let's face it; I wasn't attempting to spell "pneumonia," or "ratatouille." A sixth grader plummeting to defeat on a first round word like "cheese" can fling a teacher into the disgust zone. Miss Divine proved no exception to that rule.

I dragged myself back to my desk, still smarting from the sting of Miss Divine's invitation to take a seat, and plunked down just in time to hear that smarty pants, Mark Meehan, throw those three e's into the cheese word in all the exact right places. He barely finished and don't you know that old bell was dinging again.

After the agonizing cheese incident, my phonetic confidence plunged to an all time low. The mere mention of a spelling bee triggered gastrointestinal disturbances in my belly strong enough to measure on the Richter scale.

As in most middle school mountains imagined from tiny molehills, I survived the spelling bee blues. Sad to say though, my spelling skills have not improved much.

A few years ago, I discovered my older sister Marie suffered a very similar spelling bee trauma in the very same classroom, with the very same teacher—just two years before it happened to me. Which, as far as I was concerned, explains a lot about the disgusted look on Miss Divine's face.

"Business" is the word that stumped my sister. Or as she spelled it: "b-i-z-n-e-s-s." It's such a comfort knowing that I'm not the only sibling in my family with tainted spelling chromosomes.

Every once in a while, I fantasize about writing to Miss Divine and telling her that my sister and I own a fabulously successful "C-H-E-A-S-E B-I-Z-N-E-S-S." I can see it now. As she reads the letter, she faints dead away, and her head lands right on the old dome-shaped bell, setting off one resounding clang for the phonetically challenged at last.

~Annmarie B. Tait

Teens Talk Middle School

Bully Payback

*Those who plot the destruction of others
often perish in the attempt.*

~Thomas Moore

28

Karma on the Middle School Bus

I am the owner of my actions, heir to my actions,
born of my actions, related through my actions,
and have my actions as my arbitrator.
Whatever I do, for good or for evil,
to that I will fall heir.
~Joan Oliver

The chaotic din of restless kids filled the yellow school bus. I leaned my head against the black plastic seat, feeling every bump as the driver jostled down the snow-filled streets of the sleepy hamlet of Jamesville. The squeaky brakes signaled each stop and even though I knew the bus carried fewer and fewer students, the noise level remained high. The girl with the biggest mouth sat directly behind me. She ran her freshly manicured nails through long strands of perfect blond hair that framed her flawless complexion. Classmates buzzed around her as if she were a queen bee. I tried to keep a safe distance so I wouldn't get stung. But on this day, she tested my limits.

I ignored the annoying kicks to the back of my seat. I wanted to scream at her, "Quit it!" I slowly sunk deeper into the hard seat and said a soft prayer begging God to help me remain calm. The more I prayed, the louder she became. I searched through my backpack trying to find a book to read, anything to distract me. I only had a math book and even though I didn't want that, I opened it to the chapter on fractions and pretended I cared about my homework. Her ridicule grew intense. I felt as if I were going to implode. On the inside I was screaming, "Shut up!" but this girl would never know because I remained aloof.

I thought about the snacks that awaited me at home: a mug of hot chocolate with marshmallows bobbing at the rim and a plate of warm chocolate chip cookies. I couldn't wait for my mother's arms to hold me. I looked out the window and realized I was still miles from home and I wanted to cry. "Please, God, keep me strong," I prayed under my breath, "and make Olivia shut up."

I played with my soft pink mittens and admired my bronze skin, a suntan I kept year round—a gift from my Romanian ethnicity. I felt blessed that Mom and Dad adopted me from a horrible orphanage. I decided Olivia was just an annoyance. I smiled at the strength God gave me, but it faded quickly.

"I'll take that," Olivia sneered as she snatched my fuzzy pink hat from my head.

"Please give it back," I asked in a timid voice. I sat sideways on the seat with my feet in the aisle so I could look her in the eye. "You don't even wear hats, Olivia. Give it back." Without a moment's hesitation, she lunged from her seat and stomped on my foot, the one with a bone tumor. I felt a surge of pain shoot up my leg. "Oww! Olivia, you hurt me!" I cried. She threw my hat in my face and got off the bus. I used it to wipe the tears that flooded my eyes so the other kids on the bus wouldn't see. I was almost home.

When the bus driver stopped in front of my house, I carefully walked down the aisle. Each step was as painful as the kick Olivia delivered. I struggled over the snowbank and up my long driveway. I was so happy to see my Mom that I burst into tears. After I told her what happened, she examined my foot to see if I needed another operation.

"I think you're going to be okay," she said through a long swaying hug. "We need to talk to Olivia's parents and the school principal."

"No," I pleaded. "It will only make her mad."

"It can't be avoided," Mom said, still holding me.

"Will she be punished?"

Mom thought for a moment. "It's all about Karma. What goes around comes around."

I didn't quite understand, but Mom said in time I would. My mother insisted she would take care of everything. Even though I trusted her, I dreaded going to school the next day. I had to face Olivia in the principal's office, where she gave me a half-hearted apology. When I thought about bullies, I didn't picture one with long blond hair, twinkling blue eyes and a superficial smile. Olivia was a bully in disguise. I distanced myself from her and managed to get through the rest of the school year without any repercussions from the bus incident. I sat directly behind the driver and kept a low profile. Olivia sat in the back seat and blabbed up a storm to anyone in earshot.

All kids love the last day of school because it represents the end of homework and the first day of summer vacation. It was the best for me because of the bus ride home. Olivia was being a bully as usual, making snide comments to unsuspecting kids. On this particular day, one fifth grade boy was bearing the brunt of her wrath. He was unusually small and his ashen face looked troubled.

"What are you looking at?" she bellowed.

"Nothing," he mumbled, looking terrified.

It seemed as if he wanted to say more, but when he opened his mouth to speak, he ended up vomiting all over Olivia and her taunting smile. She was covered head to toe in the stuff, and the bus broke out in a jubilant cheer, making the weary fifth grader a hero. I, of course, was his biggest fan. As I walked up the driveway to my house that afternoon, I wasn't singing my usual "No more teachers, no more books." Instead, another thought swirled around in my head: "What goes around comes around."

~Andrea Canale

29

El Panza de Burra (The Donkey Belly)

There's always going to be somebody who'll try to
take your dignity and self-esteem.
Just never let them take your voice.
~Eric, 7th Heaven

Being chubby in middle school is not what you want to be. The name-calling and the teasing are particularly perturbing and vicious and get in the way of concentrating on schoolwork. Add to that the fact that I had just migrated to the big city from a small village in the middle of the Mexican Sierra Madre and you have all the ingredients for conflict. True to form, as soon as I stepped into the classroom, the name-calling began: "panza de burra," they would call me, which means Donkey Belly. Not the prettiest of nicknames. One kid was particularly mean; the others were not so callous. Nonetheless, this one kid made my life miserable.

I would come home from school crying every day on account of the name-calling. After a month of a barrage of personal attacks from this one kid, my father, more frustrated than me, pulled me aside and gave me my first lesson on reverse psychology. He told — no — ordered me what to do. In fact, he was very specific in his instructions.

"As soon as you see this kid tomorrow morning," he said, "you must go up to him and call him panza de burra. However," he said, "you must show no anger or emotion. In fact, put a smile on your face and act as normal as possible."

I was incredulous! This was his solution to my insurmountable problem? This was totally out of character for me. To emphasize his point, my father also told me that if I didn't do this, I would suffer further consequences from him. That is probably what motivated me the most to follow his advice. Just to make sure that I got the idea, my father made me practice the routine with him several times until he was satisfied.

I could hardly sleep that night. How could I confront this bully? After breakfast, I painstakingly went to school and guess who was right there at the playground gate? The bully! Shaking all over but trying not to show it, I went up to him and before he could say anything, I said to him:

"How are you doing, panza de burra?" I caught him by surprise.

Mumbling, he said, "You are panza de burra."

I responded, "No! You are!"

This silly exchange went on for a few minutes. In the meantime, a group of kids gathered around us listening to the verbal exchange. They all thought it was funny that I was calling the other kid by that name. In fact, he wasn't so thin himself. Before I knew it, the rest of the kids were calling him "panza de burra." To this day, that kid, now a man, has not bugged me.

I learned a great lesson from my father. The rest of my middle school years were no smooth sail, but I was equipped with a wonderful survival tool to deal with name-calling.

~Conrado Gomez

The Eye Patch

When a resolute young fellow steps up to the great bully, the world,
and takes him boldly by the beard,
he is often surprised to find it comes off in his hand,
and that it was only tied on
to scare away the timid adventurers.
~Ralph Waldo Emerson

My stretchy black leggings that reached just past the knee were about two years past their prime by the time I entered junior high school, but I still wore them almost every day. To be honest, I had about four pairs of them, but I wore one pair all the time because they were my favorite.

Up until seventh grade, it didn't matter what I looked like. I had been in a close-knit elementary school where everyone cared about each other. I wasn't prepared for battle. For the most part I didn't care about the teasing anyway; my Mom had told me it would happen and that she was picked on too as a kid. But it was still annoying and distracting on good days and hurtful and alienating on most.

Mark Something-or-other (because by this time I've forgotten his last name), sat next to me in Social Studies class that year, and every day he had a comment for me like a quote-a-day calendar. Only instead of the quotes being soul-enhancing, they were mean and hurtful.

"Nice braces. I think you got some food stuck in them."

"Do you sleep in those pants too?"

"What's with your hair, do you think it looks nice like that or something?"

"Hey scar face."

Mark scrutinized everything about me with the precision of a surgeon, and after he would scan the room for laughs. There were always some.

So I was faced with a moral dilemma. Should I fight back? My Mom told me to treat people the way I wanted to be treated, and not to put others down to make myself feel better. So how come Mark's mom didn't tell him the same thing? What was wrong with her?

My best friend since kindergarten, Jackie, was one of the cool girls in school, so she'd speak up for me sometimes. But Jackie's alphabetically assigned seat was on the other side of the classroom, leaving me on my own with this one. Every day I'd slip into my seat just before the bell, so that class started immediately. I made sure never to turn to my left toward Mark. And every day, like a sitting duck, I—well—sat there, waiting for his barrage of put-downs. I wondered why the teacher didn't intervene. What was wrong with him? If I were a teacher, I'd say something.

Then one day there was silence. "Oh good," I thought. "Mark's out today." But when I turned to make sure, Mark was definitely not absent. When he turned towards me, I saw why he was so quiet. Mark had a giant black Captain Hook eye patch on his left eye.

Today was my lucky day. Forget treating others the way I wanted to be treated. Forget the teacher for not caring about me. Forget Jackie for having a last name that began with P and for P for being so far from D in the alphabet. Forget Mark, forget his mom, forget this class, forget the film projector, forget everything!

"Nice eye patch," I said with snort. "Who are you, "Captain Hook?"

"Shut up!" was his only response.

I finally got to him! He would think twice next time he considered making fun of Shana Donohue!

Things were looking up for the rest of that day, and I held my head high on the walk back from school. My mom clearly didn't know what she was talking about. I felt great!

It was early spring when this happened, and in New England this means there's a layer of sand covering every concrete or asphalt surface. My house was probably five stone throws from the school, by a large parking lot that Jackie and I would walk through to go home. It was windy that day and the parking lot had been well sanded that winter.

As I recapped the events that happened on my side of the classroom, the wind picked up, blowing sand all around us. This wasn't so unusual since it was spring, but this day some sand blew right in my eye.

"Ouch, my eye!" I said as I rubbed it. "I think some sand got in." I rubbed it all the way home. Jackie and I parted ways when we got to my house and I went inside. "Mom, some sand got in my eye and it hurts really badly."

I rubbed my eye some more, thinking it would get better. "Mom, it hurts really badly!"

"Stop rubbing it!" she said after trying eye drops and becoming noticeably nervous about my eyesight.

But by then I had rubbed it too much. Eye drops weren't going to cut it. My mom led me to the car and drove me to the hospital. It was determined that I had scratched my cornea, and I was fitted with a large piece of gauze secured with long strips of surgical tape that spanned the entire left side of my face.

My mom mercifully didn't make me go to school the next day, after I explained to her that Mark would think I copied him. Luckily, corneas only take 24 hours to heal.

Life's always been one to teach me swift, hard lessons, and if I look back on how I came to believe the things I believe about life, I almost always come back to Mark What's-his-name and his eye patch. Without realizing it, he taught me that what goes around really does come back around, and now I keep an eye out—no pun intended—for bullies. But I never sink to their level.

~Shana Donohue

Life Lessons

Forgiveness is a funny thing.
It warms the heart and cools the sting.
~William Arthur Ward

Toward the end of the school year, a student library aide tried to hook up a DVD player in my seventh grade social studies class. From the start, he impressed me with his helpful and positive can-do attitude. Though he worked diligently to set up the system, after fifteen minutes, he saw that the brackets wouldn't allow the cord to slip into the socket. "You've worked so hard," I encouraged. "The library is blessed to have you helping them; I'm so impressed with you. What is your name?"

He beamed with joy at the compliment. "Kevin. Kevin Smith." Immediately my expression changed to one of shock and disbelief! After a long pause, he whispered, "Are you Trent's mom?"

"Yes. Yes I am."

Fear and embarrassment distorted his face. "Oh, please forgive me."

At once, my mind replayed the last six months of my son, Trent's, eighth grade year at the local public school. Since he'd attended a Christian school where I'd taught since kindergarten, changing to a public one was a new experience for both of us. I decided I'd try to get a job there, too, because I wanted to teach where Trent attended. A couple of months before, Trent had decided to enroll in a video production class offered at his new school.

To my relief, the public school maintained strict discipline; they held students to high standards. We both fit right in and enjoyed our year. Then around springtime, Trent changed. He no longer wanted to go to school. He begged to change back to our private one. Every morning I battled, threatened, and cajoled him. We'd arrive at school with him whining, "I just can't do it mom. I just can't go to school. Don't make me. Don't you understand, I just can't do it?" However, he refused to share his reasons for making such a scene before school. Many days as I prepared to face my 170 students, I thought I'd pass out from the exhaustion of the morning.

Then Trent started hanging out in my classroom and wouldn't go out to lunch with his friends. His sweatshirt hood pulled tight on his head made his melancholy look even scarier. His grades spiraled down, and he lost the special connection to his old school buddy. Unfortunately, that friend dropped Trent for another friend—it crushed him. My husband and I didn't know what to do, but we knew we needed some help.

Over the next month, we met with Trent's P.E. teacher, his youth pastor, and a church counselor. During the first session with the therapist, Trent broke down crying about a bully from school who wouldn't leave him alone. To our shock, Trent shared that he'd been kicked, thrown down, and called filthy names. The session ended with Trent feeling better equipped to handle the bully at school. If that didn't work, my husband and I were prepared to inform the principal about the situation.

Somewhat skeptical, we agreed to give Trent some time to handle the problem. It didn't take long because the bully struck the next day. His P.E. teacher saw the incident and came down hard on him, but the next day, the bully struck again in the same class. The savvy teacher said, "We're done," and she sent the offender to the principal, who suspended the student.

We all breathed a long sigh of relief. The drama, however, continued. The bully became even more belligerent to Trent. The principal took harsher action with the punishment, and finally, the bullying stopped. As the offender suffered the consequences of his actions,

Trent gradually returned to his old self. The hood came down, the scowl left, and he started hanging out with his friends again.

Before I met Kevin that day in my classroom, I envisioned grabbing him by the shirt and saying, "If you touch my son again, watch out, because I'm going to put on my boxing gloves!" The Mama Bear in me itched to take action. But when I realized that the helpful young man before me was the bully, my heart hurt for Kevin. For him to lash out so brutally, he must have his own dark struggles. He seemed to be just another student trying to find his way through the labyrinth of middle school.

"Please forgive what I did to Trent." With pain in his eyes, Kevin stared at me. "I don't know what got into me. I'm not like that! I think I just didn't have enough sleep. I acted in a way that just wasn't me. I don't know what happened. I'm so sorry."

"Kevin, we all make mistakes." I comforted him and gently touched his shoulder. "Trent and I forgive you. We know you never wanted to act like that. Now, make a change. Go down the right path and never do that again. I know you can do it."

He flashed me a grateful smile. "Thank you, Mrs. Ryan"

"No, thank you, Kevin. I'm so glad we've had the chance to meet."

When I saw Trent later that day, he told me, "Mom, when I saw Kevin in P.E., he said you were chill."

Graduation from the eighth grade is in six days and Trent and Kevin's middle school days will be a memory. I'm proud of Trent, who so willingly forgave his abuser, but wouldn't allow it to continue. He even picked Kevin to be on his P.E. team. I'm also proud of Kevin. It takes a mighty man to admit when you're wrong. Let's hope neither one of these middle school students will forget these life lessons. I know I never will.

~Suzy Ryan

The Smile that Beat the Bully

Be excellent to each other.
~ Bill and Ted's Excellent Adventure

ave you ever had a bully who scared the skin off you? The one bully who you have nightmares about? It's the face you see when you get up in the morning with your stomach all tied in knots. Rosalie Bangeter was that for me — she was a bully in every sense of the word, and I was terrified of her. She was one of the meanest girls I'd ever met, and I have a sneaking suspicion that I was not the only person in the seventh grade who lived in mortal fear of her. I'll never forget the day I saw her pulverize another student in the cafeteria. As if pounding the girl wasn't bad enough, she topped it off by dunking her head in a half-eaten tray of meatloaf and mashed potatoes.

To this day, I don't know why Rosalie hated me so much. The fact that I merely existed and had the nerve to breathe in and out seemed to tick Rosalie off, and she never missed an opportunity to threaten or ridicule me. I would hear her jeering remarks when I walked out to catch the bus home. I could feel the heat of her glare when I cowered in my seat in the cafeteria and avoided looking anywhere near her direction. I would've walked the length of two football fields to avoid coming in contact with Rosalie Bangeter if I could have, but unfortunately there just wasn't enough time to do that and still get to my fifth period class before the bell rang.

So I had to face the reality that, for two or three excruciating seconds every day, I had to walk past Rosalie Bangeter in the hall. I tried hanging out in my fourth period class a few extra seconds and walking a little slower to my locker in the hope that Rosalie would have already gone to class, but that never worked. I would still pass her. Of course, I didn't dare make eye contact with her, but I caught sight of her sneer in my peripheral vision while I scampered past. I knew it would only be a matter of time before she lashed out at me.

I was one of those quiet, timid seventh graders who talked up a blue streak at home but wouldn't say two words at school. I had a couple of close friends who were just as shy as I was, and we usually huddled together and tried to stay out of everyone's way. Deep down, I was envious of those outgoing, cheerleader girls who would be the first ones to raise their hands to do a math problem on the chalkboard. I felt like life was passing me by and that if I disappeared one day, no one at school would even notice or care.

My family lived in a small town of about three thousand people, and it seemed as if my dad knew every single one of them. What was even more astonishing was that everyone seemed to know him. One day, I asked my mom how this was possible. She thought about this a minute and then said, "Well, Jenn, your dad never lets anyone stay a stranger. He talks to everyone he sees, and then he gives them that big smile of his. I guess it's contagious because people just love him."

I wanted to be more like my dad. I wanted to get to know people and to somehow leave my mark on the world. But more than anything, I was tired of being that girl who cowered in a corner and got picked on.

I thought about what my mom had said. I knew I had to take action, but how? There was no way I could just go to school one day and start talking to everybody. Forget for a moment that they would have thought I was a raving lunatic—I knew that, as good as my intentions were, I would never be able to force the words out of my mouth. So, I caught hold of the phrase where she talked about his smile. I could smile. I mean, everyone could do that, right? I decided to try it out, but I knew that there was only one way to go to the heart of my fears. I would take my experiment straight to the biggest bully of all—Rosalie Bangeter.

I don't think I heard a single word my math teacher said that day in fourth period because I was too busy thinking about what I was about to do. Finally, the bell rang. I gathered my books and headed to my locker. My heart was pounding in my chest, and my hands were so sweaty I was afraid I'd drop my books. Somehow, I managed to shove my math book in the locker and pull out my English book. I ran my tongue over my teeth that felt dryer than the Mojave Desert. Then I did a practice smile that I was sure looked more like a grimace. I took a deep breath and willed my feet to keep moving forward.

I saw her in the distance coming toward me, looking as mean as ever. For the first time in my life, I made eye contact with her, and then I did it! I actually managed to squeak out a smile through my chattering teeth. Rosalie looked downright shocked, and then she scowled. I hurried past, sure that she was going to turn around and pounce on me. I don't think I took another breath until I made it to my next class and collapsed in the chair.

The next day, I tried again. This time, my teeth weren't chattering quite so badly. Rosalie was no longer surprised, but her snarl remained. This went on for several days, until one day, she didn't glower. I hurried past her. Maybe she was in too big of a hurry today, I thought.

The next day, she didn't glower at me either. In fact, she gave me a little half-smile for my effort. Over the next few weeks, Rosalie actually started smiling back. And then came that memorable day when I got the nerve to nod and say hi. I couldn't believe it! She said hi back! At the end of the year, Rosalie looked me up and asked me to sign her yearbook.

In the years that followed, I broke out of my shell one small chip at a time. I made many new friends and became an active participant in my classes. Looking back now, I can trace it all to that fateful day when I had the courage to smile in the face of the bully. The next time you're in a jam, give it a try—it's amazing how far a smile can go.

~Jennifer Youngblood

The Courage to Roar

The difference between school and life? In school, you're taught a lesson and then given a test. In life, you're given a test that teaches you a lesson.
~Tom Bodett

T he details of our dreams usually vanish quickly upon awakening. But, when I was twelve years old, I had a vivid dream that branded itself in my memory forever.

In it, a tiger sunk his razor-sharp teeth into my ear. I lay there paralyzed with fear, frozen in pain. All I could do was listen to my heart boom loudly in my chest. My eyes flew open, shattering the dream, but I was certain there was a tiger under my bed. I needed proof that the big cat was really gone, so I slowly lifted the bed skirt and peered under the bed. No sign of a tiger, only an old pair of Keds tennis shoes, big, fuzzy slippers with puppy dog heads, three *Teen* magazines, and a few dust bunnies.

Mom called from the kitchen, "Helen, are you awake? Your breakfast is almost ready."

"Yes, Mom. I'll be right there."

I got dressed in front of the full-length mirror. It proved to me everyday that my butt was too big, my skin was too oily and my curly red hair defied taming. My eyes were the only good feature I had going for me. They were almond-shaped, caramel-colored with tiny, golden specks that reflected the color of my curvy lashes. When I looked closer into the mirror, I found a huge, cherry-red zit sitting on the very tip of my nose. I wanted to jump back into bed and pull the covers over my head, but I knew that Mom would still make me go to school.

I slumped down the stairs dragging my backpack, and when I walked into the kitchen, my nine-year-old brother took one look at me and said, "Hey, look! It's Rudolph the Red-Nosed Reindeer."

I shot him an angry glance. "Shut up, you little dork. Mom, can we trade Todd in for a dog or a cat, or even a gerbil?"

"No, we can't," she said. "He's your brother, so you're stuck with him. Todd, apologize to Helen."

Todd gave a heavy sigh. "Okay, I'm sorry that you look like Rudolph the Red-Nosed Reindeer."

I raised my fist in Todd's direction and said, "You're gonna look like vomit soup."

Mom extended her arm like a cop stopping traffic. "That's enough from both of you. That blemish doesn't look so bad, Helen. I'll put some make-up on it right after breakfast."

I gulped my breakfast, brushed my teeth and waited for Mom to work her magic on the red balloon that sprouted from the tip of my nose. "This should do the trick," Mom said, as she opened a bottle of cover-up and dabbed some on my nose. Todd studied my face for a moment and said, "Anyone up for mountain climbing?" I opened my mouth to protest just as Mom spotted the school bus coming down the street. She quickly coaxed us out the door saying, "Don't worry, it'll be fine."

We boarded the bus and I plopped myself down on a seat near the back. I turned my face to the window, closed my eyes and thought how great it would be to rule my own world. There would be no school, no parents to tell kids what to do, no brothers, and no more pimples.

My thoughts drifted, the air became warm and heavy and my eyelids closed. My earlier dream flowed back into my thoughts, and I found myself in a jungle of tall trees.

As I picked my way through the tall grass, I had a feeling that I was not alone. I heard a growling, rumbling noise and turned to find an enormous tiger, posed in a valiant stance, gazing at me.

The sunlight filtered through the trees and flickered over his majestic body. Prominent black stripes were perfectly painted over his ivory-white to reddish-orange fur. His nostrils flared in anger at my impudence in invading his habitat. He let out a mighty roar, and I started to run.

I knew that I couldn't outrun the tiger, so I grabbed onto a golden-colored vine hanging from a tree and climbed. When I looked down in my dream, the tiger was clawing his way up the tree trunk. I could think of nothing else to do, so I opened my mouth and roared with a thunderous clap that echoed through the air. At the sound of my roar, the tiger began to shrink. I gave one last powerful blast, and the tiger shrunk down to the size of a kitten. I now felt confident enough to come down from the tree, so I swung down to where the kitten sat. I felt powerful and free.

I woke up, hearing laughter in the distance that became so loud it disturbed my thoughts. I squirmed in my seat and remembered that I was on the bus, not in a jungle.

Kids were laughing as two boys tossed Todd's lunch bag back and forth across the aisle. Todd was getting more upset with each toss. After a couple more throws, I got up and stood in front of the boy who just caught the pass.

"Hand it over," I said, giving him my best steely-eyed glare.

"Oh yeah?" he said. "Whaddaya gonna do if I don't?"

"I'll go straight to the principal and rat you out as a bully. I have lots of eyewitnesses here to support my story. You'll probably get detention or worse."

He paused for a moment, gave me a silly grin, and pitched me the lunch bag. "Take it. We were done anyway."

The bus pulled up to the school, the doors opened, and kids started piling out. Todd remained in his seat with a soulful look on his face. I walked over to him, handed him his lunch and said, "Don't worry about it, Todd. Those guys are jerks. Come on; walk with me up to the school."

We walked together quietly for a while and then Todd said, "Hey, Helen? Did you know that you look really pretty today?"

"Sure, punk. I'm positively glowing—especially around my nose." I gave Todd a playful push, and we both laughed.

~Helen Stein

Teens Talk Middle School

Finding Your Passion

Only passions, great passions can elevate the soul to great things.

~Denis Diderot

Let There Be Light

You gain strength, courage, and confidence
by every experience in which you really stop to look fear in the face.
You must do the thing which you think you cannot do.
~Eleanor Roosevelt

My heart was beating so hard in my chest I thought everyone around me could hear it. I was gulping in air as fast as my lungs would let me, and I could feel a cool shiver run down my back. I was nervous. Really nervous.

People were filing into the old, white church getting ready for the annual Christmas Pageant. Parents, grandparents, brothers, sisters, friends, teachers, and other students shuffled in from the cold and settled themselves in the wooden pews. The huge space was alive with noise as the floors and seats creaked and moaned with every movement, and the growing crowd murmured unintelligibly to one another.

From the second floor balcony, I saw my mom and dad looking around for me. When my mom spotted me, she waved enthusiastically and smiled. My dad gave me the thumbs up.

Around me, my classmates were laughing, making jokes, and squirming restlessly in their seats. Christmas break started the next day, and everyone was busy talking about their plans for the holiday and what they wanted for Christmas. While they chatted around me, I quietly sat in my chair and tried not to panic.

I had agreed to read at the pageant. No—not only read, but

read a poem of my own composition. It seemed like a good idea at the time, yet as I waited for everything to start I couldn't remember why I had said yes.

I had loved poetry from the moment I read "The Road Not Taken" by Robert Frost in my fifth grade English class. I was fascinated by the way people could convey any feeling through poems, and was endlessly intrigued by the different styles and presentations a poem could use. My first poem, "Bumpkin Isle," was published in the school writing journal at the end of the year and from that day on, I was known to my friends and teachers as the class poet.

Just before Thanksgiving, the vice principal had called me into his office.

"Nacie, I want this year's pageant to be extra special. Could you write something for it? I would love to have an original composition presented during the event."

"Sure," I said with a smile, my dreams of being a famous poet swelling and swirling in my mind. I left his office with the sounds of the cheering crowd, the roar of approval, and the adoring fans loud in my ears. This was going to be awesome.

For weeks, I worked on my poem, carefully crafting the structure, sound, and voice. I reread my Emily Dickinson and William Wordsworth for inspiration. I practiced reciting it aloud. I sent a copy to my friend Becky for her to edit, and I revised, revised, revised. By December 17th, the day of the pageant, I was ready.

Well, I was ready until I looked around and realized how many people were there. And how big the hall was. And how little I felt. How could I present a piece of my poetry to 400 people? Who was I kidding? I was just a seventh grader for gosh sakes! No one would take my work seriously! I sat in my hard wooden chair and tried to make myself disappear. Maybe they would forget I was supposed to read.

"Hey Nacie, I saw your name in the program. Good luck!" My little brother's voice rose above the din as he took his seat a few rows down with his class. I nodded feebly and wrapped my hands around my stomach, trying to keep the butterflies at bay. Then the lights dimmed, the crowd quieted, and the principal took the stage to introduce the show. It was starting.

I was presenting toward the end of the program, and because of that had to sit through an hour of absolute anxious misery. It wasn't until the girls from the fourth grade class were singing "Silent Night" that my teacher brought me downstairs next to the stage. My mind was blank, my eyes were wide, and my mouth went totally dry. I kept hoping they would never finish the song—we could make up a few extra verses to "Silent Night" on the spot, couldn't we?

Then suddenly, I was on stage with the bright white lights blinding my view of the audience and the feeling that my throat was closing up. I leaned in to the microphone and tried to speak. The only thing that squeaked out was a whispery "eek" noise. I looked down, cleared my throat, and gripped the edges of the podium. There was no turning back now.

I looked up and out into that bright, breathing space and tried out my voice again as I read the title: "Let There Be Light." My voice boomed from the speakers loudly and sounded much more confident than I felt.

The room was silent as I began my piece, and I tried to focus on the words and forget the people, even though the lights made the stage hot and my hands and knees were shaking. I didn't dare look toward the part of the room where my parents were sitting—I was too nervous. My voice echoed in the old, wooden room and my mind went into auto-drive. The words somehow came out in the right order, the lines flowed together appropriately, and I even remembered which words to emphasize. I finally came to the last line of the poem and breathed a deep sigh of relief. "And God saw that the light was good." It was over.

The room was dead silent for what felt like an eternity. Was this a dream? Was there anyone in here? I swallowed hard. Maybe no one liked it. I felt like I was going to faint.

Then out of the silence there was clapping, cheering, and smiling. I dared to find my family in the sea of faces, and found my mother wiping away tears and my father beaming. I had done it. I had shared a piece of my poetry with the world, and now that it was over I felt great. With a giddy, light-headed feeling and a silly smile I bowed slightly and walked off stage.

"Great job!" "That was awesome!" "I loved it!"

"Thank you," I said to each person who greeted me as I staggered back to my seat, relief and gratitude spreading warmly through my body.

Thank you for listening. Thank you for not laughing. Thank you for supporting me. Thank you for making my first poetry reading a memorable and inspiring one. Thank you for believing in me. Thank you for helping me take the first step toward achieving my dream.

Thank you. Thank you. Thank you.

~Nacie Carson

35

The Play

Follow your dreams and pursue them with courage.
~Unknown

According to Shakespeare, "the play's the thing," or something like that. For me, plays were definitely "the thing." Well, that—and Anthony Donelli.

I sat center stage, two rows from the front of the class between Sally McBride on my left, who was telling a story about her new dog, and Al Cooper on my right, who was tapping the eraser end of his pencil.

Sally's puppy story and Al's drum solo melted into background noise as I stared straight ahead at the back of Anthony Donelli's rugby-shirted frame. Anthony—Tony to his friends—was dark-haired and blue-eyed gorgeous. If he smiled at me or borrowed one of my pencils, even a bad math test couldn't darken my day.

"Ladies and gentlemen," Mr. Tobias began, interrupting my study of Tony's perfect ears. "As you know, each class produces a play once a year for presentation to the PTA and student body.... It's show time, folks!"

Groans and hums of excitement rippled the air around me as my heart pounded against my ribcage.

"I've chosen an old favorite," Mr. Tobias said.

I felt myself leaning forward trying to hear, my nose only an inch from Tony's coal-black locks.

"We will be performing *The Reluctant Princess*, a story of high adventure and challenge in days of yore." Yore? The man enjoyed making us expand our vocabulary.

"In this adaptation, there are fourteen speaking parts. Remember, there are no small parts. For those who don't want to be a member of the cast, there are make-up and stage crew positions." Mr. Tobias sat on the edge of his desk getting comfortable while we sweated about our futures.

"I'll call out the part and those interested in a particular role please raise your hand."

Pick me! I wanted to scream

"We'll read through the play later this afternoon, but for now let's get started."

Yes! My hand was ready to go.

"Princess Lucy," he said.

Hands shot into the air like rockets, mine among them. I prayed and strained, willing Mr. Tobias to look my way. Me! Pick me!

And then he said, "Janice Grice."

What was the man thinking? No, no, no! Not snaky Janice. Janice, the girl who decided halfway through my pajama party to call her mother and leave, along with three of my former best friends because she didn't like the pizza we ordered. She had said our house smelled. Janice, the girl who invited almost every girl to her own pajama party three weeks later but didn't invite me. Janice, who could have had any boy at school groveling with the twitch of her pinky, but set her sights on my Tony. That Janice. I was still in shock when the next role was announced, but I raised my hand anyway.

"Queen Gladys." Mr. Tobias's eyes again landed far from my out-stretched hand, and did the same until he got to the Lady-in-Waiting. "How about you, Rose?"

Grateful to finally hear my name, I nodded. There are no small parts. A heartbeat later, Tony got the part of Prince Albert. There was probably a last kiss in the final scene, and Janice would plant it on Tony. I wanted to cry.

We went into rehearsals that week and the next, with our moms supplying costumes made from long, wide pieces of cloth and painted cardboard with glued-on glitter.

Janice looked the part of the princess during our costume fitting, in a long white dress and red robe, her blond hair waving over her shoulders. A glittering rhinestone crown sat on her head. Tony was fit with a plastic sword, boots, turtleneck sweater, and shorts. He was covered in gold fabric and wore a wide belt. I wore my mother's old blue dress with a silver belt and a pointy cardboard cone-hat.

Two weeks later, we were ready for the PTA performance. I moved Janice's cape around the stage and said my line, "The king awaits your presence in the great hall, my lady."

The rest of the play, whether on stage or off, I mouthed each part. I may not have engaged my brain in long division, but I could store a lot of things if I wanted. In this case, I had memorized the entire play.

I wanted to shove Janice when Tony delivered the fateful kiss at the end, but I settled for a view of the smiling face of my father in the audience. Show number one was over. Two more shows to go.

That was Friday night. Monday and Tuesday we were doing shows at two different assemblies. I came into school on Monday morning, ready to do my job and give the role of Lady-in-Waiting a loud delivery and a deep bow.

Monday morning started with the usual rummaging around in our desks, laughing, and scratching of chairs across the wooden floor. I looked around, wondering when Janice would head Tony's way, but I couldn't spot her anywhere. I got up for a better look. Still—no Janice. No Janice!

Leaning over a long table to touch up a piece of scratched cardboard scenery, Mr. Tobias hadn't noticed anything.

"Janice isn't here today, Mr. Tobias, can I have her part?" I machine-gunned out the words hoping to say them before he picked someone else for the job.

He raised his head slowly. He had a crease between his graying eyebrows and sagging lines around his mouth. "What? Janice isn't here?" With a look of doubt and a lot of dread, he scanned the room for the absent Janice.

"She's not here?"

"Nope. Can I have the part?" I restrained myself from adding, "please, please, please!"

"I better check with the office and see if her parents have called in." He wasn't listening to me!

"Can I have her part!?" If I said it any louder, he'd tell me to pipe down. "I know her lines. I know everybody's lines."

He finally looked at me; really looked. An hour later I was trying on Janice's dress, robe and crown. They fit.

When Tony planted the final kiss that afternoon on my puckered lips, I was ready. The kiss was a little disappointing, but I liked being able to hold his hand. Janice was laid up for two weeks with chicken pox and missed having her picture taken for the Trenton Times. As for me, I still have that picture from the newspaper and the smile on my face says it all: Learn your lines and follow your heart.

~R. P. Houghton

36

Happiness Is a Gorilla Suit

Nobody can make you feel inferior without your consent.
~Eleanor Roosevelt

There is nothing—nothing—more awkward than middle school. Not blowing soda out your nose, not running smack into something (which, unfortunately, always seems to happen in middle school), not even talking to your crush while you have a huge zit on your forehead, although that is one hundred percent guaranteed in middle school.

When I was in middle school, I was so easily humiliated. With every fart, burp, bad hair day, bad skin day, or awful fashion mistake, I blushed redder and redder. In the seventh grade, I was a certified geek following my passion for film. There was an afternoon video production class that I loved. On a scorching May day, I finally thought I'd found some semblance of popularity.

I was sitting at a cluster of desks with three eighth grade guys. This was major. Even though, in hindsight, I knew they were all dweebs, I was still trying to impress them.

On this one day, I rolled up the sleeves of my cute sweater without even thinking about it. The classroom was getting hot and I was starting to sweat—very unimpressive. To my horror, Val, one of the eighth graders, recoiled at the sight of my arm.

"Ew, gross!" he shrieked, loud enough for the entire class to hear.

Had I sprung warts? I looked down at my arms in search of the problem. They were still just my dumb old arms.

"What?" I asked, panic rising in my voice.

"Your arms!"

"What about them?"

"Not even my arms are that hairy!" Val said.

The whole classroom craned their necks to see and even the teacher edged closer for a peek. I yanked my sleeves down but it was too late. The rest of the eighth graders in my cluster were laughing. That sweat I was trying to avoid? It was definitely rushing down my back like Niagara Falls.

Now, of course, when I look back I think, "C'mon Val. Really?" I let myself be bullied by a guy named Val! But back then, it was awful. And to add insult to my injury, my arms were never even that hairy. I wasn't packing a werewolf under my sweater or anything. But there was nothing grosser, or so I thought, than being a hairy girl. To my seventh grade mind, this was a crisis fit for the Pentagon.

I ran home in tears and ripped apart the strange, smelly drawer in our bathroom where my mom kept all sorts of weird products like hair remover creams and tubs of wax. Before she came home from work, I had painfully, odiously destroyed half of my arm hair, screaming as I ripped it out and holding my nose while the awful depilatory creams did their business.

Then I spied my mom's pink disposable razor. That would fix it, I thought. Three minutes of shaving later, my arms were baby smooth and hair free. I wore a tank top to school the next day. Val didn't say a word. To my horrible disgust, the hair grew back with a vengeance — dark and coarse. So I had to shave my arms again in two days. Then again and again.

I kept shaving my arms (in fact, at twenty-four years old I still do out of habit) but it was the next year, in eighth grade, when I learned that I shouldn't care so much what other people think of me.

Ironically, the thing that helped me finally figure it out was big, black, and completely covered in hair: a gorilla suit.

After Val bruised my self-esteem in video production class, I turned my eyes to the stage. I wanted to be in the drama club more than anything because my friend had spent all summer talking about the fall play. Unfortunately, I had missed auditions and the whole show had been cast already.

On the first day of eighth grade, I woke up early and hustled to school to beg Mr. Crabb, the drama teacher, for a part. They were doing a shipwreck adventure on a deserted island. He looked me up and down.

"Can you lift a person?"

I was tall but not that strong. "Um, sure, I guess. Why?"

"We've got one part open, but I was looking for a guy to cast." Great. I didn't have the arm hair anymore but someone thought I was manly anyway. Still, I wanted the part so badly. I knew theatre was my thing. "Well, I can try. What is it?"

He nodded his head at a rack of costumes. "It's on the last hanger."

I walked over with my heart hammering. I'd get a part. Everyone would see my shining face on stage. Or not. When I reached the end of the rack, I spied a hideous black gorilla suit, complete with gorilla mask. "A gorilla?"

"If you don't want it, that's fine," Mr. Crabb replied.

"No." I stuck my chin out and screwed my lips into a tight smile. "I'll take it."

I soon learned that it's lonely onstage inside a gorilla suit. Still, when we did the play for the whole school, I was so excited that I ripped my gorilla head off as soon as we were done and dashed out into the halls to meet my friends. They were laughing and joking but the rest of the school filing out of the auditorium was laughing and pointing.

"So YOU were the gorilla!"

"Duuude, it was a chick!"

"Gross!"

"Eeeeew!"

Standing there, hairy all over, I thought about Val and my arm hair. Then something clicked. Instead of running back to the dressing room, I smiled and waved. Theatre had finally given me a home and a place I could be myself. Even though I had to do it behind a gorilla mask, I had asked for a part and gotten one. This was just my first show. For the first time in all of middle school, even though I was wearing a gorilla suit, I had nothing to be ashamed of.

By my last show of the year, I was the leading villainess. I got to shoot a cap gun to close the first act of the show. As my gun went off center stage and the curtain fell, I heard kids from school clapping and laughing in the crowd.

"That was so cool!"

"Awesome!"

"That rocked!"

Awkward things like arm hair and gorilla suits happen in middle school. What I did with them, though, was completely up to me. If I can work a gorilla suit in my favor, nothing is impossible.

~Mary Kolesnikova

A Cheerleader for Life

All of us are stars and deserve the right to twinkle.
~Marilyn Monroe

'd practiced hard all summer, honing my skills. I did high kicks, straight moves and even smiled through a cartwheel. I had reached a goal I'd dreamed of since I was in grammar school. I'd been chosen to be a cheerleader! Me! I could not have asked for more; my prayer was answered. I knew it was going to be a great year as I planned on cheering my heart out for my junior high school.

Cheerleading tryouts had been difficult. Even though I had the moves and rhythm down, I doubted I would be picked. Surely they would choose the gorgeous girls rather than the girl-next-door type. Popularity had to be a prerequisite, I concluded. Although I was an honor student and well liked, I was not part of the "in crowd."

On the day the selections were made, I waited anxiously as the Cheer Director counted the votes. When my name was among the seven announced winners, I couldn't believe my ears!

Some of my friends had tried out as well, but there was no jealousy when I won the position. My attitude was one of gratefulness and humility. I could cheer and still be a really good friend.

The only drawback came in the form of a small, athletic woman more than twice my age. Her name was Miss Abbot and she was the cheerleading coach as well as P.E. teacher. Although she was a pretty thing, she had a pointed nose that would turn ruby red when she was angry. Her eyes could pierce through you like a dagger. I decided I never ever wanted to cross her.

Nothing I did that summer even won me a "Good job, Ginger," from Miss Abbot. A smile from her was a rarity. Until then, my teachers had given me praise for my efforts in keeping a straight-A average, so I treated cheerleading just like I did my studies. I hoped that, in time, I would win the coach's approval.

Cheer Camp was enlightening and I quickly bonded with the other girls. Shopping for our uniforms, taking photos, and practicing daily left little time for other activities. The school year began with a heavy schedule. At the end of each day I was pooped, yet no one, including Miss Abbot, knew what I had to contend with at home.

Diagnosed with congestive heart failure, my Mom had been sick since I was thirteen. I hated to see her suffer. My Dad was a good father, but he was an alcoholic. I rarely brought anyone home for fear of embarrassment.

It felt like I was living a double life between home and school. I worried daily about my mother's condition while I pretended everything was fine. Mom actually made it to one of our football games that year to watch me cheer. She never came again, though, as her health steadily declined.

Soon, the insecurity of my world began to show in my cheerleading. I mastered the routines, but Miss Abbot began picking on me anyway. "Ginger, what kind of cheerleader can you be if you stick your tongue out to the side like that?" She criticized. I guess I hadn't noticed my strange tongue habit. She intimidated me with those critical daggers. Her pointed nose flaring open and closed, like a bull preparing to charge its target, definitely clued me in on her disappointment. Nevertheless, the more I tried to tame my tongue, the more insecure I became.

Miss Abbot never asked me about my family or anything personal, for that matter. She could not see that I was struggling to find my bearings at a very tumultuous time in my life. She apparently had no clue as to how her words might affect a young girl's self-esteem. Miss Abbot was unaware that my Mom was dying. My performance was all that mattered to her. The cheer squad was serious business to her, for sure.

One day at practice, I was shot with another one of her lethal looks. On this occasion, Miss Abbot stopped our routine, and singled me out in front of the girls. Pointing her finger at me, she yelled, "You're still doing that thing with your tongue, Ginger! You will never be successful in cheerleading, or anything else for that matter, with your tongue sticking out of the side of your mouth. It looks stupid!"

At that point, you could hear a blade of grass grow on that field, and I felt my face turning as red as her nose. Tears welled up in my eyes, but I gulped back my emotion and agreed quickly with a "Yes Ma'am."

She was right. I'm sure it looked stupid, but now I felt stupid. From that moment on, I concentrated harder on keeping my tongue in my mouth as I led the cheers for the crowd.

Eventually the annoying habit disappeared, but the hurtful comments lingered.

In between graduating from junior high and starting high school, I lost some of the confidence I had gained. I decided not to try out for any extracurricular activities.

A year later, I got the dreaded call at school that there was a family emergency. I lost my Mom that April. She was my best friend. Three years later, my Dad passed away.

After that, I made some wrong choices in life, which nearly caused Miss Abbot's words to be true. Fortunately for me, God intervened, and He became the anchor I hung onto for dear life.

I knew that one day He would make sense of it all, and He did. Four years after graduation, I married my high school sweetheart, and was blessed with three wonderful children who I have cheered on each day of their lives.

At a trophy ceremony for my son's Little League team, I was awarded "Best Team Mom and Cheerleader ever." My husband and my kids smiled proudly at me. We joked about the award, but my success in life was evident in the faces of my family and the friends who filled my world with "good cheer." The love and approval that was mutually invested came back to me day after day. It sure didn't take a performance to see that. I could not have asked for more.

Through the years, I've thought about those hurtful words spoken to me at the impressionable age of fourteen, and how desperately I wanted Miss Abbot's approval. An utterance by someone in authority can often make a difference in how we view ourselves. It's a shame that she didn't really know how to "cheer."

Now, there's probably a lesson to be learned here, but in this case, I'd say it was more for the teacher than for the student. As for me, I can assure you that I have successfully become—with tongue in cheek—a "cheerleader for life!"

~Ginger Boda

Sliding Along the Halls of Middle School

> *As you go the way of life, you will see a great chasm.*
> *Jump.*
> *It is not as wide as you think.*
> ~Native American Initiation Rite

The buzz of the bell interrupted my daydreaming. I hastily gathered my books and shoved them into my backpack. No time for being neat. My survival depended on being invisible.

I could imagine the taunts: "Hey, there she is! Ugly Renee. Let's follow her home." It had happened before—a torturous stroll complete with cruel taunts and a few rocks thrown for the "fright" factor. Visibility was dangerous. Sliding along the wall of the hallway, I was able to avoid the pushing, laughing crowd of kids who used the breaks to socialize and sometimes tease geeks like me. I did not understand their world and they had no interest in understanding mine. That was the essence of my middle school existence—stay out of everyone's way until I could run home to safety at the end of the day.

Then I was placed in Mr. Johnson's Language Arts class. A thin, greasy-haired girl with pimples, I expected to be just another nameless face in the midst of the teacher's full class schedule. Sure, some students would never be faceless. They were part of the "beautiful" set. I belonged to the ranks of the unsure, the ordinary, and the awkward.

We stumbled in and out of classes like dust balls, so commonplace that we were barely considered a life form.

"Welcome to Language Arts," grinned Mr. Johnson. He sat on the edge of his desk and told jokes as he talked about English. I forgot to daydream and laughed along with the rest of the class.

"We are going to have some fun with language," he said as he loosened his tie. "Just wait and see."

Fun was far beyond what I desired. I just wanted to be like the other kids—running around with friends in the hallway, laughing and joking in between class. Reminded of my crooked teeth and pimpled face, I hunched down in my chair and stared at the smooth surface of my desk.

"Take out a piece of paper," the teacher continued as he leaned back and relaxed, "Write for the next thirty minutes on this topic." To this day I cannot remember the topic. I do remember writing furiously as idea after idea fought for recognition in my head. The final outcome was a short story about a haunted beach house. As I wrote, I could smell the salty air. I could hear the crashing waves and feel the pull of the sand beneath my feet. For just a moment, I forgot where I was. I forgot who I was supposed to be. I was lost in the story.

"OK, pass your papers forward," said the teacher. "Let's see what we have."

For the rest of the class time, the teacher read each individual work aloud. I braced myself for the humiliation. Instead, I was captivated by the excitement in the teacher's voice.

"He's actually enjoying this," I thought. He read each work as if it were a masterpiece. Students sat up straighter in their chairs. No one muttered nasty remarks. No one smirked at mistakes. For one short class period, students saw each other differently because what we had to say mattered to the teacher at the front of the room.

From then on, we had a writing assignment every day. The guidelines were simple; the ideas were up to us. I remember the sound of pencils scraping against paper as we eagerly filled our lined paper with words from our imagination. The reward was listening to the teacher read our works aloud.

Outside of class, I still slid along the lockers. The new confidence that I felt in my English class disappeared in the crowded hallways. With head down and my books clutched against my chest, I braved the puberty jungle and trudged from class to class.

"Hey, are you Renee?" A voice rang out from behind me one afternoon as I headed to my last class. I froze. This was it. I was about to get beat up, pushed around or worse—taunted in front of the other students.

"Hey, you," the voice persisted again. I gulped and turned. The girl held up the weekly school paper. "Did you write this story? I love it."

Speechless, I shook my head. I barely had the courage to speak at school much less write for the school paper.

"It has your name on it," the girl added excitedly, "I love it. 'The Beach House.' Haunted. Cool."

The next time I went to English class, my teacher was waiting for me.

"I hope you didn't mind," he said, "You really have something to say. Other people need to read it."

My face flushed as I stumbled to my desk. I had something to say? Me? During the writing time, I scribbled furiously. After class, I clutched the teacher's words to my heart as tightly as I clutched my textbooks to my chest. I had something to say. Me. An awkward adolescent who could barely lift her head, much less utter a word in public. I had something to say.

Eventually, I moved on to a new class in a new grade. But I kept writing. I began speaking in front of other people and enjoyed it. I developed a love for communication and drama. As I grew and matured, the awkward girl slowly disappeared. A braver, more confident woman emerged. But I never forgot the teacher in middle school who believed in every student—the jock, the cool kid, even the shy girl who stared at her desk. He believed and he listened. He made his class a haven for students and a place to grow. My time in his class is a memory that I still visit when I start to lose my confidence and slide along the walls of life.

These days, I lift my head up and face the world. Once again, I believe in myself because my teacher believed in me.

~Renee Hixson

Defining Moments

Happiness is a way of traveling, not a destination.
~Author Unknown

I used to love to run in gym class. Middle school was hard for me, but when it came to jogging around the track, I was always way ahead of all the other girls. To hear my effortless breathing in sync with my dingy-white Keds hitting the ground was such a freeing feeling from all the cares in my adolescent world. I could get lost in my dreams of someday becoming good at something and making my mom and dad proud.

While growing up, my parents' priorities didn't include their children being involved in after-school sports. My suit-and-tie step-father was fifty-eight years old when I was in middle school, and my reserved mother was no soccer mom. We weren't a hands-on kind of family that enjoyed spending quality time with one another. It took a voice of encouragement from one of my peers to help me believe in myself.

Pam and I met in Mr. Felton's seventh grade science class. I wasn't used to his style of teaching. All that was missing was a megaphone when he announced in a no-nonsense voice, "Oh, by the way, is there anyone who would be willing to help JoAnne? She isn't doing very well in my class."

I remember glancing over to see the popular, smart girl raise her hand without hesitation. Pam and I had attended different elementary schools and we were never formally introduced until that day when we made plans to start studying together. My new friend not only helped me with my science assignments, but more importantly, I learned about the deeper significance of love, acceptance, and understanding from our budding friendship.

I still remember feeling a sense of "we are all in this together" from the blissful applause of my classmates. Mr. Felton had asked me to stand up at the end of the semester to share my unbelievable accomplishment. Pam was a big part of my cheering section as I giggled proudly, "I brought my grade up from a C- to a B+."

We were only thirteen years old, but Pam seemed to know I was struggling to find my strengths.

"Oh, come on," she tried to convince me, while we hurried down the hall one day and headed off in different directions to our next classes. "We need someone to run the 600 in our track meet today—one of our team members is home sick."

Part of me was excited that she had thought about asking me, while at the same time I tried to find excuses not to go. Looking down, I pulled the bottom of my short dress out with both hands as I squealed, "I can't wear this!"

I often wore dresses to school, and that day was no exception. Being able to shave my legs for the first time was a step closer to feeling like I was part of the girlie-girl league, a full-fledged teenager.

But Pam wasn't going to let me get off that easy, and she seemed to have all the little details worked out ahead of time. "Just grab your gym clothes from your P.E. locker and I will meet you out front after school."

Out of earshot, or so I thought, my words echoed in the now almost empty corridor, "My mother won't want to pick me up after the track meet."

"Don't worry, I got it covered. My parents like you. They will take you home," she shouted back before shutting the classroom door behind her.

Halfheartedly, I whispered, "Okay, I will call my mom and ask her permission to go."

Since science was the only class we ever had together, Pam didn't even know that I loved running. But there was still a part of me that was afraid I would fail or embarrass the team if I did poorly.

There was no way for me to get cold feet now—Mom didn't say, "No." My heart flip-flopped as I started to feel excited, then quickly turned to anxious thoughts as we got closer to my first track meet.

Mingling with the other team members on the sidelines, I looked in amazement at the activities happening simultaneously around me. From the freshly chalked white lines circling the track, to the pole-vaulters, high jumpers, and long-distance runners, I felt like a child getting her first glimpse of a three-ring circus. I was trying not to let on to any of the other girls that I hadn't ever run in a race, when Pam gently nudged me. "It's your turn. I know you will do well."

Listening carefully as the coach told me where to stand, I wondered why the girls from the opposing teams were being staggered in different starting positions on each lane of the track. But it wasn't really the time or place to ask any questions. I just waited until I was told to ready—set—GO like a filly sprinting towards victory. Each time I would pass another girl, I didn't have a clue if I was winning or losing, because we had all started out in different spots. But I did hear the crowd of people shouting my name as I continued to keep a steady pace down the middle of my lane. For me, it was an exhilarating feeling to have this opportunity to run as if there were no tomorrow.

Just as I reached the finish line, Pam and some of my peers rushed over to congratulate me. Bent over with my hands on both hips, trying to catch my breath, I looked up surprised as it was announced over the loudspeaker that I had won the race.

Although distance separates our life stories now, I know in my heart that Pam and I will always share a special bond. Since that day, my life has been deeply enriched by a friendship that was meant to be—a part of God's plan. These days, when Pam and I get the chance to reconnect, it's as if we are those two thirteen-year-olds again, making up for lost time.

I may not be able to wear a size five dress anymore or run quite as fast, but etched in my soul from the middle school years is a sweet reminder that "we are all in this together." I can still hear the encouraging cheers as I face the challenges, as well as celebrate the triumphs, that my life brings.

Believing in ourselves is not about winning or losing—it's about the way we choose to run to the finish line.

~JoAnne Bennett

Anyone Who's Anyone Knows the Horah

If we look at the path, we do not see the sky.
~Native American Saying

There was a point in my life when, almost every single weekend, I would pull out the nicest clothes that I owned, put on what little make-up I knew how to apply, and strap on a pair of not-so-high heels to dance the night away with all of my friends. That time, surprisingly, was seventh grade.

I hadn't realized how many of my friends were Jewish until they each started turning thirteen and having the inevitable Bar or Bat Mitzvah. I became accustomed to the routine: Go to the service. Try not to giggle when they recite their Torah portions, no matter how off-key. Throw gummy candy when the service is done. Bring $36 in an envelope to the party for whoever was becoming a man or woman. Dance the electric slide in tube socks. Repeat.

And repeat and repeat. Countless weeks of Bar and Bat Mitzvahs and I became an expert. I could do the horah flawlessly and anticipated the rhymes for the candle ceremony. Every time I went to a Bar Mitzvah with someone less experienced, I felt like the person at the movie who spoils the plot.

"This is the part where they march around and carry the Torah," I'd whisper to the new Bar Mitzvah-goer. "Don't touch it with your hands!"

Week after week, I took pictures with my friends that were turned into key chains and wore silly party favor sombreros. I anticipated the moment when my middle school boyfriend would ask me to dance, eyes on the floor and hands fidgeting. I made sure to remove my heels, towering over him even when barefoot. Then we would dance, arms straightened, with a good three feet separating our bodies.

Inevitably, I started to get jealous. Every week I watched a new friend, sometimes someone I barely knew, be doted on. I wanted my parents to stand on the bema in front of everyone and give a speech about how proud of me they were for having accomplished all the work that went into a Bat Mitzvah. Instead, my mom, a professional chef, was cooking every day for people who weren't me, and my dad was working long hours in New York City and living with his new wife. I envied the kids whose happily married parents were planning elaborate ceremonies and parties for their kids as they entered adulthood.

I started to consider the possibility of having my own Bat Mitzvah. Although my Dad was Catholic and I was currently enrolled in Sunday school, my mom was a non-practicing Jew. If my friends, whose grades were surely worse than mine, could learn Hebrew, why couldn't I? It was an obsession. I imagined what my Bat Mitzvah dress would look like, who I would invite to the party, and I envisioned all those smiling faces in the synagogue, staring up at me as I did my haftorah portion.

What I like to call the "Bar Mitzvah" phase of my life came and passed, as we all started to turn fourteen and enter eighth grade. My desire to have my own Bat Mitzvah decreased when I realized how much work and dedication it would take for me to pioneer my own religious education, ceremony, and party. But a big part of my realization was seeing why, exactly, I even wanted one in the first place.

I was looking for faith, for family, and for appreciation. I wanted to feel part of a religious community for the first time in my life, and I wanted my whole family to congregate because of my hard work. I found other ways to get those things.

I joined the church choir a few years later. Singing had always been my passion, and it helped me feel the spirituality I was seeking. In high school, I managed great grades and tried out for every musical I possibly could. I had found a way to get that attention I craved—I could be on stage.

But every now and then, when a big, white envelope with calligraphic lettering arrives in the mail from some family friend turning thirteen, I smile and think of all the outfits I wore, the boys I danced with, and the chicken tenders I scooped onto my plate from the buffet line. Bar Mitzvahs were awkward and loud and completely over the top. But most of all, they were fun.

~Madeline Clapps

EVERYONE SENSED IT WAS DREW'S
FIRST TIME AT A BAT MITZVAH

Stay True To Yourself and Your Dreams

In matters of style, swim with the current;
in matters of principle, stand like a rock.
~Thomas Jefferson

When I was six or seven years old, I would go up to my parents and say, "Mommy! Daddy! I want to be just like that person when I'm all grown up!" My parents would just look down at me and smile. My mom would always say, "Do what you think will make you happy." I always tried to stay true to that, but as I got older, I decided that I wanted to be something else. When you find something that you truly want to be, but people around you think that you are not capable of doing it, it hurts.

When I was in seventh grade, I decided that I wanted to be a police officer, or at least someone in law enforcement. I wanted to make a difference. I barely told anyone what I wanted to be because I was afraid people would laugh at me or would give me that you've-got-to-be-crazy look. Well one day it came true!

I was putting away my clarinet after a long practice for a music contest. My band director, whom some high school students call Mr. S., was talking to another clarinet player, Eli. Eli and I both wanted to be the same thing... police officers. Mr. S. was giving advice to him. I don't know why I did this, but I spoke up and said that I wanted to be a police officer too. Mr. S. and Eli gave me the look I had been dreading.

"I don't think you can be a police officer, Nicole. Police officers have to be tough, quick, and they can't show any mercy," Mr. S. told me. "You are just too nice and down-to-earth. I bet if you pulled over a cute boy and he batted his eyes at you, you would let him go."

I stared at Mr. S. for a long time. I couldn't believe that he was telling me this. I knew I was nice, but I didn't think that would make people think I couldn't be a police officer. "I know I wouldn't do that. I would give him a ticket just like everyone else," I stated. Mr. S. and Eli just rolled their eyes at me. Eli said, "You can't be a police officer because you're a girl and girls don't have the strength to do the things that police officers do. I'm sure you are lying about ticketing a cute boy."

I wanted to defend my feelings to Mr. S., but I knew that if I did, I would be in big trouble with Mom and Dad. Mom was a teacher at the school and would soon find out. I didn't say anything—I couldn't. When the bell rang, I stormed out of the room. I didn't cry. I was heartbroken, though. It was like my dreams had been ripped apart and thrown away.

When I got home, I walked slowly to my room. I stared at all the law enforcement books I had on my bookshelf. Most of them were mysteries about Nancy Drew. I had read every one of them, and knew what I would be up against by choosing a career in law enforcement. Now it was like they were taunting me. They were grinning and telling me that I would never be like those people who make a difference in people's lives. I sat down on my bed and started to cry.

I thought back to what Mr. S. had said. I didn't think I was too nice to be a police officer. I knew I could be nice, but not too nice to be what I truly wanted to be. I was always told that being nice was a good thing. Now it seemed like it was bad. It seemed like Mom and Dad had lied to me. I didn't want to think about it, but maybe Mr. S. was right. Maybe I wasn't police officer or even law enforcement material after all. I didn't want to think that way, though. It just made my heart ache even more.

I started to think about what Mom would say to me: "Don't let anyone say you can't do something. Follow your dreams and stay true to yourself. You are too stubborn and hardheaded not to." I realized that Mom was right. If I really believed that I could do something, then I could.

All the criticism I have received from people has given me more reason to become what I want to be. When Mr. S. told me that I couldn't be a police officer, it just made me want to prove him wrong. I learned not to let other people's words get me down and make me stop dreaming. I am always going to follow my dreams—no matter what. Now, I am even more determined to become a police officer than before! Just as long as I stay true to my dreams and myself.

~Nicole R. Roberts

Going Long
in Middle School

It ain't what they call you, it's what you answer to.
~W.C. Fields

I never thought myself to be much of an athlete. From kindergarten up through sixth grade, I stuck with being a bookworm and getting As and good remarks from my teachers in all my classes. But when it came to P.E. and recess, I couldn't stop showing the "jocks" how un-athletic I was, giving them a reason to laugh at me. One time, my P.E. class was playing kickball. I kicked the ball right into the hands of one of the opposing team's members, and everyone laughed at me, crying "You stink at sports!" Moments like those got me picked on all the time.

A summer later, I found myself at a new school where I seemed like a total stick-in-the-mud, or so I thought. All I cared about at first was getting good grades and good comments from all my teachers. Except I also cared about making new friends, not wanting to end up being a loner for the rest of my time at the school. When I tried to make some friends fast, I made the fatal mistake everybody does; I tried to act cool and not like myself. I tried cracking a few outdated jokes that I thought would be funny. I tried changing my look by getting some cool clothes, which only drew attention to the clothes. Most of the attempts I made miserably failed and backfired. I was just as lonely as ever.

One day, however, I put aside my fear of being laughed at and headed to the upper field. Back when I was at my old school, I was good at only one athletic thing: tackling and blocking people when we played rugby. And the first thing I saw when I stepped on the grassy field that day was a bunch of boys playing football, some of them from my classes. Gathering all my inner strength, I walked up to the leader of the group, who was shouting all the orders to his friends, and asked if I could play with them. He scanned me for a moment, like he was trying to see right through me, and said "sure." After some brief introductions he asked me, "Are you good at blocking?" I thought for a few seconds and responded with a slightly reluctant, "Yeah."

When we were setting up for the play, he positioned me in front of him, since he was the quarterback. The other team sent their strongest player to rush the quarterback, probably thinking that the "noob," or the "new kid," would be the worst player. I got ready to block (and be laughed at) and then came the "hike!" I stood my ground, focused all my strength into my legs and arms, and braced for impact.

The other team's player collided with me at full force for only a split second, but when his weight made contact with my arms, I pushed hard, causing him to bounce off me just like one of those "super bounce" balls ricocheting off a wall when you throw it indoors. The quarterback took advantage of his opportunity and chucked the ball to a different player on our team, who scored a touchdown. Everyone was surprised by my powerful block and congratulated me.

Later, the teams switched positions and my team was on offense. As we began the play, the quarterback I defended walked up behind me and whispered "Blitz," readying himself for the play. Knowing what this meant from watching the "jocks" at my old school play football, I moved to the front of my team and waited for the "hike!" It came just as clearly as the last one did, and I pushed off with my legs and sprang forward, charging like a rhino towards the enemy team's quarterback and blocker.

Once I was within arm's length of the center blocker, I folded my arms across my chest and ran into him so hard that I knocked him onto his back. I then jumped over the stunned player, who had a look on his face as if he'd just been hit by a bullet train, and dived at the quarterback. We made contact, and that was the end of the play.

The rest of the game was similar. I was used as a blocker and center until lunch ended and my team won. From that day on, I gained a whole group of new friends who would sometimes fight with each other over who got me on their team. I also got a new nickname: "Tank."

~Nicholas Berson

Chapter 6

Teens Talk Middle School

In Like, In Love, and Just Not Into You

*Ooh, I got a crush on you
I hope you feel the way that I do
I get a rush when I'm with you
Ooh, I've got a crush on you.*

~Mandy Moore

Thirteen

I do not know how to kiss, or I would kiss you.
Where do the noses go?
~Ingrid Bergman

My life was simple before I turned thirteen. Most of my days were occupied by school, sports and the afternoon lineup on Nickelodeon. But there comes a point in every young boy's life when he crosses the great divide separating his childhood from his teenage years. Waiting to greet me as I crossed that threshold on my thirteenth birthday was something I had successfully avoided for the entirety of my twelve years of existence. At thirteen I had no choice. I would be forever forced to interact with girls.

Girls. Babes. Chicks. Women. However you slice it, boys have a natural and powerful interest in — and fear of — girls. For most boys, the arrival of the teenage years means that interactions with the opposite gender are no longer viewed as taboo. Before my teenage years, I wouldn't dare be caught with a girl unless every avenue of escape was blocked, for fear I might contract the deadly disease known throughout schoolyards as Cooties.

Cootie infections meant an inevitable onslaught of ridicule. Limericks involving a baby carriage and sitting in a tree were just some of the symptoms. However, with the arrival of my thirteenth birthday came immunity to this bug. At long last, the threat of acquiring Cooties was lifted from my shoulders and shelved with polio and the "Macarena" among ailments that no longer plague human society. Although it was now socially acceptable to converse with girls, at thirteen I wasn't exactly adept at it.

School dances were a nightmare for me. I never thought much about going to dances until I officially became a teenager. Before thirteen, I thought of dances as cesspools ripe for contracting Cooties. But soon my teenage years required that I attend my first dance, and I was terrified. I felt naked, as though I had just plunged into the jungle without taking malaria medication. Although I could see my fellow thirteen-year-olds talking to girls with no sign of Cootie outbreak, I felt it would be safer to stand against a wall and admire the object of my affections from afar.

I envied my friends who had the courage to talk to girls. The decision to move away from the wall and talk to the girl I liked was not an easy one. I don't remember how I convinced myself to take the plunge, but somehow I drifted from the wall toward where the girls were. But I was scared, and I walked as if my legs were shackled to cement blocks. Why was it so hard? I was not afraid to talk to her. She sat next to me in three of our classes. We regularly had profound, personal conversations. Well, at least I thought we did. Whenever we spoke, in my mind, I was Tom Cruise in *Jerry Maguire*:

I love you. You complete me, I would think.

Shut up, just shut up. You had me at "hello."

In reality our conversations never progressed beyond the boundaries of homework problems and asking for pens—not quite the romantic poeticism that played out in my mind.

However, the school dance was my opportunity to talk to her and declare my feelings. Here, romantic interactions seemed almost inevitable based on the pageantry of the event, yet I could do nothing but stare at her as she playfully danced with her friends.

She was beautiful. Although the dance floor was dark, she stood out of the almost subterranean blackness with the radiance of a beacon. Her smile, though aligned with braces, caused her nose to wrinkle ever so slightly. I could have admired her forever. Once, she looked in my direction and caught my glance, and I hurriedly averted my eyes.

After the weight of her stare had passed, I lifted my eyes to resume my fixation. To my dismay she was no longer there.

I thought, "Maybe she went to the bathroom, or for a drink of water, or for..."

"Hey," I heard somebody say.

She was talking to me. I didn't know what do. I was stunned. Paralyzed.

A series of wild and frightening questions flew through my mind:

"What should I do? What should I say? Should I ask her if she wants to dance? Am I speaking right now?"

"Do you want to dance with me?" she asked.

I did my best to make some comprehensible, positive reply. She grabbed me by the hand as she led the way toward an open patch of tile on the floor. Once there, she put her arms around my neck. I somehow managed to control the shaking in my arms and wrap them around her waist. We began to dance — rotating in a small orbit on the floor. My heart, exploding with each beat in my chest, surpassed the throbbing of the bass that flooded the room.

As the song progressed, she inched closer to me so she could rest her head on my shoulder. I knew what this meant. I had seen it happen before. She wanted me to kiss her. But I had never kissed a girl before. I didn't know what to do.

"If only the song would never end," I thought.

But it did. Gradually, the surrounding couples began to separate as the lights started to return. Eventually the lights came on, chasing the darkness from the room, and everybody stood like moles in the sunlight as they adjusted their eyes to the blinding brightness. As soon as I could see again, I looked at the girl in front of me. Her nose crinkled as she smiled, and she brushed her hair back into place.

"Thanks for the dance," she said.

I didn't say anything for a moment as I tried to think of some clever response. That's when it happened. She leaned in and kissed me—a quick peck on the lips—but it was the most passionate kiss of my life. Any hope I had of impressing her with a quick-witted remark vanished as I was reduced to an incomprehensible buffoon. I didn't have time to compose myself because she left with her friends soon after. I stood there in the middle of the cafeteria floor with a huge grin across my face.

That was the moment to end all others. I wanted to believe no romantic exchange that had ever occurred, or ever would occur, could supersede the one I had just experienced. However, one fact remained certain: I was infected with an even deadlier agent than the Cooties that plagued schoolyard children—love.

~Robert Pellegrino

Puppy Love

Love puts the fun in together,
the sad in apart,
and the joy in a heart.
~Author Unknown

The phone isn't ringing.
No responses to my e-mail.
I haven't gotten to see him
since school has been out.
I can't stand it any longer;
I have to at least talk to him!
So I get up my nerve
and dial his number.
No one is home,
and I'm sort of relieved.
But I'm also upset—
and disappointed.
I'm only twelve,
and I know it shouldn't matter
if I can't see him.
It's not like we'll be together
forever or anything.
So why does it hurt so much?
I can't say,

but it does.
I pull out a photo of him
and practice what I'll say
When I call back.

~Jennifer Lynn Clay

Love Life

We are all a little weird and life's a little weird,
and when we find someone whose weirdness is compatible with ours,
we join up with them and fall in mutual weirdness
and call it love.
~Author Unknown

My love life has been pretty uneventful, with the exception of one remarkable blip. His name is Andy Martin and I've been hung up on him since the fifth grade. Andy has cream-colored hair, a toothy smile, and an egg-shaped head. He's irresistible. When I was eleven, I'd sit on the bleachers at Somonauk Park, watching his baseball games.

Somonauk is our local core of activities. There are no hills and only a couple of trees so you can see the whole world stretching around your head. Like in the ending of one of those cheesy movies where the main character has some triumph and they're standing with their arms spread out looking at the blue sky and the camera is spinning all around. It's the perfect contrast to the sweaty bodies bickering over the last slice of bologna inside my house.

During my Andy-stalking days, I'd scare up a girlfriend and ride the two miles to Somonauk hoping to catch a sighting. On the stiff benches we'd weave ribbons into silver barrettes and slip them into our hair.

Sometimes, Andy took a brief break from his baseball obsession to bless me with a glance or a wave. He'd hold up the bat with his skinny-licorice arms and the way he wavered would look a little dangerous, like the bat might be so heavy he'd lose control over it and clobber his own head. But what Andy lacked in beauty and balance he made up for in personality. He was kind, a little bit quiet, and he could make me laugh so hard I wanted to throw up (in a good way). When Andy broke into a smirk after delivering some sarcastic remark, I felt like the sun was rising in my stomach.

He kissed me only once. At the time, we were officially "going out." I guess I should explain that in order to "go out" with someone, one of the two people (usually the boy) writes a note to the other one. This note tells you everything you need to know about a boy's real and true personality. You could get a straightforward:

Will you go out with me?

Or the more artistic:

If you want to go out with me check "yes"—if you don't check "no."

And sometimes, usually from the most insecure boys—the ones my mom claims will someday make the best husbands—a girl might get a note which says simply:

Do you like me?

Andy was a "will you go out with me?" type, and I readily said, "Yes." The day after our thrilling agreement to "go out" was cemented, Andy skipped baseball practice to hang out with me on the school playground.

He said, "Your shirt is nice."

I said, "I spilled milk on it at lunch so maybe it stinks by now."

He said, "No... it doesn't stink."

Andy jammed his hands into his pants.

I could hear myself breathe.

Andy glanced sideways and whispered, "Hey, let's go back here." He pulled me behind the rough brick building, pressing forward until his soft mouth hit my pursed one. Andy smelled like fabric softener. I wanted to keep breathing him in and in. Even now, the smell of dryer sheets makes me weak in the knees.

In the kiss department, I'm fairly sure I was a disappointment. I nervously sucked my lips back into my face while he searched for them with his. Still, though neither of us probably enjoyed the act of kissing, the very fact of its success felt magical. We agreed we were clearly in love and began planning our future with discussions about what we would be when we grew up. I chose comedian/waitress (my sister Peggy said all Hollywood performers pay their bills by waiting tables). Andy, predictably, would be a baseball player.

We passed notes in class with love-soaked messages like...

This class totally sucks.

I think Mr. Totesworth has a booger on his lip!

The best memory I have took place on a field trip to the Adler Planetarium in Chicago. It happened on the long bus ride there with no air conditioning. Andy and I sat together in one of the very last rows bumping along, holding hands until sweat made rivers between them and our fingers were so slippery-hot it was almost impossible not to lose our grip. Over time, the students around us shrunk and blurred until the whole world was just me, Andy, and the quivering heat. Somewhere in the background, the bus jostled our butts and belched a recurrent hum.

We kept on holding hands at the planetarium, during the black, starry movie, walking through the exhibits, (which I have no memory of because the power of that hand-holding was so strong it wiped out everything in its path) and then back on the bus again. Other kids watched us with longing. We gave them a reason to feel lonely. In my whole lifetime up until that point, I'd never felt so special to another person.

Andy broke up with me on a Monday. He used the ultimate in cowardly break-up moves—the note. But, to be honest, he'd used the same tactic when he asked me out, so at least he was consistent:

Dear Juliet, I'm sorry I am breaking up with you.

It was great. Let's stay friends.

~Andy

After the joy of being someone's true and only love, it's pretty tough to be dumped. I couldn't understand why Andy would discard our perfect future plans or how he could resist a life with me in it.

For the first few weeks after the break-up, I went on attending his baseball games and manipulating seats by him in assemblies, pitifully hoping for one more flash of blissfully sweaty hand-holding. Then I saw him talking to Paula Bernadel on the school playground. They stood so close they must have been sharing the same breath. Andy reached up and ran a finger through one of Paula's perfect curls and I heard him say, "Hey, let's go back here." He pulled her behind the building and my insides were scraped clean. Something inside broke and fell to the ground floor of my chest, trembling.

Adults think that eleven-year-old first loves are cotton candy filling the mouths of children. And they do melt. But those moments with Andy were my first tender proceedings into the realm of the heart. They offered a blink of knowledge about the realities of love when, until that time, I'd only been privy to theory. My heart fluttered to life with a grace that can be remembered better than described. And every bit of it mattered. Maybe love is always that way.

~Juliet C. Bond

46

Ben

That's why they call them crushes.
If they were easy,
they'd call them something else.
~Jim Baker,
Sixteen Candles

I'm talking to my friends at my locker,
not paying attention to much of anything.
Then, I get up and turn around.
Behind me, he is standing.
His smile melts me.
"Hi," I finally manage to say.
He waves, then walks away.
Slowly, all feeling comes back to me.
Hi? I think to myself,
angered that I hadn't said more...
hadn't kept him longer.
Later in class,
I can't help but steal a glance at him;
He's looking at me too!
I quickly turn back to my paper.
Now I lie in bed,
wishing I knew how he felt about me —
wishing I knew how I looked in his eyes.

I close my ears to all sound, my eyes to all sight.
In my mind, I see him smiling, his brown eyes glowing.
I make up my mind:
Tomorrow I will tell him how I feel.

~Jennifer Lynn Clay

47

First Kiss, Last Kiss

We always believe our first love is our last,
and our last love our first.
~George John Whyte-Melville

I t started and ended with a kiss on the cheek—the first peppered with chlorine and M&Ms, the last sweetened by the New York City night.

We were in sixth grade when it all began, when I entered into my first real "relationship" with a boy. Prior to middle school, I'd been the girl who loved boys from afar. I wrote in my journal about them (when I kept one) and constantly daydreamed about whether or not someone, anyone, would kiss me. I was a hopeless romantic even at the age of eleven.

But this was different. Ben liked me as much as I liked him, maybe more. He bought me presents and wrote me notes. We spoke online every day, for hours at a time, and were best friends. He told me all the time how pretty and smart he thought I was. The only thing missing was that all-important, all-encompassing kiss, and both of us were too shy and young to do anything to fill that void.

Until the end of seventh grade. Tired of waiting around for Ben, who was a good four inches shorter than me and a little on the wimpy side, I planned the moment thoroughly. My friend Diana was having a pool party to mark the end of the school year and I had big, kiss-on-the-cheek-filled plans.

Every night, I would get in bed and think about how it would work. I figured I had to swoop in after a hug, when we were already physically close, and just get it over with. I instant messaged my friends to discuss whether or not the plan was feasible and if he would even want me to kiss him, knowing full well he did. They assured me it was a foolproof plan, and I counted down the days till the party.

Finally, it came. After a day full of playing sharks and minnows, eating pizza, and tossing M&Ms up into the air and into each other's mouths, the time to enact my master plan had come. My mom had arrived with the top down on her Mustang, waiting for me to leave the party and return home with her.

I signaled for her to wait a moment and ran to where Ben stood, his thin frame evident even beneath the T-shirt he had donned post-swim. I walked over to say goodbye and gave him a hug. As I pulled away, my lips ever-so-slightly brushed the line between his neck and his cheek. My first attempt at a kiss. I turned away immediately and hurried off, pinching my friend in the arm as she tried to comment on what she had just witnessed.

Immediately I felt guilty, as if my mom could sense what a loose woman I had become now that I had kissed a boy. It was scandalous, but I couldn't wipe the goofy smile off my face. As I sat in the passenger seat of the convertible, looking at myself in the side view mirror, it occurred to me that this was the first time I had withheld anything from my mom.

Ben and I "dated" through eighth grade, finally breaking it off the summer before starting high school. It was hard to tell him that I was growing up and no longer felt for him what I had before, but I bravely called him — instant messenger was far too callous for the delicate situation of dumping someone — and told him I no longer loved him.

Six years later, when Ben and I were both in college in New York City, we made plans to see each other and reconnect. I made my way uptown to Columbia, taking the long subway ride and trying to suppress the jittery butterfly feeling in my stomach. I hadn't seen him in a few years, since high school, and I wondered if finally he had grown taller than me.

What followed surprised me more than anything had in recent years—a new relationship with the boy I had adored for three of my formative adolescent years. Ben was, in fact, taller than me. He had grown into a handsome guy with many of the boyish traits I had fallen in love with in sixth grade. As far as I was concerned, he was still that first boy to acknowledge and return my affections—the first boy I ever really kissed.

And so it was fitting that I found myself standing outside on a New York City sidewalk as Ben walked me back to my friend's dormitory, an awkward silence setting in as we avoided looking at each other. Our two months of rehashing our puppy love had turned sour—things hadn't worked out. And now he looked at me, the realization that he'd lost his second chance with his first love evident in his light blue eyes, the same eyes I'd peered into day after day in seventh grade science class. The same eyes I'd thought about every night before I drifted off to sleep when I was thirteen years old, planning where and when I would kiss him and trying to imagine exactly how it would be. A sadness settled over both of us as we realized, maybe for the first time, that we were really adults.

He looked up at the sky for a second, then at me. He brushed his lips against my cheek, quickly, with a little hint of that seventh grade awkwardness, and walked off down the quiet street. I haven't seen him since.

~Madeline Clapps

My First Love

No love, no friendship, can cross the path of our destiny
without leaving some mark on it forever.
~Francois Mocuriac

Jack Hines. His name will forever remain in my memory and in my heart as my very first love. I was a mere twelve years old when I first discovered my feelings for him, and he was seventeen. I think people tend to dismiss crushes from their younger years as silly and naïve, but even typing his name now, I am overwhelmed by memories of him I feared I might have forgotten. I can see his name scribbled over all my notebooks, varying from "Jack Hines, Chase Hines," "Chase and Jack," or the standard, "I Love Jack Hines," always with tiny hearts floating nearby. I can see him in his green Jeep Cherokee, pulling into the school parking lot each morning with a smile on his face. He always seemed to have a smile on his face, and then in turn made me smile.

He was grinning from ear to ear the first time I ever laid eyes on him. Our entire school had meetings twice a week where anybody could get up in front of the school and say whatever they wanted as long as it wasn't offensive. I attended a small school with around five hundred kids in total, middle school and high school combined, so these "town meetings," as they were called, always felt intimate. Jack Hines was a town meeting celebrity.

I was at my first town meeting, zoning in and out of the never-ending announcements, none of which applied to me, when there was a break in the monotonous droning of faculty members and Jack Hines took the microphone. I quickly snapped out of my daze, and focused every fiber of my being on him and whatever beautiful words were about to come from his mouth. He stood, smiling at everyone, and he seemed a little bit nervous as he coyly asked, "Do you guys want to hear a story?" I had to restrain myself from shouting, "Yes! Jack, I would love to hear a story." If you were to close your eyes, you could have heard in his voice that he was smiling, and it made him so enjoyable to listen to. He could have been giving directions to the airport and I would have been just as enthralled.

He told a story about how he snuck out of his house when he was grounded, to give his soon-to-be girlfriend, Sarah Johnston, a cupcake on the eve of her birthday. He had the whole school captivated, faculty included, and we were all laughing. Everyone kept glancing back to a beautiful girl who was laughing and blushing at the same time. I assumed this was Sarah, and wished I could be in her shoes. Jack Hines had a crush on her and that qualified her as the luckiest girl in the world.

Jack Hines's sister Kaylee was in the grade above me, and she and her friends had invited my friends and me over for a sleepover. My heart sped up when I heard about the invite. I would be going to Jack Hines's house! No, not just going—sleeping at Jack Hines's house. My mind raced with questions. What would the house be like? What should I wear? Would he be there? The last question was the most important but, alas, he did not grace the sleepover with his presence. My friends told Kaylee of my love for her brother and she thought it was adorable. The next thing I knew, the whole school knew about my feelings.

It was amazing how easy it was for me to wake up every morning and go to school, knowing that at some point in the day I would see Jack Hines, even if it was only for a moment. He was now well aware of my adoration for him, and he always made a point to smile and say hi to me whenever he saw me.

Valentine's Day was upon us, and I watched as various classmates of mine received roses and pink notes from their admirers. I wasn't

My First Love: In Like, In Love, and Just Not Into You   181 disappointed when no roses were dropped on my desk because I wasn't expecting any. I reached the end of the day and I was at my locker, packing up my books and binders for the night's homework when I heard him say my name behind me. I have never loved my name more in my life.

I turned around in astonishment, not fully believing that Jack Hines would be standing behind me, but there he was, in all his glory, smiling contagiously. He handed me a pink note with a rose, and said in his beautiful voice, "Happy Valentine's Day." I stood there smiling and blushing like a fool, and watched as he turned to walk away, feeling like someone had just handed me the key to my own utopia. My friends had been watching in the wings, and immediately ran up to me squealing with delight. I still have that note which simply read, "Happy Valentine's Day Chase, Love Jack Hines," in all capital letters.

May came around and it was time for Student Council elections. Before each grade voted on their class representatives, the whole school voted for their two presidents—one policy president and one events president. Jack Hines and his best friend, Tyler Madison, swept the polls to become arguably the best, most attractive presidents any community has ever seen. I was inspired. I needed to be a part of Student Council, so I ran and won. I stood in front of my class, acting like I was really interested in improving school policies, when I may as well have just said, "I love Jack Hines, and this is the one way I can spend time with him." I could not wait for next year. There would be meetings and events to plan, and most importantly, there would be Jack Hines.

Eighth grade was probably one of the best years of my life thus far. I saw Jack Hines all the time. He even took me to the doctor when, during a student council meeting, my eyes turned bright red and were itching uncontrollably. The doctor diagnosed me with pink eye. I looked at Jack by my side and thought, "Thank God for pink eye."

It was only fitting that one of the best years of my life had the most magical, memorable endings, one that I remember as if it were yesterday. The middle school dance took place on the night of our last final. I was looking my best, or so I thought at the time, and showing off my best dance moves, when Jack Hines strolled onto the dance floor. Faster than I could comprehend that he was there, he burst into a rendition of The Righteous Brothers' "You've Lost That Lovin' Feelin'," a la *Top Gun*. He swooped me in his arms and we danced to the song. It was so beautiful, the only thing I could do was stare into his eyes and try to remind myself that I wasn't dreaming.

Every now and then that song comes on the radio, and I smile as I remember the days when I loved Jack Hines.

~Chase Bernstein

The New Boy

Love and kindness are never wasted.
They always make a difference.
They bless the one who receives them,
and they bless you, the giver.
~Barbara De Angelis

He came in the middle of my seventh grade year,
Tall and quiet with large dark eyes.
He was the center of curiosity on that first Wednesday
Ballroom dancing in the gym at 10 A.M.
Who would the new boy choose?
I sat with my fellow wallflowers:
Lucille, the poor girl,
Her pretty face marred by crooked teeth.
Marjorie, the preacher's daughter,
A forty-five-year-old spinster in a twelve-year-old body
And me,
Too tall, too fat, too odd.
The music began and the boys rose from the benches,
I craned my neck to see which of the popular girls would be chosen,
Unaware someone was standing before me
        until he held out his hand.
The new boy had asked me to dance.

~Juliana Harris

50

Slow Dance of Love

I got started dancing because
I knew it was one way to meet girls.
~Gene Kelly

The first day of sixth grade was a real turning point for me—I fell in love. Who would have thought that a brown-haired, mushroom-cut boy with dark brown eyes would catch my attention? I leaned over to my friend Karen and asked her about him.

"Who is that boy, the one with the brown hair and green shirt?"

"Umm, that's Jon Eanes."

"Oh really?" I asked. "Jon. He's so cute!"

"No, no!" She cried. "I saw him pick his nose and eat it a few times in fourth grade. We call him 'Jon the nose-picker Eanes' or just nose-picker for short." I giggled a bit with Karen over his name, but his history didn't faze me. I couldn't stop looking at him. I remember saying to myself, "One day, Jon, you will be mine."

From that day on, my crush sat with me for nearly every class. I flirted with him constantly and even passed notes. My teacher knew about my infatuation, and often joked about it in class. Jon didn't notice these things. One day, Jon wrote on his binder and passed it to me. There, in light pencil, were the words, "I like you." I jumped in my skin and smiled, not knowing what to say or do. I didn't reply for a while; all I could do was smile. Then I somehow found the guts—not to pour my heart out—but to say "I know" in response.

The girls were so proud of me as soon as I told them. We were all giddy that day, and Karen introduced a new assignment for me.

"You should tell him to go to the dance." She was talking about the YMCA Teen Center dance held every Friday night.

"I don't think he goes to our dances." I said.

"I know, but you should ask him to the dance."

"But...." It was a losing battle.

"Jen, come on! If he goes to the dance, then he will have to hang out with you and maybe even dance with you."

"No way!" This hadn't occurred to me. "Really? You think I should?"

"Yea! If he likes you, he will go to the dance."

These dances were a big deal. Every week I would dress in my cutest outfit, pile on make-up, and have my dad drive me to the Teen Center. I somehow gathered the guts to ask Jon to meet me there for the dance, but I was deflated when he resisted. "I don't go to those things," he said.

Karen had the brilliant idea to talk to one of Jon's friends to get him to go, and it worked. The night of the dance, I was so nervous. What if he didn't come? What if he said "forget it" when his father drove him up to the curb? I worried frantically, and when I saw him standing in line, I panicked. It was a good thing my friends were there to get me dancing and de-stressed.

Toward the end of the night, my friends repeatedly tried to get Jon and me to dance. They played many slow songs, but I would stand against the wall and talk to my friends during them. When the last song of the night was minutes from playing, I deflated again. "I guess he doesn't want to dance with me," I thought. My friends came running over to me and begged me to come with them. I shrugged and followed. Then, in the corner of the gym, Karen aggressively pushed Jon towards me. He was smiling and panicking, and I was so embarrassed. Karen urged, "Just dance with her! I know you want to!"

My friends backed away. I looked at him and shrugged. He nervously came up to me, and asked if I wanted to dance. The last song,

"I Don't Want to Miss a Thing," by Aerosmith played, and I sighed. Saying yes to his request, I got close to him and put my arms on his shoulders. He was so nervous, he put his hands up on my shoulders too! I was so surprised that he didn't know what to do, and afraid my friends would make fun of him, I whispered, "Um, your hands go on my waist. Quick!" He recovered, and we both laughed when I said that this would be the talk of the school come Monday.

We danced slowly, our bodies stiff, and my world disappeared into a black mist. We were so awkward, just a couple of eleven-year-olds with a crush. When the song ended, I ignored my friends and said goodbye to him. He asked me to go bowling with him the following weekend. I couldn't breathe, knowing that the boy I liked, liked me back, and had just asked me out on a date. If the world had blown up just then, I wouldn't have minded, knowing that I had this moment to remember.

On Monday it was the talk of the whole sixth grade. Even my history teacher sighed with relief upon hearing the news. I think it was because he was sick of seeing us flirt in class.

This is a small adventure compared to the rest of my teen years, but that's just it—a small, yet memorable event. Jon and I still laugh about the moment years later in high school, talking about the "old days." Even though we're older and wiser now, and we each tell our own version of our relationship, I like to remind him that after watching couples dance all night, he still managed to mess it up. Yes, Jon, although you deny it now, you still put your hands on my shoulders during our first dance in the sixth grade.

~Jennifer Chase

Glasses Geek

It took me a long time not to judge myself
through someone else's eyes.
~Sally Field

I was in love. Just saying his name made my heart flutter. Scott Sumsion... Mrs. Sumsion... Mrs. Scott Sumsion. It was a dream, and he was mine. I wrote his name all over my notebooks. His dimpled smile and bright blue eyes made my knees buckle. He was by far the cutest guy on our middle school campus.

Scott and I met in sixth grade and our romance heated up during seventh grade when we had the same homeroom teacher. We'd smile and snicker at each other, trying to catch each other's eye during class—out of view of the teacher, of course. We weren't about to get caught and have the whole class know our heart's desires. Ours was true love to last forever, or at least until the next cute boy walked by.

It was during that same year that I noticed a blurry Scott sitting far away. His blond hair wasn't glowing as it had at the beginning of the year. I figured it was just the lighting in the room, but then I realized I couldn't see the writing on the blackboard either. Even the trees were getting fuzzy. Was the world in chaos? The straight poles I could see all over town weren't just straight poles. As I got closer to them I realized they had lights on the ends.

Then my world collapsed. The two most dreaded words in the English language came out of my mother's mouth: "EYE DOCTOR."

"NO!" I yelled. This could not be happening to my perfect world

And just as predicted after my eye exam I heard the word I feared the most: "GLASSES."

My life was ruined. I was going to end up a wallflower at all the dances and be passed up like a freak of nature. There went my dreams of prom night and moonlight smooching. Now I was going to be known as the dateless chick, the four-eyed freaky one, the less-than-zero girl. I was turning into a nerd, and not by choice. How could my parents do this to me? And as if my life couldn't get any worse, my parents insisted I get the type of frames that would hold up in gym class, in case I got hit by a ball or something. Come on, give me a break! I wasn't the kind of rough girl who beat up boys. Well, except for the time I gave Scott Mitchell a bloody nose. And who cared about that?

Why couldn't I get some cute little wire frames and look like a girl instead of looking like my dad? Come to think of it, my dad and Drew Carey looked an awful lot alike. I cried when I looked in the mirror. I hated my new glasses. I knew Scott would hate them. I was officially a glasses geek.

I took off my new glasses the second I walked through the doors at school and I would hide them in my pocket or leave them in my locker. Things went smoothly until Mrs. Johnson asked me to read something on the board. How could she humiliate me in front of everyone? I was horrified because I couldn't see. I slowly slid my glasses from my pocket and stuck them on my face. I read the sentence and threw my glasses back in my pocket. I was found out. I was going to have to live in a mole cave for the rest of my life. Mrs. Johnson insisted I wear my glasses throughout her class so I could read when called upon. Scott had seen me in full glasses geek glory.

"You don't look that bad," he told me.

I had a hard time adjusting to wearing them all day at first, but soon realized that I actually enjoyed seeing things clearly and crisply across the room.

Scott played the drums for Swing Choir and he and I ogled each other from across the room. He was awesome as he jammed and occasionally threw a drumstick in the air, almost hitting our teacher. My heart would race when he'd glance up and catch my eye before I quickly looked away. I knew he was watching the gleam in my eye; or more like the reflection of the lights in my glasses. I was hopeless.

Then, one day, I was hit square in the face with the ball in P.E. My glasses flew into the air and the left arm shattered into three pieces as they hit the floor.

Now I could get a new pair of glasses, I thought.

My mother didn't agree. I left geek-ville and I entered a new phase of triple-decker-nerdville. My mom had the audacity to make me tape them together. Not just tape — masking tape.

"I can't and I won't," I cried.

"It'll build character," She announced.

I had heard those words my whole life. At this point, I should have had enough character to sustain an entire village of nerds. How could I face everyone at school? I was humiliated beyond words as I walked down the halls.

"Cindy, you have a new look today," chimed Mr. Higginson, our choir teacher as he snickered and laughed with all the other kids.

"Yeah, it's called 'broken' by Calvin Klein. I think it might really catch on." I smugly replied, and put my head down behind the piano so no one could see me. I'm sure he didn't know he was scarring me for life. I looked over at Scott and saw him snickering. Even he couldn't help but laugh at the princess of Nerdville.

I lasted another three weeks of school, then summer hit. What a relief! I could have the summer off from being the class nerd. I begged my parents for a new pair of glasses and not just a repaired version of the broken ones. They finally relented and let me actually pick a fashionable pair. I didn't have to hide any longer.

On the first day of eighth grade, I showed up with my new glasses. Scott walked up to me and grabbed my hands.

"You look great," he said.

Oh yeah, I thought, where were you when I needed you? Where were you when others were laughing at me, when I was ugly?

I felt weird inside when he talked to me. I didn't have butterflies in my stomach and my knees stayed strong underneath me. His smile had lost some of its appeal as I noticed that my heart wasn't doing the pitter-patter dance it used to. I must have changed over the summer months.

I looked at Scott and slowly slid my hand away from his.

"Yes, I do look great, don't I?"

I walked down the hall, leaving him to gawk at my new "character."

~Cindy Ovard

First Kiss

Stolen kisses are always sweetest.
~Leigh Hunt

heard a loud knock on the front door that bright summer's morning, and then someone calling my name. "Patsy, can you come out and play?" I was the tomboy who ran with the neighborhood boys: the tall, gangly girl with the shoulder-length, unmanageable, natural-curly hair. Not that I cared. At age eleven, I looked forward to beginning sixth grade at summer's end.

Just recently, I'd noticed the slight swelling that infringed on the flatness of my cotton T-shirt, especially if I stood very straight and stuck out my chest. Somehow I felt wild and wicked when I did that, and kind of disappointed that no one else seemed to notice my advancing adolescence.

I bounded across the living room and swung the door wide open. My friend Larry, who lived next door, stood on the front porch step. He grinned and then asked, "What should we do? Ride our bikes?"

"Yes!" I replied emphatically. "Let's go check out that house my grandpa is building."

We hopped on our bikes and took off down the street, skidding around the corner to the right, and turning into the building site. My grandpa owned a lumber mill located a block away that my dad managed while Grandpa kept busy with building projects around town. In fact, Grandpa had built the house my family lived in.

I thought watching houses being built was like working a three-dimensional puzzle, with the architect's plans serving as the picture on the puzzle box cover. Larry and I had been checking out the progress of this house for several months. Although the framing was done and the roof on, the doors still needed to be hung and the windows set.

We dumped our bikes in the dirt and entered the house through the open door frame. The 2-by-4s emitted the pleasant smell of fresh-cut wood. No construction workers were around. Newly installed plasterboard gave the floor plan new definition, and we began to wander through the bare rooms. I casually roamed into the back bedroom and into the closet, with Larry trailing behind. Dead end. I turned to leave and there we were—face to face.

"It's time to go," I said.

"Wait a minute!" he said. Then he leaned over and kissed me smack-dab on the lips. He immediately bolted for the bikes so fast you would have thought the house was on fire. I hesitated, then followed his path to the front door. Up the street I saw dust flying, tires kicking up gravel bullets, and Larry speeding down the block. He disappeared around the corner without a backward glance. I'd been left behind.

I stood still for a moment, shaking my head, dazed by his spontaneous act. I took the back of my hand and wiped off my lips, as if that would make the memory disappear. I couldn't fathom what had happened. All I was sure of was that I had felt the lips of another on mine. As swift, as unanticipated, as abrupt as it had been, there was no denying it. I had just experienced my first kiss.

I shrugged my shoulders, jumped on my bike, and headed home, knowing that something had changed. I finally got it. I wasn't just a tomboy anymore. I was a girl!

~Pat Stockett Johnston

Love Crazy

If you think you've found that one that you really love...
make sure they love you back.
~The Ataris, "Choices"

I like Jacob.
Jacob likes Kayla.
Kayla likes Jacob. Tons of heartache for me.

Lizzie likes Joshua.
Joshua likes me.
Heartache for Lizzie and Joshua. Nothing for me.

Mitch likes me.
He's public enemy number one.
Heartache for him. Anger for me.

Adam likes me.
I hate his guts.
Heartache for him. Nothing for me.

Euan likes me.
Euan is my friend.
I'm scared eight hours a day.

Fred likes me.
He gives me the creeps.
Heartache for him. Creeps for me.

~Arin Anderson

Twelve Boyfriends...
and Never Been Kissed

Patience is also a form of action.
~Auguste Rodin

My first boyfriend was Tom. I was in fourth grade. He was really cute and for the first time the boy I liked actually liked me. In the middle of the soccer field, he asked me out and I was the first girl in my school to have a boyfriend. We shared awkward glances, sat next to each other on the class field trip to the Detroit Zoo, and, oh my God, held hands! But the fairy tale ended when I broke up with him after two weeks because my friends—well—wanted me to.

Then there was Jim. Middle school had just started and every kid was trying to re-establish their social status after the class size more than tripled from 60 to 200 kids. I remember sitting in English class with my hair perfectly curled, but my nose running from a bad cold like a green faucet. Of course, this was the day the most popular kid, with his brown hair and green eyes, was making googly eyes at me. Whenever I turned my head around he'd be looking at me, smiling. I was too afraid to go to the back of the room and make the embarrassing loud noise of clearing out my nose, so I decided to continue using my hand as a wet Kleenex.

We left English class and my girlfriend said, "I think Jim likes you."

"Really?" I said, absolutely shocked, while wiping my nose.

"Yeah, he wants to ask you out!" she exclaimed.

And the next day Jim and I were boyfriend and girlfriend. Two weeks later I dumped him, because I knew there were more fish in the sea.

So I dated some boys I liked, and other boys because my friends were dating their friends, and others that I was repulsed by. Go figure. As I was become a J. Lo incarnate, dating everyone and anyone under the sun and dropping them just as quickly, my friends were discovering the mystery of older men.

One day in seventh grade, my girlfriend Jacki came into school. She always had her long, blond hair perfectly straight. Today she felt, for some reason, that she was having a bad hair day and needed to put her hair up. When she pulled back her perfect locks into a high ponytail, we immediately saw what she was trying to show off: a small, light purple bruise on her neck was on display for the entire middle school to see. Jacki had a hickey. She wasn't called a slut or a whore; instead all the girls were jealous she was romancing an older man who actually kissed her!

In seventh grade, though, I was losing my looks to a bad case of acne, braces, and pre-pubescent breasts. My endless track of boyfriends was slowing down. Then I met Tony, an eighth grader. He wasn't exactly Mr. Popularity, but I was completely smitten. After weeks of courting on AIM, we finally decided to start dating, but by the time we finally admitted we liked one another he was going to high school and I still had never been kissed.

I had a few more "flings" in eighth grade, and then came Steve. He was in my grade and super cute with his shining brown eyes, big smile, and brown hair with natural blond highlights. He was a soccer player and made me laugh without even saying a word.

We decided to date, for real this time. We had been dating for three weeks, the longest I had ever dated anyone. We were so serious that I bought him a box of jellybeans for his birthday. My mom even knew about him—she was the one who paid for his birthday gift. Everyone was teasing us, "When are you going to kiss? Have you guys made out yet?" I was so nervous! I had to prepare for the big birthday day.

A few days earlier, my girlfriend, who was probably nearing third base with her older boyfriend at that point, was trying to teach me how to kiss. I was so confused. Do I peck? Do I use my tongue? What is his tongue going to feel like? What do I do with my tongue? Will I be good? What if my breath stinks?

The big moment arrived. At the end of school, on his birthday, we went outside to say goodbye; with all eyes watching us we gave each other an awkward... hug. The next day I dumped him. He started crying. I was relieved; now I wouldn't have to deal with the stress of kissing him!

I finished middle school with all As and twelve boyfriends in my pocket, but not a single kiss to cherish on my lips. I didn't have my first kiss until spring break of my freshman year of high school. All the waiting made it utterly romantic. The cute older boy with blond curly hair and a tender touch kissed me under a Jacuzzi waterfall in Sedona, Arizona.

While other girls' reputations were already tarnished from rumors of making out — or further — in the middle school locker rooms, I came out of middle school with my reputation and bragging rights intact.

I learned that physical love can be unkind to girls, and that it is better to wait and maintain an innocent, "prude" reputation than experiment too far too early. It may be embarrassing at the time, but waiting for the right moment will make the kiss more romantic — and the memory so much sweeter.

~Andrea Feczko

Teens Talk Middle School

Being Happy with Yourself

Self-love seems so often unrequited.

~Anthony Powell

More Than Good Enough

He who trims himself to suit everyone
will soon whittle himself away.
~Raymond Hull

It seems like the second you step into middle school, you get judged. Not by other people, but instead by yourself. It's like a constant buzzing going on in your head — an endless circle of thoughts composed of questions for yourself like, "How does my hair look?" or maybe, "Would answering this history question make me look like a snob?" and the always persistent, "Am I good enough?"

I made the bulk of my friends during the first month of school. I always talked to a wide group of personalities, so I knew people who listened to music that screamed at you, people who wore heels bigger than their feet, people who listened to hip hop (which I am much more inclined to listen to, although I never told anyone), and ones who looked like they walked straight out of one of those teen novels, fully equipped with tubes of lip gloss and pink purses.

Then I knew a boy — his name was Brian. He almost always had his earphones placed firmly in his ears (but heard and responded to everything I said), wore what he called "vintage shoes," and was an active member of the Boy Scouts. He was the guy who was different from everyone else. I thought people's stares would faze him, but they didn't. In fact, Brian welcomed negative comments and simply questioned others about the way they lead their own lives. Something about him always made me feel nervous but oddly at ease: Brian never judged me or said anything about the way I looked or what I said. Looking back, it made me nervous because I wasn't used to it.

When I wasn't with Brian, I was constantly trying to be like the people I would speak to. My grades started to slip, the loud music I listened to started to give me headaches, and I was spending the little money I had on clothes and shoes. In short, my life was a complete mess. It was clear I had caved into the pressure of middle school. It was like I was in a hole and I just kept digging.

One day, somewhere in the middle of the third month of school, I was sitting behind Brian in Algebra class. I had just gotten back a polynomial test with a big red sixty-eight percent scrawled across the top. That test was the worst grade I had gotten in at least five years. I was usually such a good student—I did not understand what was happening to my grades.

Before I had the chance to shove the paper in my bag so no one would see it, Brian turned around with a neutral expression, a one hundred percent test in his hand.

"That's because you focus too much attention on what other people think about you," he said to me, gesturing towards my not-so-stellar test. "For someone so smart, you act like such an idiot when it comes to other people." I wasn't even sure how to respond.

"What's that supposed to mean?" I asked.

"It means that you never act like yourself. I always see you change the song you're listening to when certain people walk by. And you never answer questions in class that I'm sure you know."

"That's not true," I lied.

"Yes, it is. Just stop caring about what people think. Don't try to change yourself; you're just fine the way you are when you talk to me," he said before turning around to face the blackboard.

I could feel my mouth hanging wide open, but I couldn't concentrate long enough to close it. Had Brian just told me that I shouldn't try to fit in? I thought this was middle school, where people had to make friends if they wanted to make it through high school. Yet there Brian was, sitting comfortably in his own little world, with perfect grades and a collected life. And then there was me—breaking down on the inside, horrible grades, and a generally miserable life. I must have been missing something.

I realized that Brian was right. It was time for me to listen to the music I wanted to listen to, dress the way I wanted to dress, and to take control of my middle school life regardless of what my other classmates thought of me. I realized that if you're not happy with yourself, you can't have a happy middle school experience. So I took Brian's advice and started to act like myself, and I noticed that I was more than good enough. Finally.

~Jackson Beard

Eighth Grade Giants

Confront your fears, list them,
get to know them, and only then will you be able to
put them aside and move ahead.
~Jerry Gillies

There are plenty of things to think about when you start middle school—locker combinations, rotten teachers, too much homework—so sharing a building with a whole lot of eighth graders was the least of my worries. Well, at first.

Being a rather tall eleven-year-old, you'd think I would have no problem passing older kids in the hallways, but it wasn't so. The biggest kids in school were not just huge: they were, to me, terrifying.

Picture this—a bunch of innocent sixth graders strolling down the corridor when, lo and behold, a gang of gigantic thirteen-year-olds pops out of nowhere and thunders past, banging into lockers on the way! Not to say that all the eighth graders were this violent, but a good number of them were simply too large and loud for my liking. Admittedly, nearly half of them were my height or shorter, but even those students sort of scared me. I mean, some of the guys had facial hair! Getting stopped or beaten up by one of these kids was my worst nightmare.

Strangely, none of my friends seemed to share this fear. They courageously strutted past the older kids while I cowered in the corner. Still, I hardly ever saw the eighth graders and spent most of my time studying with my eleven-year-old classmates.

One day, my fun-loving instrumental teacher invited my friend Kristina and me to hang back during last period and hang out with him in the school's assembly room. We readily agreed and ran upstairs to grab our belongings. But when we returned downstairs, we heard the din of chattering voices blaring from inside the room. We peered in through the grimy windows and gasped. Lounging on the cushioned chairs, sitting on the edge of the stage, and even lying on the carpeted floor, were about one hundred eighth graders.

Kristina looked at me and I looked at her. Despite her bravery when it came to them, she was no more a fan of the older kids than I was. We weighed our options. If we went back to class, we'd have to suffer through forty-three minutes of pure boredom. On the other hand, if we entered the room, we could be seriously injured, or worse, humiliated in front of a huge crowd (all middle schoolers know that embarrassment costs much more than physical injuries).

While I was still deliberating, Kris pushed open the door and shoved me into the crowded room. I almost screamed when several heads turned to stare at the unwelcome eleven-year-old in the corner, and I grabbed Kristina's arm and pulled her in after me. The door swung closed as most of the older kids disgustedly turned back to their private conversations.

I just felt so out of place! They wore Abercrombie-labeled tight-fitting shirts and miniskirts while I stood uncomfortably in my over-size sweatpants and muddy sneakers. Their mascara and lip gloss shone on their mature faces. When several turned around to glance at Kris and me, I felt like I would die from the attention. I could almost read their expressions: "Oh, it's just a couple of sixth graders. Let me go back to my own conversation." Still, that hurt.

Shivering, we turned to our music teacher, whose name was Mr. Guild.

"What?" he asked, chortling, "You thought I had a free period?"

"Mr. Guild, they're scary!" I shrieked, "What were you thinking?!"

He chuckled and motioned to a few nearby girls. "Hey, get this! Claire over here's afraid of you!"

It was the last thing that would make me feel better.

Some of the girls were kind of nice, though. They didn't say much, just murmured phrases of indignation. You'd think it would calm me down, but I still had my doubts.

One girl passing by was enthusiastically blowing on an oversize, multicolored paper pinwheel. I stared as she forced all the other kids to puff on the wheel, making it spin faster than ever. I couldn't help but grin.

The girl turned and offered us a blow on the pinwheel, which we gladly took. Mr. Guild then explained my fear of older students, and the girl, Annie, grabbed my wrist and began leading me around the auditorium and introducing me to intimidating clusters of kids.

"EVERYONE, THIS IS CLAIRE AND SHE'S SCARED OF YOU!" Annie screamed to her friends. Afterwards, she took it upon herself to educate me in the art of being an eighth grader. First, she instructed, I had to make a pinwheel to share with all my friends and change my favorite color to black.

Escaping from this frightening lesson, we hastened to the corner where we found ourselves face to face with (oh boy) a girl with hot pink hair. When would this nightmare end? Actually, she was the nicest girl we'd encountered that day. Surprises never cease.

Once we were semi-alone, I asked Kristina if she thought we'd be identified as sixth graders if another teacher came to investigate the loud noises emanating from the stage. After all, although we'd probably blend in with the students, I was a little nervous that both of us would get in trouble with our guidance counselor, considering we weren't enrolled in this particular class.

"Liz," Kristina grinned, pointing to the massive pile of backpacks near the stairs, "there's your giveaway." I immediately understood. In the heap of dark blue, red, camouflage, and black knapsacks, the smallest bright lavender one seemed to pop out. I groaned and mentally added "get a cooler backpack" to my list of things to do, then removed it. Why be like everyone else when I could be, well, me?

When the bell finally rang, Kris and I were the first ones out the door. And I knew that even though I might not be the coolest future eighth grader, I wasn't going to change for anyone.

Anyway, I guess the current eighth graders aren't so bad after all.

~Claire Howlett

Carly Conquers Confidence

*It is the chiefest point of happiness that
a man is willing to be what he is.*
~Desiderius Erasmus

I met Carly on the first day of school. I was employed by a community organization that provided an in-school program for middle school girls. This specific age group was targeted in hopes of changing their thinking and their ideas about healthy eating, self-esteem, relationships, bullying, and substance abuse.

I couldn't help but notice her. She was sitting by herself at the back table. I recognized her, not as someone that I knew, but someone I had been. She was wearing dark, oversized clothing, her head was down to avoid eye contact, and she was a little overweight. I remembered that combination of shyness and low self-esteem, with a healthy dose of poor body image, all too well.

My first class was healthy eating. I engaged most of the class in the discussion. Carly appeared to be listening, but she didn't participate. The following week also included a discussion on food choices—with no participation from Carly.

The third week, we moved on to body image. I gave the definition of body image as the way we perceive the way that we look, often distorted by our thoughts that we are too fat, short, tall, or a multitude of other problems. I noticed Carly looking up periodically at me, but not meeting my eyes. We also discussed how our perceptions are influenced by the media—magazines, television, and movies. I asked the students if they knew that pictures of models were often computer-enhanced. Some were surprised and others had heard it before. I told them they were trying to emulate perfection that even the models couldn't achieve.

Then, I asked the students to name something about themselves that they didn't like. Was it something that could be changed? Most said they felt they were too fat and could probably diet, exercise, or eat healthier. We also discussed how changing hairstyles, wearing complementary colors, and even different clothing styles can make us feel more confident. We took it further by discussing how talents, test scores, and hobbies could boost self-esteem.

Carly looked up. I decided to push her a little for a response. However, her response was, "Everything about me should be changed." I pushed more for specifics. She settled on saying she was too tall and fat. Her voice was low and somewhat muffled. It was a start, I thought.

Our next class was on self-esteem, including how body image plays an important role in our confidence to try new things. I decided to tell my story of how I had been very shy and had low self-esteem at their age. I felt that I missed out on a lot of things for fear of being laughed at or failing. Carly looked up throughout the entire class. We were making some progress.

At the end of class I complimented her on the green shirt she was wearing. It was a nice change from her usual dark ones. She looked down, embarrassed, and mumbled thank you.

We moved on to other subjects during the next class and Carly continued looking up. A few times I caught her eye but she looked away. After class, she hung back. I engaged her in general conversation. Finally, she asked if I had a copy of a healthy eating pamphlet that I had shared in an earlier class. She mumbled her thanks and left.

Two weeks later, Carly came to class in a light blue shirt and jeans that appeared to actually be her size. I asked if she had lost weight. She said she had been walking every day. A slight smile came across her face. "I have lost four pounds so far," she said. She went on to add she had been following the healthy eating guide, along with the walking.

The next week, Carly answered two of my questions regarding how bullying affects its victims. She looked around at her classmates and seemed surprised that they didn't laugh. She was making headway in gaining confidence.

One day, I noticed she had a library book on poetry with her. I asked her after class if she enjoyed reading poetry. She surprised me with her response:

"Yeah, but I write a lot of it too."

I asked if I could read some. She handed me a composition book. I casually flipped through its pages. It was full of poetry. "May I keep this till next week?" She smiled and nodded.

Over the next several days, I read Carly's poetry. I had expected it to be full of sadness and dark subjects. Instead, it was all about hope, dreams, and nature.

She was very talented.

I spoke with her English teacher and inquired about writing programs. She informed me there was a writing class available every Tuesday after school. They also encouraged poetry writing. I was scared I wouldn't be able to convince Carly to go.

I told her how impressed I was with her writing. She appeared embarrassed but very pleased. I mentioned the writing class and she had heard of it. "Can you stay after school?" I asked, hoping the answer would be a positive one. She said she lived just down the road and could stay. I said that I had planned to sit in on the class next week, since I enjoyed writing, hoping to encourage her attendance.

"Maybe I will go see what it's about."

After that first time, she began to attend regularly.

At the end of the nine-week grading period, I received a new group of girls. Carly would stop by occasionally, just to say hi. I continued complimenting her obvious weight loss and asked about her writing. She always seemed pleased. Toward the end of the school year, she came to me with the school newspaper in hand. On the front page was a picture of some of the writing club members. It was in recognition of their recent writing contests and awards. Carly had received first place in poetry.

Her face beamed.

"I could have never done it without you," she told me.

"No Carly," I said adamantly. "You had it in you all the time, hidden away. You could have chosen not to use the tools that I gave you to find it."

Carly is going to high school next year. She has lost about twelve pounds and her dark, extra large clothes have been replaced. Carly has made an incredible physical transformation, but it is her new-found confidence and outlook on life that will take her far.

~P. A. Perry-Armes

Searching for Perfection

Self-respect cannot be hunted. It cannot be purchased. It is never for sale.
It cannot be fabricated out of public relations. It comes to us when we are
alone, in quiet moments, in quiet places, when we suddenly realize that,
knowing the good, we have done it; knowing the beautiful, we have served it;
knowing the truth we have spoken it.
~Whitney Griswold

Much of my childhood felt out of my control, as painful events seemed to define my life. My parents were divorced by the time I was nine and my only sibling, my brother, was six years older than I was and left home as soon as he could. My grandpa was often very sick, and my elementary school years were a blur of unhappy events. When I was young, I responded to my anxiety by eating. I ate boxes of cookies and chocolate whenever I could, trying my best to eat away the stress.

By the time I was in seventh grade, I had gained weight. I wasn't fat, but I was nowhere near the size 2 bodies my closest friends had. Cosette was a dancer, Kylie was a diver, and Olivia was naturally very petite. I felt awkward around them—large, ungraceful, and disgusting by comparison. My weight had bothered me for some time, but I never did anything about it. I was focused on my grades and after-school activities, which were singing and acting. Neither of those provided me with much exercise.

For one reason or another, the summer after eighth grade I decided to try running. I can't exactly say how it all began, but my drive and determination kept it going. I started going to the gym daily, beginning with less strenuous workouts: run five laps, walk five laps. After a few days, I would switch another lap from walking to running. I started with about three miles a day and as time progressed I noticed slight changes in my body. My hips got smaller, my thighs tightened. I changed my eating habits to fruits and grains and protein bars. I felt myself changing and, for the first time, getting into shape. The feeling was new to me and I was in love with it. I continued to work harder and harder for it. And then it became an obsession.

Eventually, I increased my running to ten miles a day. The pressure on my legs was so unbearable that I developed shin splints that quickly became stress fractures. A trip to the sports doctor told me that I had to stay away from running for about two months. Terrified that my lack of exercise would cause me to gain my weight back, I stopped eating. I counted calories and wrote everything down on a tiny note card that I hid in my bathroom drawer. I researched the number of calories in different amounts of foods. If I went out to eat, I checked the calories for the restaurant's meals online. I would not allow myself to consume more than 800 calories per day. Swimming and biking replaced my usual running schedule, and pounds were coming off of my body faster than I could believe.

By the time school started again, I received compliments from everyone I knew. I was suddenly fitting into skirts and jeans that had been far out of reach a year earlier. I remember specifically one day at school, one of my teachers said to me "if you lose any more weight you'll just disappear," which I took as a compliment.

For the most part, tricking people into believing that I was merely losing weight through exercise was effortless, but fooling my mom required some extra work. She would hand me large platefuls of dinner, and I would tell her that I needed to eat at my desk so that I could do more homework. I would then shovel the entire plate into a plastic baggie. I knew that I could not throw the food away in my own house—my mom would surely find it. Instead, I hid the plastic bags in my backpack and threw the food away at school the next day. I would even go so far as to sneak cookies and other snacks from the pantry just to throw them away. Not only did my mom believe that I was eating normally, sometimes—when she noticed the missing cookies—she accused me of sneaking too much unhealthy food. She was so convinced that I was eating that she took me to the doctor's office to have several blood tests done to see what was wrong with me.

As I continued to starve myself, I began to love it even more. Feeling empty somehow made me feel purposeful, yet I never felt empty enough. I cut back even more. I stood as I watched television in order to burn more calories. But every time I looked in the mirror, I would cry because I saw myself gaining weight. The more I looked at myself, the more fat I saw.

Often nutritionists say that people starve themselves to have control over something in their lives; my experience with anorexia, though, controlled me more than I could have ever known. I stopped thinking for myself. I stopped caring about being with friends or family, as long as I could exercise. I counted calories in my head over and over again, making sure I had not gone past my limit. I weighed myself several times a day, each time terrified that the number on the scale would go up. Even my dreams were ridden with this disease; I would wake up in the middle of the night sobbing over a dream where I had binged on cake or pizza, terrified that the dream would actually become reality.

Eventually, I saw a nutritionist, and the problems I was having were slowly resolved. The majority of the forty pounds I had lost came back, but I was happy with my body. I still run and eat healthily, but I would never go back to starving myself. In the beginning of it all, I convinced myself that I could handle it—that I could maintain control.

I hope that nothing in my life ever takes control of me like that again. I lost who I was to what I looked like, and I think that is a painful lesson many girls learn the hard way. Yes, we all have parts of ourselves that we would like to change. Whether you think you have fat thighs and a big butt, a not-quite-flat stomach, or chubby arms, nobody sees herself as one hundred percent perfect. It isn't about changing your body until it's perfect, though. It's about changing your attitude to learn to love yourself inside and out.

~Samantha Harper

59

In Between

Yesterday is history.
Tomorrow is a mystery.
Today is a gift.
~Eleanor Roosevelt

Too young to have a real job,
Too old to play with toys,
Not tall enough to shoot the hoops
With towering high school boys.

Too young for going out on dates,
Too old to have a sitter,
Not shaped just right to wear the clothes,
With all the sparkling glitter.

Prom is just a distant dream,
And make-up is a chore.
I'd rather stay in bed all day
'Cuz school is such a bore.

I watch the older kids drive cars
And dream of my big chance
To make the winning touchdown,
To learn the latest dance.

Everyone is asking
"What path will you pursue?"
"What college will you go to?"
I haven't got a clue.

Life is so confusing
For each and every teen,
For everywhere we turn to look
We're caught there in between.

I learn a little more of life
With every single day.
I learn to handle ups and downs
And all that comes my way.

The problems come and problems go
I bounce back from the pain.
I learn to share the laughs and tears
And see the steps I gain.

This is a time of growth and hope
Of being just a teen,
Of planning all my distant dreams,
The years of in between.

~Cynda M. Strong

60

Cakewalk

Winning isn't everything,
but the will to win is everything.
~Vince Lombardi

In sixth grade, when I was a nerdy, gangly, awkward girl who got brutally teased for being weird, I became obsessed with winning something. I entered raffles and drawings, tried to make bets with everyone I knew, and repeatedly called the local radio station in a desperate attempt to be the hundredth caller. I didn't care what I won; I just wanted to win something so that I could feel like a winner. Unfortunately, I never won anything, so I started to think that winning wasn't possible for me. I was destined to stay a friendless loser forever.

My dream was to win the middle school spelling bee, and I am still convinced I could have done it, but my chances were ruined by an elderly middle school principal who desperately needed a hearing aid. Tragically, I was disqualified in the first round by the old, deaf man who claimed that I spelled D-R-E-A-M, as B-R-E-A-M. I was furious. I threw a fit on stage and had to be escorted out. Things got ugly. I mean, come on, who would spell Dream with a B? How idiotic can you get? Obviously I knew how to spell dream. That was an easy word!

After this sad and unjust defeat, I officially gave up. I knew it was not my fate to win anything, so I stopped trying. Then my mother took me to the Hospital Fair. Every year in our town, our hospital hosted a festival to raise money for new equipment and supplies. Everyone in town looked forward to it. It wasn't like a real fair with a midway or rides. Basically, it was a gigantic yard sale, some games put together by local church ladies, bake sales, arts and crafts booths, and stands selling BBQ chicken. I liked the petting zoo best, because I liked to watch the goats pull down people's pants with their teeth, and I always looked forward to buying a lemon half with a peppermint stick stuck in the center.

The year I was in sixth grade, it poured and some of the activities had to be moved inside the school gymnasium. My mother had been asked to bring a Pistachio Dream Whip cake, which was green and disgusting, to the cakewalk. Since it was raining, she thought I might enjoy watching the indoor event. I am pretty sure that cakewalks no longer exist, so I should explain what one is. Several people bake a variety of cakes and line them up on a table. Each cake is assigned a number. People enter the cakewalk and pay a fee to play. Then they stand up on a stage and walk around in a circle, like fools, while bad music plays. My cakewalk was set to Michael Jackson's *Thriller* — the whole album, not just the song. Then, just as in musical chairs, the music stops and the players halt on a square taped to the floor. The church lady in charge of the cakewalk pulls a number from a hat and calls it out. The person standing on the square with that number wins the cake of the corresponding number. When they win their cake they are out of the game and get to go home to joyously eat their cake and the game continues until all the cakes are gone. The thing with the cakewalk is you never know what cake you're going to get — some cakes are better than others. They're all donated by local women — some of them are good bakers, and some of them make Pistachio Dream Whip cake.

When we arrived at the cakewalk, my mother dropped her cake off on a table laden with every kind of cake imaginable, most of which were gross confections I would never dream of eating. Except one. There amidst the Bundt cakes and the Red Velvets was the most beautiful sheet cake I had ever seen. It was the cake I imagined every year on my birthday—a smooth, white, rectangular fantasy, covered in pastel colored icing roses with little green sugared leaves. Usually on my birthday I got a lopsided layer cake gooped with canned frosting. Not that I minded, because it's very nice to have someone bake you any kind of cake, but I secretly longed for the professionally decorated cake that number eighteen surely was.

My Cake of Dreams was made by a lady who had taken a professional cake decorating class and prided herself on making fancier cakes than anyone else's, so not only was the cake spectacular-looking, it was also homemade—not some cardboard-tasting store cake. Store-bought cakes were not allowed in the cakewalk. Luckily, sixth grade girls were. As soon as I spotted number eighteen I knew I wanted to spend my allowance, a whopping three dollars that I had saved up, on participating in the cakewalk. My mother thought I was crazy, but I was insistent.

"You know, your chances aren't good. It's like gambling. You hardly ever win, so just be prepared to be disappointed," she warned.

I decided to take my chances. As the music started, I concentrated on number eighteen. When I got close to the eighteenth floor square I would slow down. I almost knocked some people out of the way to get to it in time. Each time we stopped and I was on a different number I prayed:

"Please don't let me get stuck with the German Chocolate, God. I hate German Chocolate, and not the Pistachio Dream Whip either, because I could have just stayed home and had that mess. Please let me get number eighteen."

Seven cakes were given away and number eighteen remained.

"So this is Thriller...."

I stopped on number eighteen. I prayed harder than I had ever prayed in my life. I started to bargain with God, thinking that he owed me one for the spelling bee incident. The old lady pulled a wad of paper from the hat and it took her what seemed like fifteen minutes to unfold it. Then she had to pull her glasses down. It looked like she couldn't read the number.

"Please let her say number eighteen! I have to go to the bathroom and I feel like an idiot on this stage and I really want the pretty cake. Please let it be me."

"NUMBER EIGHTEEN!" said the woman.

I almost had a heart attack. I didn't move for a few seconds. Did she really say that? Did God actually hear my pleas? YES! I floated, as if in a dream, to take my beautiful, perfect, icing-rosed Cake of Dreams.

I WON THE CAKEWALK!!!

This was easily one of the finest moments of my entire life. We ate the cake for a week and I got all the roses. I couldn't believe my luck. Sometimes I still can't, and whenever I get discouraged and think that winning isn't possible, or that my dreams can't come true, I remember the cakewalk and know that no matter what, I am a winner.

~Victoria Fedden

Sweater Girl

A man's errors are his portals of discovery.
~James Joyce

I couldn't take my eyes off her. She sat on the bleachers in jeans and a chunky cream sweater. Her blond hair fell perfectly on her athletic shoulders. She was beautiful, even in the eighth grade, and she never had a reason to talk to me. I didn't know her name, but I was convinced I had to be just like her.

"All right, ladies, to the red line," Coach N. said as she blew a sharp whistle. The pretty girl was so cool, the noise in the gym didn't even affect her. She just kept staring off into space.

As I dribbled a ball up and down, I considered all the ways I wasn't as gorgeous as her. I was not slender like a model. I had chicken legs, according to my sister's boyfriend. Chicken legs covered in brownish-blond hair. I checked the ball to Angie, my best friend, whose mom let her shave her legs because she thought Angie might feel embarrassed in gym class. My mom just kept saying she didn't think I was ready.

Above my gross legs, I wore blue shorts that I had to roll up at the waist three times because I was so tiny. Some people might think that's cute, but the V-shape it formed down my front side was not. I also wore a baggy gray shirt with a bear's face on the front and the words "Bair Middle School" below it. I hated this uniform. The small-size shirts weren't long enough to cover the V my shorts made, and the medium-sized ones were too baggy.

When the dribbling drills were over, we lined up outside the locker room to wait for the crowd of eighth graders to finish dressing. One tall, muscular girl walked by our line to talk to her friend who stood next to me. She asked what grade I was in. I told her seventh. She laughed and said "Girl, you look like you belong in fifth grade!"

If I were brave, I would have told her that I was actually in high school level Spanish and eighth grade level math. But I didn't.

In the changing room, I twisted like a pretzel to get half my gym shirt off and pull on my regular shirt. Then I shimmied out of the gym shirt. All of this was necessary to hide the fact that Mom wouldn't buy me a training bra, and I was too embarrassed to buy one myself with my allowance.

Two weeks passed by, and I hadn't seen that girl again. But I remembered her when Mom took me clothes shopping. When we got to Marshalls, I went straight for the long racks of sweaters. I picked out a couple in purple, my favorite color, but I HAD to get a cream-colored one. It was a plan: Wear the sweater, be gorgeous, and have the boys, especially Zack, like me. Finally, I found one. It was a cream-colored chunky sweater with big "C" and "K" letters, standing for Calvin Klein.

When Mom came over to my section, she asked to see what I wanted. I showed her the clothes. She immediately said no to the cream sweater. She hated brand names and thought it was too expensive, even for Marshalls. I begged and whined. She just didn't understand why I needed this sweater, and I couldn't find the words to tell her how much it meant to me. Eventually, she said I could have it only if I gave up the other sweaters. I pouted and stamped my foot, but put back the purple sweaters.

That night, before I took my shower, I quickly grabbed one of the pink disposable razors Mom kept in the bathroom. In the shower, I shaved a small rectangular patch, no bigger than an inch, off my right leg. It looked good and felt smooth. I held the razor and thought about doing the rest when my dad banged on the door and told me I was wasting water. I got out and hid the razor in my towel, pulling on pajama pants to hide my secret.

The next day, I walked into the gym wearing my sweater and feeling bold about the bare patch of leg hidden under my jeans. Because we were all watching a video, we didn't have to change. I kept stealing looks at Zack and smiling at him over on the boys' side of the red lines. He had fluffy blond hair and a goofy smile. He was the cutest boy in our class. He must not have seen me because he didn't smile back.

That weekend, because my mom thought I was mature enough to do my own laundry, but not mature enough to shave, wear a bra, or date, I washed the sweater with my other clothes and threw it in the dryer.

By Wednesday, I couldn't wait to wear it again. Even though the temperature had warmed up to the 70s, I still put it on. But something wasn't right. It had bunched up, and I had to keep pulling it down to make it reach my waistline. It didn't look cool; it looked like a little girl's art smock.

"Mo-om! Something's wrong with my sweater!" I told her.

"Oh, Britt. Don't you know by now not to put your nice things in the dryer?" She touched the fabric. "Look at it! It's all stretched out!"

I sniffled as I ran my fingers down the lines that made it look pleated right above the bottom seam. "Can we go to the store and get another one tonight?"

"No, we cannot." Mom had her car keys out. "That sweater was not cheap. You'll just have to live with it and remember not to put everything in the dryer. Now go change before your father takes you to school."

She left. I went to my room and looked in my closet. I looked at my sweater. I had nothing to wear but this. I felt miserable all day at school.

That night, as I was doing homework, Mom came home. She handed me a Marshalls bag. "Here."

Inside was a purple sweater, one of the ones I had picked out last week. It hung from my hand like a jewel and seemed to sparkle like one. "Thanks!"

The phone rang. "Bobby, can you get that?" Mom yelled to my

brother. Then she turned to me. "There's supposed to be a cold front next week. No wearing it till then. Okay?"

I nodded. Bobby walked toward the kitchen.

"And what are you going to do with it when it gets dirty?" She reached out for the phone, but Bobby shook his head.

"Wash it and lay it OUT to dry," I said, and snatched the phone from Bobby.

"Hello?" I answered.

"Britt? It's Zack. From class." Ohmigosh.

"Hi!" I managed to say.

"Do you have the social studies homework from today? I was sick."

"Yeah. It's the workbook pages 34-37."

"Okay. Um, thanks. Bye." Click. He hung up.

"Bye."

I took the sweater and hung it up carefully in my closet. I thought about picking out something for tomorrow, but now I didn't care. It felt much cooler to be noticed by Zack when he wasn't even at school looking at my clothes. I pulled out a skirt. Uh oh. What about shaving? I put it back. Oh, well, I thought. No use shaving—there's going to be a cold front anyway.

~Britt Leigh

Snapshots

Never be bullied into silence.
Never allow yourself to be made a victim.
Accept no one's definition of your life;
define yourself.
~Harvey Fierstein

There in the narrow hallway, squished between lockers painted a hideous orange and seniors wielding calculus books, I had never felt so alone. It was a lonely year. No one wanted to welcome the skinny, home-schooled girl who wore turtlenecks, jumpers, and matching barrettes, and had braces and glasses. Especially not twelve- and thirteen-year-old girls who already wore make-up and short skirts. They must have had a field day with the girl who was still in the dark ages of fashionable apparel. I had been so proud of the matching clothes that I had bought with my mom for school, and especially of the skirts that I had sewn on the sewing machine all by myself. I had sewn other things, but never anything like a whole skirt before. Corduroy jumpers, red plastic barrettes, a skirt of pink fabric with beautiful blue and pink roses, a turtleneck with scattered mittens and scarves, a pair of pink jeans with a matching blue and pink sweatshirt we had bought at the outlets at the beach. They didn't quite make me fit in with the crowd of junior high girls.

We were only a little over a month into school when it was time for the annual seventh grade school trip to a local retreat center. It was anticipated with excitement by the entire class for the sole reason that we wouldn't have classes for three whole days. The fact that we could wear jeans and shorts also had the female population excited. Angela was one of the other nine girls who had been placed in the cabin with me.

On the first day, she had motioned me over to where she was standing. "Hey, Sara. Come over here, I want you to look at something," she said with a welcoming smile that drew me to her. She leaned over her opened duffle bag and pulled out jeans, a tank top, and a sweater.

"Here, I want you to wear these clothes today. They'll look so much better than the ones that you have on." She pushed them into my hands.

They felt so heavy. Right in that moment I wanted to hand them right back to her, no — throw them back at her, and yell, "I don't want them!" But I moved, as commanded, to the bathroom and tried them on.

Later, my own clothes lay in a heap on the dirty, cracked bathroom floor. Her clothes didn't quite fit me right. She was shorter then I was and so the wide legged jeans were too short too. They were also lower at the waist than what I was used to. The velvety camouflage tank didn't quite meet the pants.

Voices traveled from the main room of the cabin into the bathroom.

"I am so glad that we get to wear jeans on this trip!"

"I know. It so stinks that we have to have a dress code. All my friends at public school get to wear jeans."

"I'm going to wear my hair like this tonight. What do you think?"

"Yes, that is so cute."

"Gosh, isn't she done in the bathroom yet?"

I stared into the mirror nervously and pulled the green sweater she had also given me over my head. At least with the sweater I looked less weird than I did before.

A knock sounded on the door. "Hey, are you done in there yet? Come out, we want to see what you look like."

"I'll be out in a minute."

I glanced in the mirror again, and my eyes focused on the showers reflected in it, then on what I was wearing. I didn't like it. I wanted to put on my own clothes and run out of the bathroom as fast as I could. There was a weird feeling in the pit of my stomach that I couldn't identify. I took a deep breath to brace myself. They didn't even smell like my clothes. There was a strong scent of perfume clinging to them. The only scent that I ever wore was soap.

I opened the door tentatively and was surprised to find her still standing right outside the door, leaning up against one of the sets of bunk beds. She smiled, "Well, it's certainly an improvement. You look much better then you did before. Didn't I tell you that it would work?" Several girls playing cards on the wooden floor nodded in agreement. Others took a momentary hiatus from conversation to stare at me and then offered their affirmation as well.

"I have to get my camera. We have to take a picture of this," she exclaimed like it would be a moment that would be lost forever if she didn't capture it.

Just then, the bell rang to announce dinner time. A flurry of activity began as girls grabbed their purses and hairbrushes for quick touch-ups.

"Hurry up!" she said impatiently, grabbing my arm and pulling me down the stairs. "We have just enough time before dinner starts. Here. Stand right here." She positioned me on the tree-lined path leading down to the dining hall and yanked my glasses off my face. "There, much better." Everything around me turned into a blur as the camera snapped.

I wore the outfit all evening, letting it fall onto the same dirty, cracked bathroom floor after the night's festivities. I wanted it off. It felt too weird to wear it—too unnatural. She wanted me to wear some of her clothes again the next day, but this time I refused.

I would wear her clothes again one more time that year—I remember exactly what they looked like: a pair of flared velour pants and a blue, silky blouse with pearl buttons. I remember those pants and that blouse so well, because that was the day I realized that I wasn't Angela, and most of all, I didn't want to be her. I wanted to be Sara, geeky as she might be.

I wore Angela's clothes because I wanted to have friends and I wanted the other girls in my class to like me. But after I wore them, I decided I wanted to make my own decisions and wear the clothes that I wanted to wear. I wasn't happy trying to be someone else. I never became popular, or became the girl with a lot of friends. But from then on, I always knew that the friends I did have were friends with me for me. Not for the clothes I wore, and certainly not for how cool I was.

~Sara E. Rowe

20/20

I was once afraid of people saying,
"Who does she think she is?"
Now I have the courage to stand and say,
"This is who I am."
~Oprah Winfrey

"Laura Lynn," Ms. Elliott called, her deep throaty voice bouncing off the cinder block walls and smacking me in the face.

"Yes?" I tried to sound innocent. I was innocent, but I felt the heat in my cheeks as if I'd been caught snooping around my older brother, Jim's room.

"Take off your glasses."

"I c-c-c-can't," I said. My voice seemed all bumpy. My words felt like they were climbing the rock-climbing wall at the gym. No one talked back to Ms. Elliott, yet there was no way I could remove my sunglasses.

"Why not?" Her voice was more imposing than Darth Vader's as she strolled down the aisle of oak desks toward me. Ms. Elliott was no taller than 5'1", and her short brown hair with the middle part was plain and almost masculine. She always wore boots with stacked wooden heels that lifted her several inches in the air, and she stomped down the rows of desks like a drill sergeant. She wore a red and silver paisley necktie, crisp white shirt and a black vest — haberdashery is the word the fashion magazines would use to describe her style, but she always dressed like this, not just when it came back into vogue. It was rumored that Ms. Elliott even smoked cigars.

"I-I-I had surgery," I squawked, like a duckling learning how to quack. This was humiliating. I couldn't believe I had announced my operation to the whole class, although enough people had asked about my sunglasses, and gossip at our school traveled faster than a gurney rushing towards the emergency room.

"Remove your glasses," she demanded.

I knew Ms. Elliott suspected that all middle schoolers smoked pot and I knew she wanted to see my eyes to make sure I didn't have the slanty, narrow orbs of a pothead. But please! I was about the booki-est bookworm there was, and everyone in the eighth grade knew it. I would never do drugs! I wasn't even cool enough to be bad news. I knew it was her job to keep an eye out for erratic behavior from her students and I'm sure there was some weird rule against wearing sunglasses in school, but Ms. Elliott was going to be grossed out and completely disgusted if she made me take them off. Underneath the dark shades, I looked like something out of a horror movie!

My eyes had been problematic since birth. I'd had two eye surgeries by the time I was three. I had used medicated eye drops for as long as I could remember and glasses since the time I was five. Glasses to correct the fact that I was cross-eyed. Glasses that made me look the part of the geeky, smart kid I had become. In eighth grade, my eye doctor felt my eyes were ready to withstand another surgery and the medical advancements with lasers almost guaranteed my eye muscles could be corrected. Translation — with one more surgery, my eyes would look straight ahead, and I wouldn't need glasses anymore.

To gain the prize of freedom from spectacles, I had to endure the surgery, which was the scariest thing I'd experienced in my life. I don't remember much about the ones I had when I was little. I could only recall wisps of memories of baking pies for my dad in the pretend kitchen of the children's hospital ward and throwing off my surgical cap in disgust at how ugly it was (even back then I could detect hideous fashion). But this time, I got it. I knew I would drink something to make me sleepy and while I was sleeping, surgeons would serrate my optic muscles. Creepy!

Fortunately, I have a strong sense of faith, and I just kept praying and praying that I wouldn't go blind and the surgeons would do their best. I got to stay home from school for three days, but my eyes were bloody. The parts of my eyes that were normally white were pure red, as if someone took a red marker and colored in all the white parts. I had to sleep with a towel on my pillowcase because bloody tears leaked down my face while I slept. As a child I loved reading *Hansel and Gretel*. In my copy of the book, the witch was described as having red eyes. Now I looked just like that witch!

Ms. Elliott stood directly beside my desk now and I knew I was trapped. I mustered up my courage and slid my Ray-Bans slowly down my nose, looking her directly in the eye, as if accepting her dare. After all, she asked for it. I could tell she wanted to look away, but Ms. Elliott was too tough for that. She held my gaze, despite a slight spasm on her lips.

"I h-have a note," I muttered. Dr. Stroble had written a note permitting me to wear sunglasses in school, saying I might be drowsy and unable to handle heavy reading homework.

Ms. Elliott held out her hand in anticipation of the piece of paper. I rummaged through my straw tote bag, the one I got for my birthday, and served her with the note.

"I see," she announced and marched slowly to the front of the room where she proceeded to teach as if the whole incident had never occurred.

But it had occurred, and it was the only setback of my surgery. From that day forward, everything changed for me. I took all of my old pairs of glasses to the donations box at Lenscrafters. I figured if someone else could wear my old specs, good for them. And somehow when those old pieces of plastic were tossed in the donations box, so was my nerdy persona, never to be seen again. It was completely liberating. My operation was a success, and I saw the world in a whole new way. Not as the stereotyped glasses-wearing bookworm, but as me, myself, a girl who loved to read and dance and listen to music and play the piano and climb trees and talk on the phone — the person God created, not the label the world had placed on me because of my glasses.

Without my glasses, I could finally see and be seen for who I truly was.

~Laura Smith

A D-Minus

I have had more trouble with myself than
with any other man I've met.
~Dwight Moody

I remember my Landon Junior High School seventh grade math teacher's name very well. It was Mr. Young. He stood out, because the kids made fun of him. He was missing one of his fingers and always pointed at students with his middle finger.

For some reason, I was not very good in school. English and Math were my worst two subjects. There was just something wrong with me, inside my head. No matter how hard I tried, I just could not figure out why I didn't understand what all the other kids found so easy to learn. I do not think there was ever a day that I went to school that I was not afraid.

One day, I was told by Mrs. Winters, the head matron of the Children's Home Society Orphanage, that if I got one more E on my report card, I would be taken to the Juvenile Court in downtown Jacksonville, Florida. She would tell the judge to send me away to the "big prison for kids."

I tried really hard for weeks to learn how to multiply, do fractions and compound things. I just could not understand how to make different parts of numbers into whole things. My brain could not do it, no matter how hard I tried.

The day before report cards were to come out, I already knew that Mr. Young would give me an E, just as he always did. After class ended, I went to Mr. Young and told him that the orphanage was going to send me to the "big prison," if I got another E on my report card. He told me there was nothing he could do; it would be unfair to the other kids if he gave me a better grade than I actually earned.

I smiled at him, turned, walked toward the door and then I stopped. I looked at the teacher and said, "Mr. Young, you know how all the kids make fun of you, because you're missing your finger?"

He looked at me, moved his mouth to one side like he was biting the inside of his gum and said nothing.

"They shouldn't do that to you, because you can't help not having a finger, Mr. Young. Just like I can't help not being able to learn numbers and stuff like that," I said.

Again, he said nothing. He just looked down at his desk and began grading papers.

The next day when I got my report card, I tucked it into one of my books. While on the school bus, I opened the report card envelope and looked at my grades: Geography B+, Mechanical Drawing C-, English D-, History C-, Gym B+, Art C, Math D-.

I stood up, placed the report card against my heart and immediately fell to my knees in the center aisle. Everyone on the bus began to laugh as I cried uncontrollably.

That math grade was my favorite grade I ever received in my whole life—not because I wasn't sent to the big prison for kids, but because I knew that someone in the world finally understood what it was like for me to be missing a finger inside my head.

~Roger Dean Kiser

Blowing in the Wind

Always be a first-rate version of yourself,
instead of a second-rate version of somebody else.
~Judy Garland

I shivered from both excitement and chill. My P.E. shirt was much too large for my teeny-weeny running shorts, the ones that clung to my teeny-weeny non-running legs. Regardless, I let the shirt hang limply over my shorts, hiding them from view and making me look hilariously pant-less. Instead, I focused on the challenge at hand. It was my goal as a Del Mar student to high jump 4'6". I had crashed into the bar on the first two attempts, and now I was on my very last attempt to conquer the bar.

As I swallowed some air and began to run up to the bar, I heard my friends on the sidelines, hooting. Instead of the typical encouragement promising that I would make it over, that I could do it, they shouted in unison, "YEAH GANGLY!" Despite my concentration, I broke into a wide and infinitely appreciative grin.

I've always been that kid in P.E. that no one wants on their team. I defied the stereotype of being fat and sweaty and was, instead, undesirable because of my gangliness. I had size ten feet, and if my legs grew any more, they would wrap around my neck and strangle me. Even as one of the taller girls in the grade, it was natural for me to slink around with my head dangling and arms flailing by my sides. When a gusty wind came hustling by, my friends instinctively reached out to anchor me.

My nickname, "Gangly," was one of the few fitting things, when, in seventh grade, I was caught desperately in the throes of my pubescent growth spurt. It was an instant hit. As the nickname began to catch among my friends (though, with my athletic prowess, I would surely fumble over it like a football and never be able to catch it), I would poke my head, turtle-like, from my cocoon of excess cloth and answer, "Yes?"

On occasion, nosy teachers had taken me aside and asked in all seriousness if I was eating enough. Each time, I would grouchily assure them I was fine, irritable because they were keeping me from lunch and my tantalizingly cheesy sandwich. These same teachers would throw dirty looks at the people who called out, "YEAH GANGLY!" when I stood up for a report or answered a question. What those teachers couldn't understand is that I wasn't offended by the nickname. It's like calling a redhead "Carrot-top" or "Ginger." There was no reason I shouldn't have been proud of who I was, no matter how graceless, uncoordinated, or dangerous in the presence of scissors.

I was receiving harsh looks of doubt on the day of the track meet, especially when my fellow athletes saw me stumble off the bus for the meet. I always loved being able to gleefully shout "Yes!" when asked if I was going to the meet. Of course, as I flailed forward and raised a limp, dangling hand for a high-five, it was obvious that I was going to the meet as a high jumper. I was joyful that I had finally found a sport where gangliness prevailed; the high jump, where the objective was to barrel up to and leap over a bar.

My friends, who were quite aware of the runners' and shot-putters' skepticism over my ability, screamed for me, the infamous Gangly and I felt more athletic than ever. I smiled over at them and continued to run up to the bar. Just as I propelled my feet off the ground, whipping them up to the sky, the cheering took on a different note, one of wisdom and advice: "PUT ON SOME PANTS!"

I flipped my ankles over my head as my body arced over the bar and landed with a hum onto the mat. I waited, sprawled upside down, and heard nothing. No clatter of the bar hitting the ground.

No disappointed sigh from the crowd. To me, this emptiness was overflowing with pride. I had made it over and was now in the Top Five, something that had never happened for me in sports. I was ecstatic. Ganglies: 1. Buff People: 0.

"YEAH GANGLY!" came my friends' voices once more. IT was the only thing they could say, for as I kicked my legs over the bar and flipped onto the mat, shirt over my head, it was quite clear that there were, indeed, shorts beneath my very large P.E. uniform.

~Brittany Newell

66

In Between Is Okay

Life is not easy for any of us. But what of that?
We must have perseverance and above all confidence in ourselves.
We must believe that we are gifted for something and that
this thing must be attained.
~Marie Curie

"There's the sign," my mom said. "'State School for the Deaf and Blind.' We're here." I could see well enough to make out the large red building looming before me.

As a twelve-year-old kid, I felt nervous coming to a new place to live, only going home on weekends. Why did I have to come here?

Until a year ago, I thought of myself as being like other kids. I hadn't noticed I held the book closer to my face than they did to read. At the beginning of sixth grade, I found out I was different.

I walked home from school alone on that dreadful day. Tears stung my eyes as my teacher's words raced through my mind.

"You can't be class president. You're blind."

I looked down at my feet dragging through the gravel and at my blue coat sleeve as I wiped my eyes. "Why does he think I'm blind?" I wondered.

My partial sight had never kept me from doing what other kids did. I watched TV, skipped rocks on the pond, and played tag with my friends.

After the election, I felt as if I didn't measure up to the sighted students. I wasn't good enough to compete in their world. My identity shattered because being partially sighted seemed to mean I wasn't capable. To top it off, teachers in public school decided I needed extra tutoring. That was why I was headed to the school for the blind.

Reluctantly, I entered the girls' dormitory.

The dorm mother greeted me. "Hello, Pam! Rachael, Elaine!" she called down the hall. "Come meet your new roommate."

I didn't see the girls until they came into my close range of vision.

"Hi," I spoke hesitantly.

I didn't realize both of them were totally blind until they each felt for one of my hands. They both talked at once. "We've been excited to meet you and make a new friend. Come let us show you our room." I had a glimmer of hope as I said goodbye to my parents. Maybe I would finally find acceptance here.

Having been around sighted people, I was surprised that I could see more than most of the girls in the dorm. At times, I assisted them and aided them with their homework, guiding them places and describing to them the colors of their surroundings and the big items I could see. I told them about the full green trees, brilliant sunrises, fluffy white clouds, cute outfits others wore, and decorations on walls. This gave me a sense of fulfillment and joy. In return, they gave me love and support.

At age fourteen, in my third year at the school, another dorm mother, Mrs. Benton, pulled me aside. "Since you're lucky enough to see better than the others, and want to be so helpful, you can be in charge of the table at meals and serve the girls." Her sarcasm was lost to me.

"Sure, I'm glad to help," I said with enthusiasm.

I enjoyed this job until she used it against me.

One night, in the dining hall after dinner, the girls at my table started clearing the food. Lindy, a totally blind teen, picked up a brimming bowl of fruit and juice to take to the cleanup tray.

"That's too full," I warned her. "Take something else."

She grabbed it anyway. I smiled at her determination. When Lindy spilled it all over the floor, Mrs. Benton ordered, "Pam, clean it up!"

"I'll be glad to help her," I offered.

"Lindy is blind and you can see," Mrs. Benton argued.

"So what if Lindy is blind?" I exclaimed. "She's still able to help clean up her own mess."

Mrs. Benton's voice escalated into a scream.

"You - will - clean - it - up!"

While I picked up pits with squishy fruit and mopped the sticky floor, she kept yelling at me. My cheeks burned as the house parents and all the dorm students, including my boyfriend, listened in awkward silence. Lindy didn't say a word.

I left the dining hall as soon as I could. The cold air hit my hot face. I saw Rachael following me.

"Hi Rach!"

"Pam, are you alright?"

A lump filled my throat and I couldn't speak.

"Let's walk," Rachael suggested. She took my arm.

Finally I said, "Why did she do that, Rach? I don't mind cleaning up some of the mess because I'm in charge at dinner, but Lindy's not helpless. I was embarrassed."

"I know. I'm sorry." She squeezed my shoulder. "Pam, sometimes life seems unfair and people don't always understand." I was amazed that Rachel sounded wise beyond her sixteen years. "Don't let Mrs. Benton get you down," she continued. "You've got too much going for you for that."

"What do I have going for me?" I heard self-pity in my voice, but at the time I didn't care. "I don't know who I am anymore. I don't get a fair chance with the sighted kids since I can't see well enough," I complained. "Now that I'm here, I'm being persecuted because I can see too much."

"It has to be hard for you. Remember that TV advertisement you described to me; the one about the girl who is partially sighted, like you, reading a large print book? The caption said, 'Help the hurt that doesn't show.' You must feel misunderstood."

"My dad says it's like I'm in the middle. That's exactly how I feel. I'm glad I can see some things though. It can't be easy for you, Rach, not seeing at all."

"I have never been able to see, so I don't miss it. People can shut their eyes and comprehend total blindness easier than partial sight." She paused. "So what if you're in-between? You're perfect as my friend." She sighed. "You're not the only one picked on by Mrs. Benton. She doesn't feel sorry for me either even though I can't see. It doesn't matter how much sight we have or don't have. I think she rails on us because we're independent."

I thought about her words. "You're right. It makes no difference if I see less than some people and more than others. That's who I am."

"You're a fun-loving person and that's what counts. Besides, who would read to all of us if you couldn't see?"

I grinned. "Thanks, Rach."

At that moment, my boyfriend Mitch ran up to us.

"Hey, Pam I'm mad at the old bag for humiliating you like that." He took my hand. "It'll work out. I've got a funny way to get even," he said conspiratorially.

The next night, Mitch and I were talking on a two-way radio. Mrs. Benton heard his voice and burst into my room.

"You know boys are not allowed in the girls' dormitory," she hollered.

She frantically ran around the room looking under beds and behind closet doors. I stifled a giggle when she peered out the window and glanced down at the ground. She never did find the boy, but we all had a good laugh. The joke was on her and I felt better. Through all these experiences, I began to understand that I am okay, in-between as I am.

~Pam Bostwick

Teens Talk Middle School

Tough Times

Turn your wounds into wisdom.

~Oprah Winfrey

67

Misplaced Kisses

You cannot do a kindness too soon,
for you never know how soon it will be too late.
~Ralph Waldo Emerson

ute boys were often the cause of fights between the girls in my tightly knit group. When one of us confided to the group about our newest crushes, someone else in the group would ultimately claim that she had liked him first. It was hard to keep track of who was off-limits, with our hearts bouncing from one crush to the next. The Taylor boys were no exception. We often talked about the three brothers: Ryan was in eighth grade, T.J. was in seventh, and Joey in sixth. All of us girls liked one of the Taylor brothers at one time or another.

It wasn't until April started "officially" going out with T.J. that any of us could claim any of the Taylor boys as a real boyfriend. It was a whirlwind romance. Over the next few weeks there was plenty of hand-holding and even a good amount of kissing, mostly at the park behind April's house. But all of that wasn't enough to keep April from thinking that maybe it was too hard to have T.J. as a boyfriend. He went to a different school, lived across town, and was virtually silent when she could get him on the phone.

April and T.J. broke up a few days before Easter, but all of us remained friends.

On Easter Sunday, the Taylor boys and I were at April's house. T.J., Joey, and Ryan all helped to raid April's family's Easter baskets of all the good chocolate. We laughed, played games, and just had a great time before the boys left on their bikes.

April, Beth and I took our normal walking route that evening. We stopped for a corndog at the grocery deli, and then walked down the street to the Mini Mart for a big soda. We had to walk fast from place to place, since it was sprinkling a little and threatening to really rain. We bumped into a few of our other girlfriends hanging out at the Mini Mart. We stopped talking and laughing when we heard sirens and watched as an ambulance rushed by.

Police cars followed the ambulance down the street we were standing on. We ran across the street, and joined the crowd that was forming. It was chaos, with the flashing lights and the rain getting heavier. I saw a truck on the wrong side of the road. I saw a bike, twisted, in the middle of the street. I saw Ryan. I saw Joey. They were sitting on the side of the road, heads in their hands, breathing heavily. We called their names and they looked up at us. Were they crying? Suddenly, April was running and screaming and pushing a cop away from her. She ran up to the crumpled figure lying next to the bike and knelt next to T.J. "No!" she yelled as the cop pulled her away and she wiped the blood on her hand across the front of her white shirt.

I felt like I was watching something on TV. The darkness broken only by the red and blue flashing lights gave T.J. an unreal quality as he lay there, not moving. I could faintly see the blood next to him that April had put her hand in.

I couldn't believe that blood was from T.J. I saw a man, head hanging low, talking to the police. Was that the guy from the truck? Was he driving too fast? Was he drinking? I didn't want to think of T.J. crossing the street in front of traffic, like he'd done so many times before. I didn't want to know the details or if he had bolted in front of the truck a second too late.

We couldn't even think about how. We could only cry and hold each other on the side of the road, asking each other why this happened. Why? Ryan and Joey left to meet their family at the hospital after they loaded T.J. into the ambulance. My friends and I went to

April's and waited by the phone for more information. All we knew that first night was that he was still alive, for now. We stuck by each other for as long as we could before going home.

T.J. wasn't able to stay close to home. His condition was severe enough that he was transferred to a hospital three hours away. He held on to life but stayed in a coma. Our parents tried to prepare us. They told us he might not make it, and if he did he wouldn't ever be the same. None of that made any sense to us. My friends and I were sure that T.J. would be back with us in no time, riding around in the dirt lot with a new bike or hanging out in the bowling alley. We tried to force life to seem more like before, even arguing over who was T.J.'s real girlfriend.

April and Jessie were yelling at each other one afternoon. April had said her break-up was a mistake, and she still thought of T.J. as her boyfriend, but Jessie was sure that T.J. had been planning to ask her out. I couldn't take it any more — I screamed at both of them that T.J. was hospitalized in another state and comatose. He had just had a bolt screwed into his head to keep his skull together! He wasn't going to be going out with anyone for quite a while. Fighting over him when none of us could even talk to him — because he wasn't even able to speak — seemed ridiculous. When Jessie accused me of wanting T.J. for myself, I stormed out and cried. I didn't know how to fight about the things we always fought about and worry about T.J. at the same time. I didn't talk to Jessie for days.

Three months later, enough time had passed that arguments faded away. April requested a trip to the hospital for her birthday, and I went along. We knew that T.J. was out of a coma and slowly getting better. I didn't understand until we were in the hospital room how slow that healing process could be.

A whole new person lived inside the T.J. I used to know. His eyes no longer held the spark of mischievousness. In its place was a simple innocence, punctuated by the fact that he was now much like a baby, learning everything from scratch. If he was in his wheelchair, his head was strapped to the back of it, keeping him looking up. He couldn't do that on his own yet. The little bit of communicating he could do came in the form of hand signals with his one good hand—one finger for yes, two for no. He could also blow kisses.

That afternoon, April asked T.J. to be her boyfriend. After a while, T.J. held up one finger and April and I smiled and laughed. We asked for kisses. T.J. obliged us both. My best friend and I were happy to get those sweet kisses from our cute friend. We knew there would be no fights about misplaced kisses here. When it came to T.J., we knew. We were just lucky to get them.

~Tina Haapala

A Letter of Support

Most of our obstacles would melt away if,
instead of cowering before them,
we should make up our minds to walk boldly through them.
~Orison Swett Marden

Dear Friend,

I recently was told that you were diagnosed with a brain tumor. You are probably feeling tired, sick, sad and scared. I am very sorry that you have to go through this experience. I understand what you are going through.

I have been battling a brain tumor for over a year now. Having this experience has taught me many things, but one thing I have learned a great deal about is friendship. I now know that I have wonderful friends who will stay by my side and still be my friends through anything, even when I can't remember things very well, or my head is shaved. My friends and I may even have grown closer during the time of my illness. Even my friends' friends that I don't even know have reached out to me.

When I was in the hospital, a lot of my friends came to visit me, even though the hospital was a couple of hours away. My friends gave me things that they knew I would really enjoy. One of my friend's mothers brought me a ten-pound cheesecake because she knew it was one of my favorite desserts. Every time I would open the refrigerator, I would ask, "Who's that cheesecake from?" because I couldn't remember. So finally, my dad put a note on the box that said,

"Brought by Michele Ward." I kept wanting to know who it was from because it was important to me to know who had come to see me and who had brought what. Things that friends do for one another are worth remembering.

One time, I was eating lunch in the cafeteria with some people at school. After I finished eating my food, several other people and I got up to take our trays up and throw them away. I was the first one back to the table, so I sat down. A few moments later, the other girls came back. My best friend Carleigh came up to me and said, "You were sitting on the other side of the table, Quinn!" I couldn't even describe to you how foolish I felt at the time. My short-term memory was that bad! They had a little laugh, but I know they understood that after my surgery I had a harder time remembering things like that. Until my memory problems improved, they helped me remember things.

Another thing I really adore about my friends is that they don't treat me like I'm sick. They will help me out if I need it, but they don't give me any pity. Some people will just treat me like I can't do anything. Even if I know I'm allowed to play physical games, they'll treat me like a China doll. When people do that, it makes me angry.

This year, I owed a lot to my teacher—Mrs. Joyce Davis. I consider her a good friend of mine. I had Mrs. Davis in third grade, but she moved up to fifth when one of the old teachers left. Before she agreed to move to fifth grade, she told the principal that the only way she would go to fifth grade is if I were in her class. I think she really cared about me and wanted to help me out in any way she could. Some years ago, Mrs. Davis was in a bad accident. She has been through a lot and I think that has helped her be sensitive to others' feelings. She would always notice when I was feeling bad or upset. Mrs. Davis is very special to me and to many other people. I have also been through a lot and I think I try to follow her example of noticing when other people feel bad and trying to help them.

I also got a very special gift from a friend. There is an eye doctor I know in town who tested my vision after my first surgery. His name is Doctor Ozzie Reynolds. One day not too long ago, Dr. Reynolds sent me a poem. Inside the folded piece of paper was a one hundred-dollar bill. There was a note on the poem that said if I could memorize the poem, I could keep the money. The poem is called "If" by Rudyard Kipling and I've been learning some each night. He gave me the poem because it was very special to him and he wanted to share it with me. Now, the poem is special to me too.

In the past year I've learned many things. I've learned about cancer and about tumors and about different kinds of doctors and about how you can't get a good meal or a good night's sleep in a hospital. But the most important thing I've learned is how blessed I am to have such good friends who love and care about me.

Stay strong and keep thinking good thoughts.

Your friend,

~Quinn Scarvey

[EDITORS' NOTE: This letter was written in 2003 and won the Andre Sobel River of Life Foundation award. The competition required the story be written in the form of a letter to a friend going through a similar experience. The topic was, "What I've Learned About Friendship" through having cancer.]

A Mental Cancer

People are like stained-glass windows.
They sparkle and shine when the sun is out,
but when the darkness sets in their true beauty is revealed only if
there is light from within.
~Elisabeth Kübler-Ross

It was December of my sixth grade year, and Mom wanted Quinn and me to run in the "Reindeer Run"—a one-mile "fun run" for kids. Quinn was an athletic, gorgeous, golden-haired nine-year-old; I was her stumpy, awkward-footed older sister. While I was twenty months older, Quinn had always been skinnier, just as strong, and nearly as tall. It was a no-brainer who should be running in front.

Yet on this sunny December day, my sister found herself doubled over after a mere five minutes of jogging. Mom and I exchanged a glance—where was the girl who clambered up doorframes and ate sugar straight from the packet? Where was my energetic little sister? I didn't know it then, but this was the first sign that my family dynamic was about to change. In a month, my sister would be diagnosed with a brain tumor.

In my experience with my sister's illness, I don't know that I learned anything too different from anyone else—though I have my own story to tell. One lesson that I have had to repeatedly learn over the past six years is that, as it was put by B.C. Forbes, "Jealousy... is a mental cancer." Even though Quinn has had to endure six brain surgeries, memory loss, impaired vision, learning disabilities, and countless other side effects, I have been jealous of her just as many times as she has been to the doctor. Relatives we had never met came out of the woodwork, sending money, gifts, and cards that were addressed to her nine times out of ten. People at church, school, people I babysat for, people I hardly even knew all seemed to have a newfound reason to talk to me—about my sister. When Quinn was home from school because of chemotherapy and wanted something, all she had to do was ask, and she received.

I knew deep down that she was suffering from things I would never know the magnitude of, yet jealousy swelled inside me. While I was in no way ignored by my friends and family during this time (all were very supportive), I wanted the attention Quinn got—minus the whole "head about to explode" thing. Yet at some point, when I was feeling sorry for myself, it dawned on me that no matter what people gave Quinn, no matter what material items she now possessed, no matter how focused the spotlight now was on her, she would have traded it all to have the one thing I still took for granted: my health. I realized that the jealousy I felt inside was unhealthy, both for my own sanity and for my relationship with my family.

While the jealousy never left me, and even lingers to this day, I have learned to fight this mental "cancer" by giving to my sister. Yes, giving her the very thing everyone else was giving her—attention—is what has helped me to overcome my jealousy, because it made me realize that she deserves what she is given. This is probably the most important advice I could have been given six years ago: "Yes, you will be jealous. No, life isn't fair, but that doesn't mean you can't overcome your jealousy to be there for your sister."

I learned that life isn't always going to be about me, and I am a better person for that. A few years ago, when Quinn was taking a chemotherapy drug that made her tired and nauseous, she, Mom, and I were on our way to one of my favorite places: The North Carolina Renaissance Festival. We were almost there when Mom and I heard a noise: Quinn was about to blow banana chunks all over the backseat. We pulled over into someone's private drive, which featured, among other high-class things, a flock of chickens pecking about. Immediately after hurling, Quinn argued that we needed to go to the Festival because I really wanted to. I argued back, "No, you don't feel well!" In addition, Quinn had thoroughly banana-chunk-ified her jeans, so we were going to head back home for the day, but, for whatever reason, somebody wanted us to be at that Festival because Mom unearthed a pair of sweats from the back of her cluttered car. Quinn changed in the driveway while Mom stood in front of her. I stood guard against the scrappy chickens.

It ended up working out, but later that night, Quinn told me how much it meant to her that I was willing to give up my yearly smoked turkey leg because she didn't feel well. It was her appreciation for my actions that made me realize her guilt at being the reason I had to give things up, whereas I always felt guilty for being able to do things she couldn't. This was another important thing I realized during my sister's illness.

My sister is the kind of person I try to emulate, and I hope (one day) my children will, too. If I can instill in my kids one-tenth of the courage and love their Aunt Quinn has shown me, I will consider my life a success. This is how I hope to use what I have learned during this experience for the service of a better world—I aspire to be a living example of what my sister has taught me. I also think that because of my experience over the past six years, I have something a lot of adults wish they did—the ability to empathize with people who are going through difficult situations. After watching my family struggle through many tough times, I have realized that you don't need to know what to say—you just have to say something.

~Spencer Scarvey

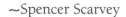

Best Friend Gone Forever

While we are mourning the loss of our friend,
others are rejoicing to meet him behind the veil.
~John Taylor

The year that I transferred to public school, one of the first people I met was a girl named Sarah Parker. Since we were both new to Darby Middle School, our sixth grade guidance counselor, Mr. Madison, paired us with each other for a private study hall to help us feel more comfortable at school and improve our grades. Sarah and I became best friends.

It was hard for us to invite each other over because her parents were strict and kept her from doing fun things like going out for ice cream or studying with someone else. Sarah was still a happy and enthusiastic child who was easy to get along with. Both she and I loved to read. One of her hobbies was drawing and she liked to write about cartoon characters. She was an amazing artist.

Lunch table cliques and bus-seat bullies are fixtures in most sixth graders' lives. A family or home that is restrictive can only add to the pressure of school. Now, when I look back, I'm glad I reached out to Sarah and had my friendship reciprocated, albeit fleetingly. We were about halfway through the school year when it happened. With no indication and without telling anyone, Sarah killed herself. Up until the last day I saw her, I had no idea she was sad or depressed.

The day after her death, my history teacher was waiting for me when I got off the bus. He said that Mr. Madison wanted to talk to me.

Mr. Madison took me to his office and told me to sit down. He didn't make any small talk before discussion—he just said that one of my friends was no longer with us. My thoughts were very far from Sarah. And then he said her name.

At first, I thought he was kidding, but then I saw the truth in his eyes and it hit me. I would never see her again and we would never share our special moments of girlhood giggles and laughter. My soul felt broken for the next week or so. My other friends and I cried a lot that week. Little by little, things like the sound of her voice became harder to remember. I was recovering and moving on. I knew that Sarah was in a better place, and that we would never really know what was going through her mind or what drove her to do it.

She was an amazing friend. I will miss her.

For people who have experienced the loss of a friend, or for those who will encounter it, you just have to keep one thing in mind. When these things happen, you do not have to accept them—just live with them. That person who you cared so much about will always live in your heart.

~Carmelle Wasch

A Boy Named John

Death leaves a heartache no one can heal,
love leaves a memory no one can steal.
~From a headstone in Ireland

There are moments in your life that you will remember forever. Over time these memories may become fuzzy and altered, but the important parts always remain intact.

I had no idea that Saturday night would be so important. I had no idea that it would be this moment that I would later treasure with all my heart. I had no idea it would be the last time he would make me giggle.

One Saturday night, I ventured to my friend Katie's house. Our night started off normally. We watched a movie, ate pizza and talked about boys like twelve-year-old girls do. We were in the middle of arguing about who was hotter, Chad or David, when Katie's older brother, John jumped out from behind the couch and scared the living daylights out of us.

I had always been a big fan of John. Throughout elementary school, he had served as a constant entertainer for us younger girls. Somewhere in between second and third grade, boys had lost their cooties and become something of interest to me. John was one of those boys. I developed a huge crush on him one day during carpool when he shared his Starbursts with me. If nothing else, John was definitely an added bonus to being Katie's friend.

"We should totally have a séance," John suggested moments after scaring us. "That'll really scare you."

I'm not completely sure why a fourteen-year-old boy wanted to spend his Saturday night with a Ouija board, two scented candles, and two twelve-year-old girls, but he did, and Katie and I were intrigued. So we sat in a tiny closet, hand in hand, attempting to decide who we wanted to bring back from the dead.

"Elvis, definitely Elvis," Katie suggested.

"Stupidest idea ever," John replied.

"You're stupid," Katie responded.

John shook his head and turned to me.

"Wanna see something cool?" he asked.

I nodded, thinking perhaps John had some sort of trick up his sleeve. That, and I couldn't turn the boy down. I sat waiting to be impressed, when there in the crowded closet John lifted up his butt and farted right into the candle. In the movies or in an immature boy's head, the fart would have ignited a large flame. In real life all that happened was a suffocating odor quickly took over the small closet we were sitting in.

"Disgusting!" Katie yelled as she slapped her older brother. "That's it! This was such a stupid idea." And with that, Katie marched off. I, on the other hand, had found the entire thing to be amusing and was balled up in the corner laughing.

I don't remember what happened next. I'm sure I eventually followed Katie to her room. Her mom would probably later bring us a snack and we would stay up too late talking about nothing in particular. I probably agreed with her when she talked about how weird her brother was, while I was secretly naming our future children. In the months that followed, Katie and I drifted apart, partly due to my inability to keep in touch with friends and partly because the two of us were entering that angst-ridden adolescence.

And then one day I got a phone call about a boy, a thing called a brain aneurysm, and finally a funeral. Later, I found myself, thirteen years old, standing in a cemetery, listening to someone play "When The Saints Go Marching In," knowing that I would never see my crush, Katie's brother, again. I would recall that Saturday night and the disgusting odor that suffocated me as I lay laughing in the corner of a dark closet. For a brief moment, the tears stopped. For a brief moment, I smiled at the simple memory of laughing with John. It would be gone later as I sat with Katie watching home videos of her and her brother. I'd forget it when I saw their mom in the grocery store, sad and grieving, yet continuing on with everyday life.

Years would pass and the memory would be pushed further and further away. But every once in a while, without notice or reason, I remember a boy who made me giggle until my stomach hurt, and I'm taken to a time and place where it seemed like each of us had all the time in the world.

~Kathleen Ingraham

Simon Says...

There are some defeats more triumphant than victories.
~Michel de Montaigne

I t was the first day of summer. I was done with elementary school, and I was on top of the world. My best friends and I lay sprawled in my front yard, the gentle sun warming our backs, the grass tickling the bottoms of our feet, ice cream dripping from our cones onto our grinning faces. In my mind, it couldn't get better than this. As I drifted into a lazy nap, I vaguely heard my mother's high heels clicking down our front walk. I sat up, expecting lemonade or something of the sort. She was carrying no drinks, but her face was just as sour.

"Al," she pointed towards our house, "I've got to talk to you."

I usually know when something's wrong. I get a sinking feeling in my stomach, and my throat feels as if it's closing. Sometimes this feeling can be helpful, but right then, I wished things had been left unknown.

"Ali..." my mom sighed as we approached the front door. "Simon has leukemia."

Simon Sharp is my stepfather's nephew. Even though we aren't related by blood, Simon was one of the most amazing people I had ever met and meant more to me than any blood relative ever could. In some ways, he was a normal teenage boy — he loved video games, pizza, all the normal teenage stuff. But he was more special than that. He liked to ride his bike around Celebration, Florida — playing his saxophone at the same time. He ate his pizza covered in mustard. He was the kind of person who is impossible to forget once you meet him.

I stopped in my tracks. The lump in my throat got bigger and my stomach got heavier. My eyes shone with disbelief. "But he'll live, right?" I whimpered.

"There's no way to know for sure. He has a pretty rare case though," my mom tried to fake a smile. "Don't worry."

I guess my perfect summer wasn't so perfect after all.

Day by day, Simon seemed to be getting weaker. His appetite sometimes vanished for long periods of time. The doctors tried countless treatments, but each resulted in a worse reaction than the one before. Throughout his treatment, Simon suffered anaphylactic shock and two strokes, all because of the medication that was supposed to be helping him.

Somehow, with all of the odds against him, Simon went into remission, which is sort of like a break from the cancer. We were hopeful, knowing it might even lead to a full recovery. The whole family was thrilled. Sadly, he relapsed about a year later.

It was around then that we had received our "Simon Says..." T-shirts. On the front, in big blue letters, it read, "Simon Says..." and when you turned it over it read, "Cancer is a detour, not a stop sign." I proudly sported it at sleepovers and wore it all around my house. Somehow, that sentence showed me that no matter how hard the cancer fought against him, Simon and his loving family would do whatever it took to push right through it. We wouldn't give up. What impacted me even more is that it referred not only to Simon's battle, but to everyone's who has ever had a seemingly impossible challenge in their lifetime.

Not too long after we got our shirts, Simon came down with pneumonia. Because of the chemotherapy, his body couldn't fight it off. In his final days, Simon's twin sister, Sophie, wouldn't leave his bed, just like when they were infants still in the crib. On November 14, 2007, when he was just fifteen years old, Simon Sharp passed away.

Simon touched countless people with his unique personality, kind soul, and extreme persistence even in his time of need. It was hard for everyone to let go, but somehow we were able to. I think it's because we can wear our T-shirts everywhere we go and proudly say, "Simon Says..."

~Ali Edelson

The Struggle with Meds

The greatest discovery of my generation is that
a human being can alter his life by altering his attitudes.
~William James

"T hat's disgusting," I said to myself as I coughed up the awful stuff I was forced to swallow.

"Come on," my mom said, while trying to shove more of the nasty-tasting substance down my throat. "Just take this and you'll be done for the day."

Let me explain what's happening here. I was born with Attention Deficit Disorder, or ADD, which makes it hard for me to pay attention and focus. My mom was trying to get me to take my ADD medication. I didn't know how to swallow it because I was still young. So my mom would break open the capsule of the pill and pour the medicine inside into some frosting and make me eat it. I had to eat that stuff until I learned to swallow my pill, and I hated it because the frosting mixed with the medicine tasted like moldy cheese that had been sitting in the sun for two months.

My trouble with medication began when I first started school. "He is a great student," my teachers would say, "but he has trouble listening in class." I was later diagnosed with ADD and had to start taking medication to control it. I was little then and had no idea how to swallow pills. Thankfully, I learned later how to do it and no longer had to eat the disgusting frosting concoction my mom made.

The taste, however, was not my main problem. After taking the medication for a little while, I started feeling depressed and tired. This was a major problem, because the pills were still necessary to help me pay attention. But now they also made me feel awful all day long. The pills did help in school, but the side effects were destroying the rest of my life.

So I stopped taking my medication sometime during middle school. It felt great to act like my old self again. It didn't last long though — my parents saw a drop in my grades as soon as I went off my medication. I guess you could say I was stuck between a rock and a hard place.

I went to many doctors who prescribed many different medications for ADD. I honestly thought that the doctors were all idiots, even though I knew they cared. Still, all of them made me feel miserable. I couldn't decide if it was more important to take my medication or not, and I doubt I'll ever really figure that out. I mostly went on and off the pills throughout school while trying to find another pill that wouldn't make me feel terrible.

I think ADD is both a gift and a curse. I'm kind of glad and angry that I was born with it. I have my share of problems, but I also have learned to accept it, and that only makes me a better person. I've learned to accept myself for who I am, even though I may not always like who that person is.

~Justin Lynema

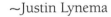

Before and After

There is no education like adversity.
~Disraeli

The sound of gunshots woke me up in the middle of the night. I turned to my alarm clock. The red numbers read 2:00 A.M., blurring my vision. "Ah man," I said, realizing that I had to wake up for school in five hours. Now I wouldn't be able to sleep. I wondered who was shooting the gun outside, and if this had something to do with the day my cousin brought a silver pistol to the room we shared. Looking down to his bed, I heard our black iron bunk bed screech. I screamed, "Ricky did you hear that?" When he didn't reply, I worried that he was dead. I jumped down to the freezing cold floor and my feet felt as if I were standing on a bag of spikes. "Ricky!" I yelled frantically, but he still did not budge. I put my hands on his shoulders, moving him over. Finally, after what seemed like an hour, he awoke.

"What the hell are you doing?" he said. I started to say that I was worried, but I didn't want him to think I was "soft," so instead I said I needed to ask him a question.

"It's two in the morning; wait until tomorrow," he yelled. I went back up to bed, with the boulder of my cousin's death off my shoulders. I closed my eyes, which felt like they had been open for decades.

I awoke to the sound of my clock. It was 7:00 A.M. My bed felt like it was made of bricks, but my body wouldn't move. I knew I had to get to school.

I washed my face, brushed my teeth, and then put on the blue slacks and white button-down shirt that we were required to wear. Walking out of the living room, I realized that I was the only one awake in the whole five-bedroom apartment. Twelve of us lived there, and out of the ten that attended school, I was the only one ready. My aunt and uncle were the two exceptions who didn't have to get up.

As I opened the big, metal door, the wind rushed into my face, giving me chills. I walked to school quickly, trying to avoid my friends who refused to go.

My best friend, Kenneth, spotted me. "Darren!" he yelled through the morning sky. Running up, he said, "Where are you going?"

"To school. Can't you see the book bag, stupid?"

"Why are you going?" he yelled. "Your aunt doesn't care if you do or don't."

Annoyed, I just walked away from him, not giving him an answer. It was true; I could do anything I wanted and not get into trouble, at least not with my aunt and uncle. "Why am I going?" I asked myself, as I walked up the school steps. It was simple—I needed school. School was my way to get out of the ghetto. It was what would give me a better future.

I walked into my class and sat at my designated desk. Everyone was quiet and their eyes were red. My teacher, one of the toughest people in the world, stood up in front of the class with tears flowing down his face. I looked at the desk next to mine and realized my friend Jose, who usually sat there, wasn't at his desk. Jose always had my back in everything.

"Where is he?" I whispered to Ashley, to the right of me. She started to cry, and I suddenly realized that my friend would not be in school that day—or ever again.

"He was shot and killed last night," she sobbed. I felt my eyes start to water. One of my closest friends was dead, and memories of death in my own family started to run through my head like a movie

I couldn't forget. Anger filled my body and I became tense. I walked out of the class, through the frigid streets and up to Jose's apartment. I found his mother weeping in her room. I could not look in her eyes. She hugged me and told me that he was gone and we sat there together, crying.

In the funeral parlor, it was quiet and smelled like old people. Tears were in everyone's eyes. My friends were there, anxious to get the people who did this. I, on the other hand, only wanted to make my life better before something like this happened to me. I stood up in front of everyone and gave a testimonial. "Jose was always there for me. I love him and know he is going to a better place, to heaven. Many people want to get the people back who did this to him, but we have to let it go. If we don't, it will be a constant revenge circle and life will end for all of us. It's time we actually started to work and go to school. Higher education is the key for us to live in a more civil society. There is a struggle of poverty and violence in the African-American society as a whole, and we need to change that."

As I walked back to my seat, I got stares of disbelief. I looked at Jose's mother, and she looked at me with agreement. I knew she was proud of me, and I knew life had to change. "Rest in peace, Jose," I said as I walked out of the church.

That was all in eighth grade.

• • •

I wake up to the sounds of raccoons bashing through the metal garbage can and birds chirping. Looking across at my roommate, Ramin, I realize that I'm late. I quickly rummage through my clothing to find something suitable for school. Now I live in Swarthmore, a sleepy suburb of Philadelphia. I put on a wrinkled shirt and blue jeans so I can run down the street to catch the yellow school bus with all the other teens in the neighborhood. I attend Strath Haven High School, where I am an ABC scholar. The ABC program takes academically-inclined inner city students and brings them to live in a better school district. The brakes of the bus screech as we stop in front of the main entrance. I slowly walk into the school and down the stairs to my English class. My new school is difficult, but it assures me that my hard work will soon lead to college, a great job, and hope for the future. I am one step closer to my goals.

~Dan Haze Barten

Losing Mother

They say that time heals all wounds but all it's done so far is give me more time to think about how much I miss you.
~Ezbeth Wilder

The death of my mother was difficult, but to hear it announced over the intercom by the principal made me literally shrink in my chair. I'm sure he thought it was an act of comfort or kindness, like when he saw me in the hallway and gave me that oh-so-special greeting of, "And how are you today?" But for me it was just plain awkward.

It was bad enough that everyone in my entire school still had their mothers. The proof was all around me: they had lunches made lovingly by a mother's gentle hands. Where there were once holes in my fellow seventh graders' socks, now thread kept those little toes in place. And then there was always the dreaded my-mother-told-me-this or my-mother-told-me-that. But perhaps the worst of all was the long stare one friend gave another, or the obvious push or kick, meant to remind the culprit that she shouldn't say the word, "Mother," in the presence of the mother-less.

It's true that all the teachers in the school did the best they could. Even the school secretary, who was known as being equally mean to everyone regardless to their current plight, gave being nice to me the old college try. When I was sent to the office for supplies, she actually jumped from her desk and practically ran to the supply closet, something virtually unheard of. Not only was she grossly overweight, she was one of those people who didn't feel as if students were real people with real emotions. She was the type of lady who told her kids to go to bed at 8 P.M. and actually thought they did it. So you can imagine how I felt when I got to the office and she practically ran me over to get to the box of staples and packs of lined paper. "Marshawna," she said ever-so-slowly, as if she didn't plan to say anything more.

I had become accustomed to such slow and careful annunciations of my name since Mother's death. The school secretary did manage to come up with something to say to me in this instance, though. She asked me how my father was doing, in a manner that indicated she couldn't imagine the death of a spouse after twenty years of marriage. I told her he was just fine, as I had become accustomed to saying when I suspected people were digging for information. Besides, it would have been goofy to have to explain how everyone was doing to someone who didn't seem to have a heart.

The hallway was long, but the trip down it was far too short. Once I arrived back in class, I noticed that everyone was looking at me. There were two women standing in front of the class. "What?" I wanted to ask my wide-eyed sea of peers. Why was I now the center of attention? Before I could, Mr. Carracci introduced the two women as members of the PTA. They had come to present me with an award on behalf of Mother, who was a stay at home mom and always did the PTA thing. So there stood these two tall women with a freshly printed certificate in one of their hands. "For her fine work with the PTA," one said, with what I believed to be a sincere tear in her right eye. Mr. Carracci then motioned the class to clap as they all did in unison. I walked to my seat with the certificate.

Eventually, the attention faded. By the end of eighth grade, there were other kids in school with other problems that seemed to shift the focus. Although I loved this "getting back to normal," I also grew to appreciate what each person at my middle school had done to comfort me. It was awkward, sure. But it was also their way of saying they cared. My friends gradually started talking about their mothers around me again. When sent for staples and the like, the secretary hardly glanced in my direction. She only motioned for me to get my own supplies from the supply closet. And after hearing that awful news broadcast loud and clear to the whole school, I was careful never to give the principal a reason to announce my name on the intercom again.

~Marshawna Moore

Recovery Is Beautiful

Adversity is like a strong wind.
It tears away from us all but the things that cannot be torn,
so that we see ourselves as we really are.
~*Arthur Golden,* Memoirs of a Geisha

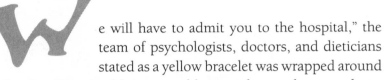

e will have to admit you to the hospital," the team of psychologists, doctors, and dieticians stated as a yellow bracelet was wrapped around my frail wrist. "Your health is not stable enough to go home and you are experiencing serious side effects of malnutrition."

It had started with a diet. I hated myself and the word "FAT" ran through my head every minute of every day. I was thirteen years old, and weighed 115 pounds at 5'3." Over the next eight months of eighth grade, I gradually ate less and less to the point where I was eating next to nothing. I obsessed over food because it was the one thing I had complete control of in my life. For some reason, skipping meals and throwing out school lunches made me feel powerful.

I was obsessed. Nothing else in the world mattered other than being skinny. I'd strip down and sneak into my parents' bathroom for a peak at the scale, sometimes forty times a day. If the numbers went up, I'd scream and cry to the point of hysteria. I'd jump on the scale as hard as I could. I'd throw it across the room. I wanted nothing more than to run twenty kilometers, then bike off another 4,000 calories. If the numbers went down, it still wasn't good enough, and

I wouldn't eat anything—not even water or gum. I refused to lick postage stamps or take pills—they would all make me fat.

Unless I could see prominent veins in my arms, I was too fat. I was only satisfied with myself when there was a deep hole in the pool of my collarbone. I'd catch myself lying down flat on my back to see how sunken my stomach was compared to my hipbones. If I couldn't see all six ribs, I wasn't skinny enough.

Everyone wanted to help me but it only made me angrier. I had put up a wall and isolated myself from everyone who cared. "Smart move," my dad screamed with tears welling up in his eyes, "killing yourself at thirteen." I didn't understand what everyone saw. All I saw in the mirror were rolls and rolls of fat. I was too fat to deserve any help.

I started seeing a psychotherapist who told my parents that their job was to feed their child—just like feeding a newborn. Still, I wouldn't swallow. One bite would ruin everything. A lady in the emergency room at the children's hospital asked me why I was so thin, rather bluntly, almost casually telling me that I was going to die if I kept eating the way I was. Yeah right, I thought. Anorexia only existed in stories meant to scare people. If I had anorexia, I'd know it.

I felt constant hunger pangs, and the sensation of emptiness manipulated me into skipping more and more meals, challenging my body to go past different stages of fatigue. When I felt hungry, I felt drugged. No previous success felt as good to me as this weight loss and I was addicted to the feeling. All happiness slipped away and my whole being was devoted to losing another pound. I would look in the mirror and say to myself, "Okay. You look better. Don't eat or else you'll ruin it."

I wanted to get my life back and become the happy girl I'd once been. A small bit of Megan was still there—not yet demolished—and she wanted to see her life transformed. But the demon inside me said, "You don't know how. What's the use?" I felt like I was stuck in a box with the lid pulled down tight, shutting myself in my own misery. This eating disorder was eating away at my brain to the point where being healthy didn't matter.

Finally, everything caught up to me. I felt like I was dying. I couldn't drag my body another step. My heart was racing, I was hallucinating the scent of foods, my hair was falling out in wads, my chest ached, and I could hardly breathe. Every time I stood up, my world went completely white and I was so scared. But I couldn't even cry because I was so dehydrated that my eyes would burn and no tears would come. I ended up in the hospital, this time for a while.

Anorexia is like a drug addiction. You don't believe you actually have it until it's almost too late. There's a constant battle between you and the voice telling you not to eat. For too long, that voice always won.

I weighed just eighty-eight pounds. When my heart rate and blood pressure were assessed, the nurse's mouth dropped. After that, I was no longer allowed to walk. There was too much risk of a heart attack or seizure. I was hooked up to a heart monitor and IV. Nurses brought me four meal supplements a day, but I still thought I was fat, so I poured them down the drain. I was making myself sicker and sicker. Patients surrounding me were facing cancer and epilepsy, while I was suffering from something I did to myself. I felt selfish and guilty.

Two weeks into my stay, the doctors decided I needed more acute care in an eating disorder program. I thought it was the worst possible thing that could ever happen to me. They wanted to take away everything that I'd worked so hard for. There were endless trays of food and I had no choice but to clear them all.

It was in the hospital, fighting anorexia with five other girls when I learned the true meaning of friendship. Those girls understood exactly what I was going through and we worked through every meal together. The laughs, the tears, the highs and lows—we went through every state together. They are the best friends in the entire world and I couldn't have ever gotten better without them. We inspired each other, held hands, and fought back against one of the most powerful mental illnesses affecting teenage girls in society.

Looking back on it, things started to change the moment I stopped eating because I had to, and started eating for myself. Things got much easier when I came to the realization that no one was trying to ruin my life—they were trying to save it. Everyone was cheering me in my race to beat the eating disorder, but the essential first step of recovery was to accept it. I had to want to get better.

It was the hardest two and a half months of my life, but I did it. I worked very hard to get my life back. All of my friends and family were waiting for the happier and healthier me to return, and they supported me on the rollercoaster ride of recovery. I know that they'll always love me and accept me no matter what shape or size I am. They will never judge me, and they'll always be by my side during hard times. I'm no longer afraid to let them in.

The success of beating this thing sends shivers down my spine and makes me feel like dancing and letting the whole world know what I've accomplished. When I look in the mirror I can say that I am a strong and inspiring person to those around me. That's when I feel beautiful.

~Megan Carty

A Final Goodbye

Maybe part of loving is learning to let go.
~From the television show The Wonder Years

"Is he okay?" I hear my mom ask. "Call me as soon as you know something." My mom hangs up the phone.

"Mom," I whimper. Only a tiny whisper escapes my mouth. I wait until she steps softly into my room to continue. "Is Paw-Paw going to be alright?"

She sighs and shakes her head "I don't know Chelsea... I don't know." I scoot over and she climbs into bed with me. I think back on yesterday. I remember the white walls, the white floors. I smell the twisted smell of disease. I remember my grandpa's face, tired but smiling. He was always smiling.

"He'll be out in two weeks." The doctor had reassured us. Doctors, I have learned, don't always know the truth.

I snuggle into the blankets and force myself to think of something else. "He's fine, he's fine, he's fine." I repeat. "Two weeks, just two weeks and he's home."

I can't control my thoughts; they swirl around my mind, around my room, around my desk to my journal. I think about what I wrote the night before.

I can't help but think that was the last time I will ever see him.

"He's fine, he's fine, he's fine." I drill the thought into my head.

The phone rings.

"I'll be right back honey," my mom whispers, and gets up to pick up the phone.

I lie still, my thoughts racing faster than my heartbeat. Then I hear something downstairs and I know what it is. It is the worst sound I have ever heard. My mom is sobbing. My mind goes numb. It's amazing how the body knows when there's too much emotion and needs to turn off.

"Michael. Chelsea." My mom barely chokes out. We cautiously step into the hallway.

"Oh God, oh God." She can't say it. She doesn't have to. We understand. "Paw-Paw, he..." She takes a pause to remember to breathe. "He died ten minutes ago." She lets out her sobs. I knew this was coming, but I don't believe it. How could this happen? I don't cry yet. My brother and I sit shaking our heads, staring at my mom.

Then it hits me. It hits me like a hammer in my gut. I think back on my life and how my grandfather was always there. There was never a recital or concert where I didn't see him sitting in the audience smiling back at me. I think back on summer picnics together at the beach. I hear him beaming with pride, saying, "How did I get such a beautiful granddaughter?" I can't take it any longer. I feel tears running down my cheeks.

I hold my mom on the couch, her head buried in my hair. When she sobs, I feel her whole body shake. I can feel the despair seeping into my skin. It's like I am inside her, feeling all of her sorrow, remembering all of her memories. I feel it in my soul, and I feel it in the air. I have never known this complete despair. I'm scared.

It's Thursday morning and I'm going to school. It's too sunny for such a sad day. The birds are chirping. My grandpa loved birds.

"Don't think about him, Chelsea." I tell myself. I walk in to school and am bombarded with hugs and sympathetic smiles. My friend Caroline tells me, "Now, it makes you sad, but eventually you'll look back on your grandpa and you'll smile." I cling to that with hope that it will come true. But none of them understand. How can they understand how much I have lost? They only think of my grandpa as an old man who they've never met. But he was so much more. Can't they see that?

The day is a numb, gray, blur, except for lunch. The usual drama of the day piles up and I can't handle it. I feel tears trickling down my face once more. I can't believe I'm actually crying in school—I'm disgusted with myself. Everyone stares at me, but I don't care. I don't care about anything. I just want to crawl into my grandpa's arms and fall asleep. I'm not sure how Caroline could be right. How could thinking about him make me smile? Whenever I think of him I remember how much I miss him. For the first time in my life, I feel lost.

• • •

Today is the funeral. I see my cousins immediately when we arrive at the funeral home. We embrace each other to keep ourselves from falling apart. We don't have to say a word; our eyes say it all. I decide not to go see my grandpa's body. I don't want to remember him as a cold, lifeless mass. Emma and Michey wait with me in the room next door. I notice there are tissue boxes everywhere. Thank God. I think we've already gone through three. As other people arrive, my heart warms to see how many people cared about my grandpa. I hug everyone, crying in their arms—even people I don't know. I like this crying better. Everyone is full of sympathy and offers me a shoulder and a reassuring voice.

After the ceremony, we go to the cemetery. It's torturous watching them lower the coffin into the ground. I can't comprehend that my grandpa is in that wooden box. The Rabbi says we must help bury the casket, because it's a sign of respect. I don't want to be respectful if it means trapping a loved one in the cold ground forever. But I take a handful of dirt and raise it over the grave. It feels cold on my skin. I grip it tight. I think about my grandpa, and how lucky I was to know him.

He was such a wonderful person, a role model for all who knew him. I deeply believe he is somewhere—who knows where—watching over me. This thought comforts me. I hurt so much, but I know it's the price that comes with loving someone. I don't regret for a second loving him as much as I did. The reward of love is so great that it overshadows the loss. I slowly let go of the soil. It thuds on the coffin. I realize at the same time I'm letting go of Paw-Paw, letting him go on to whatever awaits him. With every grain of dirt that falls, a tear rolls down my eye. I know this is goodbye.

~Chelsea Watson

My Worst Day Ever

Sometimes the littlest things in life are the hardest to take.
You can sit on a mountain more comfortably than on a tack.
~Author Unknown

The worst day of my life fell on a Wednesday. It was early November, and my father and stepmother, both of whom I considered wicked, had uprooted me yet again and moved me from a nice small town to Madison, Wisconsin. This was the seventh home I had lived in since my birth and the third move that had taken place in the middle of a school year.

I slept fitfully in my new room and was awoken at 4 A.M. when someone began pounding on our front door and leaning on the doorbell. This is exactly what I feared about moving to the big city—vandals waking us in the dead of night to steal and plunder. I crouched on the floor in front of my bed, covered all but my eyes with a blanket, and held my ten-pound Cairn Terrier out in front of me. I don't know what I expected Dusty, my Toto look-alike, to do in the event of an actual emergency but she was my only friend now and therefore sworn to serve and protect.

It wasn't a burglar—they seldom knock. Our phone hadn't been installed yet so my aunt had driven to our house with the news that my grandfather had been hospitalized with another heart attack. My father rushed to his bedside while I lay awake praying for my grandpa and dreading further the day that was to come: the day when I would have to face another first day at another new school.

It came, as unwanted as it was, with sunshine and balmy temperatures even though a storm raged inside me. My grandpa was stable and my dad was home in time to deliver me to my first day at Schenk Middle School.

I had always been a good student, but jumping into the middle of the eighth grade year made me feel like I didn't know anything. I was behind in some subjects, ahead in others and just plain lost in one. I collected my books from each new teacher and cowered in the back of each new classroom so I could tune out the lesson and let my mind drift to what my best friend, Sheryl, and I would be doing if I hadn't been thrust into this place.

Lunch came and I seated myself at the end of a table, removed from the other kids who were already entrenched in their own groups of friends. I was extremely uncomfortable with myself in eighth grade (isn't everyone?) and tried to avoid eye contact with the stream of students around me. My discomfort was due in part to the fact that, when my parents divorced, I lived with my dad while my brother lived with our mom. I knew all about baking a TV dinner for thirty minutes at 350 degrees with the dessert and potato uncovered, but I was uneducated in the world of styling products, curling irons, tweezers and other female rituals.

Someone from the other end of the table decided I was due some attention. "Hey, you new here?"

I reluctantly answered, "Yes." My eyes never left my ham sandwich.

"Well, go back where you came from." The girls all laughed and congratulated themselves on their great wit.

I prayed for a miracle to send me back home where I had friends. Friends who had stood at the back door of my last school and waved goodbye to me on my last day.

Suddenly, a wad of chewed bread hit the side of my face. The rest of the table found this hilarious and joined in the fun. By the time the lunch monitor stopped them, my long brown hair was littered with peas, bread, butter, and peaches, and my face was traced with silent tears.

We were sent, all four of us, to the principal—my first and last visit to a principal. I don't remember his name but he was dark and scary and seemed angry with me, as if I were a new troublemaker he had unwittingly admitted into his school. He read us the riot act for having a food fight and then asked for phone numbers so he could call our parents. I still didn't have a phone and therefore didn't know my phone number. My assailants laughed at my admission that this thirteen-year-old didn't know her phone number and the grand guardian of the school just sat back and let them.

When the day finally ended, I had to pay for a public bus to take me to my general neighborhood. Struggling with my new key, I let myself into the unfamiliar house, where Dusty met me at the door wagging her whole body. I smiled at her and gave her a hug, thankful that someone still loved me and needed me. We made peanut butter crackers and I told her all about my horrible day. She agreed with everything I said, as canine friends do, and comforted me just by being there to listen.

When my parents returned home some hours later, I was immediately reprimanded for my trip to the principal. I didn't bother trying to explain. It was bad enough I had lived it; I didn't care to relive it with my parents. I begged to be home-schooled but my parents declined. They thought my school was wonderful. I sulked over my chicken dinner and hoped for any sign of leprosy or whooping cough that would keep me out of school. Dusty benefited from my lack of appetite.

As the evening wore on, I noticed that something was wrong with my little dog. She was panting and coughing constantly, and seemed to have trouble catching her breath. I sat with her through the night as she continued to gasp. I dreaded leaving her the next morning, but my stepmother said she would take Dusty to the vet. I couldn't focus on school and rushed home to check on my canine companion. Dusty didn't meet me at the door. A chicken bone had splintered off from her chicken dinner and punctured her heart and lung. She died at the vet's office.

A 4 A.M. heart attack, a noon food fight, and a dinnertime

decision that killed my only friend within one hundred miles. The worst day of my life.

I wish I could say that was my only bad day and suddenly the kids liked me, but that's not what happened. Although I stepped out of my shell and tried to earn some respect by singing in the middle school talent show, it only backfired when my voice cracked and I was taunted for the rest of the school year. After, I wouldn't participate in the grade-level science fair, I squeaked by with a C in English, and I actually faked the measles for two weeks by scratching and holding the thermometer up to a light bulb. All so that I could stay home and have some relief from the horror of eighth grade.

Middle school was filled with bad days, but then a miracle happened. A miracle called high school. A miracle where students from three other area middle schools were poured into a several-thousand-member student body and were all suddenly small fish in a large pond. A pond where there was room to grow and stretch and swim with fish who like you and swim away from those who don't.

I met my best friends in high school and still talk to some of them regularly. I discovered that my voice was worth something and that the high school director had taken notice of my eighth grade solo. I was promoted to advanced English and science after my freshman year.

To this day, I try to glean some good from those days at Schenk Middle School, but I can't. I was hurt and friendless, but I did survive. I think that is the main goal of middle school: survival. If you can tolerate the evils of eighth grade and come out the other side scarred but alive, you have succeeded. So I charge you, whoever you are reading this, to survive! And if you have a chance to put an arm around the awkward new girl, then please do so for me. By lending a shoulder to cry on and an ear to listen, you may turn the worst day of her life into the best, simply because she met you.

~Becky Tidberg

Teens Talk Middle School

That's My Family

*Families are like fudge...
mostly sweet with a few nuts.*

~Unknown

Coach Dad

My father gave me the greatest gift anyone could give another person, he believed in me.

~Jim Valvano

I was always told that no matter what, family will always be with you, which was very true. But I guess you could say this: my dad took it to a whole new level.

It started in kindergarten. Mom and Dad thought it would be fun to get me signed up for some sport and that it would be good for me. So when the soccer signup sheets went home, my parents had them filled out and sent back in by the very next day. And then there was an even better part—Dad would coach. I can't even begin to describe how excited I was that Dad would coach.

The season went by and I had warmed up to the idea of Dad coaching even more. He and I were convinced that soccer was "my" sport. So he signed me up for summer leagues, only to find out that Dad wouldn't be coaching. This led to massive devastation.

I'd repeatedly told him, "Daddy, you have to coach!" And he'd respond with something like, "I wasn't asked to" or some other excuse that I only saw as another reason to ask.

I don't know what did it, but after much begging and many tears, Dad was assistant coach.

The coaching thing stuck, I guess, because when I was in first grade, soccer season rolled around again and Dad was coaching.

He was loud, and I'd get mad at him for yelling at me. One game, he even promised me he wouldn't yell. When he broke his promise, I stopped in the middle of the field and yelled back, "YOU PROMISED YOU WOULDN'T YELL!!"

But I never stayed mad for too long.

When fourth grade rolled around, we were finally old enough to play basketball. After tryouts, and when I found out which team I was on, Dad coached that too. But it wasn't the same as it was in kindergarten. I would get mad if he tried to correct me; he'd get mad if I didn't listen.

Soon, it was getting to the point where I didn't want him to coach.

But he did.

This went on through fifth grade, sixth, seventh, and all the way up to eighth. We'd argue, and there'd be the occasional "I hate you," a few tears here and there, and the times I promised myself I'd never talk to him again. Yet, no matter how many times I told myself, "Don't talk to him! You're mad at him remember?" I'd talk to him anyway, and the fight would disappear.

It got worse as I got older, because I realized I didn't love basketball, and I didn't love soccer. I didn't have a passion for it any more. And I always felt like nothing I did would be good enough for him. It seemed as if nothing would please him. I felt especially angry when he'd talk about how great the other kids did on the ride home and say little or nothing about me. Or, if he did talk about me, he'd mention all the negative things. Even though he meant it as constructive criticism, I didn't take it that way.

When eighth grade rolled around, I joined basketball. Much to my dismay, I ended up having a fun time on the team, and argued with Dad — more than ever.

But when soccer signups came, he let me sit this year out. He told me it was because he didn't want to coach anymore. Dad didn't want to coach?!

Our last basketball game was a sad one. It was the last time he'd be known as "Coach Dad" to me. He brought it up, with much sincerity and sadness, and I'd just smile and say, "Oh, I know," and brush it off, determined not to show him that I might actually be upset that he wouldn't coach any more.

The season ended, and "Coach Dad" had, in a way, "retired."

All sports-related activities had ended for me. Well, except for one — the Sports Recognition Night. My school did it every year — the coach would call up the player, say something about him, the player would get a shirt, and then they would sit down. They handed out about six awards that night.

I was totally dreading the whole thing. First of all, I wasn't expecting any awards, and secondly, I really didn't want to hear what my dad would say. But I was glad that sports were finally over for me.

As the ceremony wore on, the different coaches talked about the players and told funny stories. The audience laughed, applauded, laughed, applauded, and the night went on like that for some time.

Then, came my turn.

I stood up, pretended not to care, and tried to play it cool. I took my grand old time getting up to the stage. "C'mon, hustle!" Dad cried jokingly. The audience laughed. I couldn't help but smile, since he'd been yelling that to me for the nine years he coached me.

When I got up to the stage, I prepared myself for the story he had written. I had known for a fact that Dad had written a pretty lengthy story. In fact, he had written about two instances.

He began. "You know, when I first started coaching, I knew it would be hard on Adam—" His voice faltered. "I knew it would be—" His voice faltered once again. His lip quavered and he put his hand up to his eyes. The audience gasped.

My mouth dropped and my eyes welled up with tears. Why? Because Dad was doing something I'd never seen him do, something I never imagined he was capable of doing because, well, he was Dad.

Dad was crying.

He set his paper down, looked at me directly in the eyes, and said the six most meaningful words ever spoken: "I am so proud of you." He and I broke down crying and he grabbed me in a big, strong hug. I left the stage, still in tears, but somewhat happy.

Throughout those nine years, even though I said I hated him and didn't want him to coach... I wouldn't have traded it for anything. I felt like I had finally lived up to his expectations, but I knew all along that I had, in everything I had done.

I knew this because he loved me enough to give up his time to coach me.

And he loved me enough to say how much he loved me in front of everyone.

~Adam Patla

80

You Don't Get It

Children begin by loving their parents;
as they grow older they judge them; sometimes they forgive them.
~Oscar Wilde

"Y ou don't get it," my daughter, Betsy, reminded her dad and me when she was frustrated with us. She was in middle school and had strong feelings about protecting her image. She was easily embarrassed and impatient with the unintentional blunders of her parents.

When I bought her a pair of nice slacks, she rolled her eyes and complained. "You don't get it. These aren't 'in,' they're 'nerdy.'" To prove her point, she insisted I come to school on Parents' Day and notice the styles of the students' unwritten dress code. I saw the other girls wearing dark corduroy pants... and understood.

On the subject of underwear, the word "bra" was Betsy's forbidden three-letter word. One Saturday, while shopping in a mall, I asked her if she needed some bras. "Mom! Shhhh," she replied, as though I had shouted foul language. She stooped her shoulders, quickly glanced at the other shoppers and whispered, "You don't get it. People will hear you say that word and I'll just die."

The day arrived when Betsy hit her limit of being embarrassed by her parents. She called after band practice saying she needed a ride home. Her dad was in the middle of painting shelves but said he'd rush over to get her. He didn't have time to shower and change out of his work clothes, so he wore his stained and sweaty shorts and shirt. When he arrived at the band room, it was teeming with students waiting for rides. He stood alone in the doorway, perspiring and grungy, and searched the crowd for his daughter. Then he heard Betsy's familiar voice yell out to the group, "Hey everybody. Someone's dad is here."

He got it.

~Miriam Hill

81

A Parent's Guide to Middle School

Hot dogs always seem better out than at home;
so do French-fried potatoes; so do your children.
~Mignon McLaughlin

Middle school can be a scary place. Not for eleven-year-olds, who are itching to leave the warm and fuzzy confines of elementary school, to eat lunch with kids who shave, but for parents who have to accept that their child is growing up and entering a world where lockers have combinations and hormones lurk around every corner.

Fortunately, the middle-school curriculum is carefully structured, and the staff professionally trained to help children bridge the awkward period between the elementary years and high school. For most parents, however, the middle school experience is not a bridge, but a dark and mysterious tunnel that morphs our sweet babies into surly adolescents and makes us wonder, "Is it cocktail hour yet?"

As the mother of a recent eighth grade graduate, I've learned a few things that I hope will shed some light into that developmental tunnel and make the next few years a little less terrifying:

1. The weight of your child's backpack has no relationship to the amount of homework he or she has been assigned. An eighty-

pound child who drags home forty pounds of books and papers will still claim to have no homework.

2. Kids who say that they have no homework should be required to clean their rooms and organize their backpacks. Faced with this alternative, middle school students will often display remarkable powers of recall and suddenly remember that they have a science project due tomorrow.

3. Never pull up to the front steps of the school when you are driving your child to or from middle school. No matter how heavy the backpack is, your child would rather walk an additional half block than risk having anyone discover that she has parents — especially parents as weird as you.

4. Despite all appearances, middle school is not populated by little boys and twenty-five-year-old super models. Girls just mature faster... much faster.

5. Shut up and drive. When the backseat is full of seventh grade girls going to soccer practice or to the mall, the chauffeur gets the inside scoop. Do not try to inject yourself into their conversation or sing along with Avril Lavigne. Just keep your eyes on the road, your hands on the wheel and your ears on the backseat.

6. Know that even the most academically-gifted middle school girl cares most about just three things: what she looks like, what her friends look like, and what her friends think she looks like. In three years, the situation in the Middle East will still be a mess. Your kid can catch up on global events when she doesn't have to worry about pimples.

7. If you want your middle schooler to eat breakfast and get to school on time, assure her that her hair looks great. Really. It's fabulous. It will get greasy if you touch it anymore. Now, eat some cereal and get out of here.

8. Don't worry if your child says she's "popular." Although the term "popular" can be a euphemism meaning that your daughter dates the high school track team, a child who boasts that she is "popular" is generally just... popular.

9. Attend your child's athletic events, but do not speak to other parents or cheer audibly. Never offer encouragement to your player by calling out "Run like a big boy!" or "That's Mommy's precious goalie."

10. When middle school boys and girls talk about their peers "going out," this does not mean that they go to the movies, hold hands, or even speak to each other. These pairings are created by girls through a series of elaborately folded notes, text messaging and third-party conversations. Relaying these messages and folding the notes take away time from other activities like homework and room cleaning. Parents should encourage platonic friendships and learn how to refold the notes.

11. Four eighth grade boys + twelve Dr. Peppers = one trashed TV room.

12. Discourage parties. See number 11. Forbid boy-girl parties unless this sounds like your idea of a swell Saturday: Your daughter runs upstairs in tears and locks herself in her bedroom, other girls leave in a huff and the boys stay until the chips run out. Analysis of the evening's events online and over the telephone detracts from homework and room cleaning for the rest of the school year.

13. When you attend parent-teacher conferences and your son or daughter's math teacher says that she's a joy to have in class, don't look shocked and ask if you're in the right room. Simply smile and say, "Thank you."

~Carol Band

Jonny and Me

When you look at your life,
the greatest happinesses are family happinesses.
~Joyce Brothers

My family sometimes talks about "Before Jonny" and "After Jonny." But I've never known life without my special brother.

Not that we're not all special — at least that's what my parents say. We are fifty-four weeks apart, which to some people means we're "Irish Twins." And in a way, we really were like twins when we were little.

Now we're pretty different. That's because Jonny has Down syndrome, or as my mom calls it, "A Little Extra" — an extra chromosome on his twenty-first pair. I finally understood this when we made DNA models with gumdrops and pretzel sticks at school.

Jonny isn't really all that different, but his differences are enough to make him stand out in a crowd. Over the years, I've seen a lot of different reactions from people in all sorts of situations. But while I've heard stories about kids giving disabled kids a rough time, I've never seen that in the places where we've lived. In fact, Jonny seems to bring out the best in the people he meets. Now, when he walks down the halls of our high school, he's greeted with tons of high fives and cries of "Hey, Jonny!"

For a while, in middle school, I even worried that Jonny was more popular than me. When I told my dad how I felt, he said that

Jonny had a long road ahead of him—and that he needed all the confidence he could get in his early years. Someday, my dad said, those people high-fiving and "Hey Jonny-ing" him would be the same people who might give jobs to him and other people with disabilities. My dad told me that soon middle school would be over. He said that what I was feeling was normal for a girl with an older brother in the same school and, as he often liked to repeat, "This too shall pass." I used to hate it when my dad said that, but as I get older I start to see that he has a point.

And it did pass—my mixed feelings about Jonny's popularity. Now I'm happy for him. I'm happy we live in a town where he can have a lot of friends and I'm proud of our school where four years ago a senior girl with Down syndrome was voted Homecoming Queen.

While my mom and dad have had to work hard to help Jonny reach his potential, they've worked as hard to help me reach mine. Jonny and I share a love of Broadway musicals and both of us hope someday to work onstage.

Seeing Jonny's life unfold has helped me see that there's a plan for mine as well. Just like Jonny's Down syndrome, our love of music and acting are things that were present in us the day we were born.

My parents say having a baby is like getting a gift from God. As they grow up, that gift is slowly unwrapped until we see what's inside.

Jonny's little extra was obvious the minute he was born. Unwrapping my package may have taken a little longer, but if there's one thing Jonny has taught our family, it's that each of us is a little different. But what's most important are the ways in which we are the same.

~Madeleine Curtis

The Letter

*To us, family means
putting your arms around each other and being there.*
~Barbara Bush

I found the letter a couple of weeks after we buried him. It jumped out at me, fluttering to my feet as I thumbed through an old photo album. Although it was addressed to me, I couldn't remember reading the letter. Crumpled and yellowed, it was written by my grandfather two weeks after my birth. In the opening paragraph, he joked, "Gee, I probably have been a bit presumptuous about your ability to read; so if you can't read yet, please encourage one of your parents to read this note to you." The rest of the page welcomed me into this big, beautiful world—and expressed the hope that we would be seeing a lot more of each other.

And we did see much more of each other. I saw "Pop-pop" every year at least twice. With Grandma by his side, in his Tennessee drawl, he welcomed us into their house each time my family made the nine-hour drive to Washington, D.C. I loved their house. It was one of the oldest ones in the neighborhood, which meant that it had a backyard. My younger brother, sister and I used to play beneath the ancient oak trees and explore the bamboo forest at the far end of the yard. The house itself had its own, special smell—a bit sweet—that was familiar and safe. My sister and I slept in my Mom's old room, and Pop-pop often read us stories before bed. I fell asleep many times to the sound of his voice—strong and permanent, protecting me.

By Thanksgiving of my year in eighth grade, things had changed. We visited D.C. earlier than usual that year. We didn't drive; we flew. And we didn't stay in their house like we usually did. Instead, we stayed in a hotel nearby. When we visited the house, Pop-pop wasn't there to greet us at the door. Grandma yelled from the kitchen for us to come in. As we entered, I noticed that the good smell of the place had been replaced by the sterile scent of cleaning solution.

Mom had warned us that Pop-pop was sick, but we had no idea what to expect. How could we be ready for something we'd never seen? His bed was in the living room on the first floor—a hospital bed in the corner of the room. A moveable toilet, white and plastic, glared from the foot of the bed. Oxygen tanks stood in the opposite corner of the room, half hidden by the door. A stranger sat next to the bed—Pop-pop's nurse, or "Hospice," but I didn't know what that meant. Pop-pop could still mumble things, swallow and sip through straws okay. But his skin was white and clammy, like someone who's been in the water a long time and grown cold. His breathing was labored. I was scared. The house, the smells, the people—the scene seemed a twisted dream.

We had Thanksgiving dinner in the house, in the room next to Pop-pop's as he lay dying. We all tried to count our blessings as we ate, but I did not feel thankful. By then, it had become clear to me that this was final. The day before, Pop-pop had stopped swallowing, and when you stood near his bed his eyes couldn't focus on you. He was dying and we were waiting, going through the motions of having a holiday, of being thankful.

As we ate, part of me was furious that we hadn't seen it coming. After his diagnosis, it was like a bad horror movie—when flashbacks reveal that the killer was hiding in plain sight all along. Pop-pop died of pancreatic cancer. This too-late diagnosis made his summertime symptoms make sense. I remember in late August, Pop-pop was late for breakfast. After we had all eaten, my grandma successfully coaxed him out. When he reached the table, Grandma put down his breakfast. He just looked up at her and leaned back a little, like he was catching his breath, unable to open his eyes. He was in pain, unable to really speak, and very weak—but none of us knew why. Grandma started to panic, shaking him and yelling his name. My siblings and I were swarming around the kitchen table, miming my Grandma's alarm, all of us unsuspecting that he was terminally ill.

I kissed his cheek before we left for the hotel that night. At around 1 A.M, the phone in our hotel room rang. My Mom answered. The conversation was short, and she got up in the dark, dressed, exchanged a few words with my father, and left. We all knew what the phone call meant. I was wide-awake, staring at the ceiling.

At the funeral, I watched as the simple pine coffin was lowered into the ground. Next to the grave, there was a pile of dirt with a few shovels. I was the first to throw a shovel-full of dirt onto the coffin—to bury him. As the dirt landed on the wood with a sick thud, I knew that now it was real, that he wouldn't come back, that he couldn't come back, and that I would never see him again. A huge sadness washed over me, and I cried and cried, burying my face into my mother. She cried, too.

His death changed me. For the next year after he died, I went into a fierce depression. I was furious and wounded. Things around me just didn't seem to matter. There was no one person or thing to target with my anger. The worst part was that I felt like no one else my age knew what I was going through or what I knew—that life is so fleeting, painful, and pathetic, some sort of a sick joke. I was hurt that the world didn't stop and notice that a great man had died. Things went on, almost as if he'd never existed. I still went to school. We still visited D.C. The sweet smell had returned to the house, but Grandma wanted to leave. "It's too big," she said. While we were there, I kept expecting to see Pop-pop walk right in through the front door.

I look at myself, and I see a hole—one that I desperately have tried to fill and cover up. But I think we are supposed to miss the people that we love. I don't think that we are supposed to mend.

Instead, his death also reminds me that the time we have on this planet is fixed—and that, perhaps, we only get one shot. I continue to admire Pop-pop's courage and his strength, and I aspire to be as good a person as he was. Each time I think about how much sadness life can bring and how stressful the day-to-day can be, I also take a moment to appreciate that life is beautiful, too. I think this was something Pop-pop knew. I aspire to adopt his willingness to love and find happiness from moment to moment.

~Mariel Reed

Timeless Moments

The great gift of family life is to be intimately acquainted with people you
might never even introduce yourself to, had life not done it for you.
~Kendall Hailey

People dressed in white rushed down long glossy hallways that smelled like rubbing alcohol. Hospitals were places that I tried to avoid. They were always full of sick, complaining people, or crying family members. I slumped down in one of the wooden chairs in the waiting room. The rest of my family was sitting beside me, all except my mother. She was the reason we were here.

My mother was the comic relief and happiness booster in our family. But lately, she had been acting moody and irrational. Unfortunately, there was a very good explanation for the mood swings. She was pregnant. I was thirteen years old, and already a big sister to two other siblings. Why did we need another one?

My mother and I were as close as can be. We watched movies together, painted each other's nails and even gossiped about friends. When other kids were embarrassed by the silly things their moms did, I joined in doing silly things with my mom. She wasn't just my mother—she was my best friend. But, I wondered, with a new baby in the family, would she forget to do all those cool things with me?

I wasn't sure I could be a big sister to another baby, anyway. What if this new one was annoying and pooped all the time? I folded my arms and looked at a clock that was on the wall next to me. It was seven in the morning. We hadn't been there long, but my mom had been in the hospital for hours already. My dad was the one that took my mom to the hospital at four in the morning. At six thirty he had called my grandparents and asked them to bring me and my brother and sister.

My dad kept pacing back and forth between mom's room and the waiting room. Then, finally, he told us to follow him. My brother and sister jumped up to follow, but I lagged behind. This was it. This was the moment everyone had been waiting for—seeing the baby. I wasn't so sure about this. I could understand why my brother and sister were so excited about the baby because they were new at this whole big brother/sister thing. But me, I was the old one. There was nothing too significant about this moment for me.

We filed into the room where our mom was. She was lying on a hospital bed covered with a blue blanket, her curly hair wild around her face. My family crowded around her before I could even see what the baby looked like.

"Who wants to hold your new baby brother?" my mom asked.

My brother and sister fought over who should be allowed to hold him first while I just leaned against the wall.

"Erica," my mom called to me, "would you like to hold the baby first?"

I soon found myself sitting in a leather armchair while my dad placed my new baby brother in my arms.

At first, all I saw was a bundle of blue. Then, I saw a tuft of blond hair. I pulled down the blanket a little and came face to face with a chubby blue-eyed baby. A little hand broke free from the bounds of the blanket and tried to grasp my finger.

"His name is Ben," my dad said. Ben's smooth face broke into a toothless smile, and I found myself smiling too.

"Hello, Ben," I said. His soft fingers held mine tightly and his eyes sparkled with curiosity and tried focusing on my hand. Maybe he wasn't so bad after all. I couldn't help but feel a warm, elated feeling rising in my heart. From the firm way he was holding my finger, I could tell that he knew I was his sister. He needed me, and deep down maybe I needed him too.

"I'm your big sister," I said.

Even though I thought that being a big sister again wouldn't be as special as the first time, it felt just as special. I found myself thinking that this baby deserved a big sister just like any other baby. Just because he was the youngest of four siblings didn't make his birth any less significant.

I leaned down close to Ben's ear, and even though I knew he couldn't understand me, I whispered, "I'm going to be the best big sister ever."

~Erica Kinne

Busted — The MySpace Story

Hmmm! Teenagers. They think they know everything.
You give them an inch, and they swim all over you.
~Sebastian, The Little Mermaid

Almost a year has passed since my daughter turned thirteen and got the ultimate gift from her grandparents — her own computer. To say she was psyched would be an understatement. She couldn't wait to set up shop, surf the latest fashions, and e-mail and IM her friends from the comfort of her multi-colored, poster-crazy, gum-wrapped bedroom.

The computer came with rules, rules, rules. Never talk to anyone you don't know, no chat rooms, and no MySpace. My daughter, Leah, would sigh (pretty loudly), roll her eyes (she is a master at eye-rolling) and say, "Mom, we've been over this. I know." So all was well; Leah was officially a teen with all of the infinite possibilities of the Internet.

Sometimes as I entered Leah's room, she would quickly minimize a screen and turn to me. "What?" she'd ask guiltily.

"Just checking in," I'd say, or "hello!"

She would patiently wait for me to leave, and as I shut her door (at her request) I'd hear those fingers frantically hitting keys in happy rhythm.

One afternoon, I walked into Leah's room as she was typing a long instant message.

"Who's that?" I asked.

"Some boy from Chicago," she replied.

"Some boy from Chicago???" I asked. "How do you know a boy from Chicago?"

She stopped typing and looked at me. "I really don't know."

And so the lectures began again. "Don't talk to strangers! How do you know that's really a teenage boy? I thought you knew the rules!"

One day when Leah was at school, I surfed the web. I had been hearing so much about MySpace in the media, and I wanted to plug in our zip code and see who popped up. I heard that teachers did this to see which kids have accounts and to make sure they are being safe. In no time at all, I saw lots of familiar faces. So many kids had their own MySpace pages. I snooped further.

It was easy to read comments and click on pictures. I saw the kid in dark glasses with a shirt pulled up to her nose and a hat pulled down to her eyebrows, a girl in a dance pose, a boy standing on his hands.... As I clicked, I learned which kids were friendly and which ones weren't. There was that girl with dark glasses, that dancer, and that acrobat again and again.

As I read comments from the dancer, and then the kid with dark glasses, a horrible feeling swept through my body. I leaned a little closer to my computer screen as reality hit. That was no kid in dark glasses—that was my daughter!—the girl who knew she wasn't allowed to have MySpace!

My emotions ran the gamut. They went from shock to anger to disappointment, to wondering what I would have done at thirteen. It's not that I couldn't understand that she really wanted a MySpace, but knowing that she did it behind my back when it was against the rules was wrong.

And although I was tempted to stomp down to the bus stop, violently waving a copy of her MySpace page, I decided there was probably a better way to handle my discovery.

I went ahead with Plan B. I created my own MySpace page and carefully selected my photo. Did I want an angry face or a happy one? A headshot or the whole me? I finally decided on a headshot—just a simple picture of smiling me cropped to a circle with one word written down the side: BUSTED. I then left Leah a "friend request" on her MySpace page, along with a message: "Busted. I thought I could trust you." I knew when she signed on and found my picture waiting, she would know her MySpace days were over.

It didn't take long for Leah to arrive home from school, grab a snack and disappear into her room. I waited for her to come flying down the steps, but it seemed awfully quiet up there. Finally, she came downstairs. She walked right past me.

"Uh, hello???" I said. "Is there something you'd like to say?"

"I'm sorry," she replied. "I really am."

So we talked. I told Leah what bugged me the most is that she knew she wasn't allowed to have MySpace, and she did it anyway. I understood she must have really wanted it, but she never even tried to talk to me about it. I explained that MySpace has been called the "candy store for creeps." I hated the thought of absolutely anyone out there being able to look at her picture, talk to her, and above all, hurt her in some way. A friend of hers recently had her whole page sabotaged by a former BFF—since this BFF knew her password, it was easy to get on her page and fill it with racist comments and mean images. It just seemed like there was so much potential for harm.

A lot of trust was lost that day and by the way, so was Leah's Internet connection—right after she deleted her MySpace. She went a long time with no Internet at all. Recently, Leah came to me and sat down.

"Mom," she said, "I'm asking this time. When can I have MySpace? I really want it."

"Ugh." I responded.

"I'll be safe. I know there are bad people out there."

I waited a few minutes before answering. "You can have it now, but it comes with rules. Set your profile to private, only talk to your friends, and know I'll be looking."

"You'll be looking at my page?" She was not liking this.

"The Internet isn't private," I said. "Anyone can look at MySpace, because your space isn't really yours when it's online. And Leah?" She looked at me. "Please be careful."

Leah's connection to the Web was restored, along with her MySpace and my trust. Her fingers can be heard tapping away within the colored confines of her room. And maybe we both know now, a little better than before, that the most valuable communication comes from connections within families—even more valuable than the infinite possibilities of the Internet.

~Carol S. Rothchild

Reprinted by permission of Off the Mark and
Mark Parisi. ©1996 Mark Parisi.

Possum and Soda Spit

A sister is a gift to the heart, a friend to the spirit,
a golden thread to the meaning of life.
~Isadora James

"What? Laura's going to be home the night of my party?" I shrieked. My sister was the last person I wanted around the night of my slumber party. I was really looking forward to having the house all to myself while my friends were over. After all, it was my birthday! Trying to get my mother to understand, I said, "Gosh Mom, can't you find someplace for Laura to go, like cousin Ellie's? Having her here will ruin everything!"

I had finally talked my parents into letting me invite a few of my teammates from the soccer team as well as a few school friends. I had been waiting for this night for weeks and now I had to contend with my older sister being around. It was completely unfair.

"Now Emily," my mother said to me, trying to calm me down. "Laura will stay out of your way and in her own room. Besides, I don't understand why you're so upset about her being here. She's older than your friends and probably doesn't want anything to do with them anyway."

"That's what you think," I pouted. "She'll hang out and want to talk about something yucky like boys, or the soccer finals, or something other than what I like to talk about. It's going to ruin the whole party!"

"Laura being home during your birthday party will only ruin it if you let it," my mother responded to my whining. "You need to get a better attitude young lady, or there won't be a party at all!"

I stomped out of the room and into my bedroom, throwing myself down on the bed and banging my fist into my pillow several times. Frustrated and angry, I thought about how unfair this was. It was my birthday and I didn't want Laura around! She was going to steal all the attention and ruin the party. And how dare my mom say I needed a better attitude. Laura was the teenager with the attitude, not me!

My anger was getting the best of me as I threw my glasses on the floor and buried my face in my pillow to hide my sobbing. "I hate my life," I thought. "Why do I have to have an older sister anyway? Why couldn't I have been an only child?"

When my weeping finally slowed, I recalled all the anguish I had gone through making my guest list. The plans had finally come together and I had been so excited when I made the list of friends I wanted to invite. This was going to be a special party because it was my last before entering my teenage years. The friends who attended were the most important factor in the success of the party.

Rachael was invited because she had the best CD collection and Kanitha because she always told the best stories. Of course, Shannon expected to be invited because she was very popular. These were my favorite friends, but suddenly I felt nervous and scared. I started to worry that the girls from the soccer team wouldn't get along with my school friends. On top of that, I had to put up with my sister being there and ruining everything. It just seemed so complicated!

I pulled my long blond hair back in a clip and tried to wipe off my red, puffy eyes. My heart thumped fast in my chest. Realizing I might have made a mistake planning this slumber party, I sat holding my head in my hands, trying to figure it all out. Again, I felt the hot tears stinging my cheeks with frustration at my situation.

The days passed slowly but finally the time for the party arrived. The air was filled with excitement while I waited for my friends to come. At last I was going to have the special birthday party I had been waiting for. I could only hope that Laura would stay in her room.

The scavenger hunt I had planned went well. The girls all returned to the living room with their treasures, ready for the next planned activity. Suddenly, my friend Meeka noticed movement behind the curtains by the window. As we stepped over to see what it was, a baby possum came running out from behind the curtain, heading straight toward Shannon! The screams and hysteria were deafening and I had no idea what to do. I stood motionless until Laura ran in to see what was happening. When she entered the room, the possum scampered toward her. At the very last second, Laura opened the front door and allowed it to run out.

Thank goodness! If the possum had hidden in another room, bitten someone, or gotten into the food, it would have been a total disaster! We all sighed with relief and laughed at the fact that Kanitha would probably soon be telling the possum story with exaggerated facts at the next party she attended, although we still didn't know how the possum managed to get in the living room in the first place.

Later that night, we were all in the kitchen getting snacks. While giggling and talking about the possum, a full bottle of soda spilled on the kitchen sink and drizzled down onto the floor. What a mess! At first I was horrified and was sure I would get in trouble, but once again it was Laura who came to the rescue.

Instead of making a fuss about the sticky soda, Laura laughed, found some straws, sipped some soda into a straw and then spit it at one of the girls. The soda spit landed right in Rachael's hair. For a moment, I was nervous. How would Rachel react? I was just about ready to yell at Laura and tell her to leave, that I knew she'd ruin my party and everything I'd planned. But, to my great relief, Rachael spit soda right back at her! Everyone joined in on the fun and the "spitting party" lasted for quite a while.

When it was over, the entire kitchen and everyone's pajamas were sticky and wet, but the laughter and fun that everybody experienced was definitely worth the mess. Laura took the blame when my mother came in and even helped mop the floor. I was pleasantly surprised that my sister could be so much fun and fit in so well with my friends.

The next day after everyone had gone home, I told Laura how glad I was that she was there to help with all the surprises. While I picked up the final pieces of trash from the party, I thought about how much fun we'd had. I knew for certain this was a party my friends would remember forever.

Finally, the house was cleaned up. I went to my parents to thank them for letting me have the party and allowing me to invite the friends I had wanted to come.

My mother asked, "Did you have a good time last night?"

"I sure did, Mom," I answered. "Everyone got along really well and there were some great surprises too."

"Oh really?" responded my mother. "Like what kind of surprises?"

I got a silly grin on my face when I said, "Oh, like possums, soda spit, and older sisters." My mother had a puzzled look on her face, but thankfully didn't ask the obvious questions. As I skipped out of the room still with my smile spread across my face, I was beaming and thinking that being twelve and having an older sister wasn't so bad after all.

~Nancy Maggio

Daddy

Dad, your guiding hand on my shoulder
will remain with me forever.
~Author Unknown

I had just turned ten years old and I was celebrating my birthday. It was a great party. My friends, family, and the person who always made me laugh—my Daddy—were there to share this special day with me. Everything was going well until my mother took me aside and told me that she had two important things to tell me that would change my life. She sat me down as soon as everyone left the house—only my mother, my little sister and my Daddy remained.

She started by telling me how lucky I was to have such a loving family. She kept on telling me stories about when I was younger, how my Daddy always took care of me when she went to work, how happy she was when she found out she was pregnant and how she screamed her head off when she saw me for the very first time on the sonogram. She kept going on and on, and, at times, I joined in with memories of my Daddy too. I mentioned the day my friends started asking me about my unique hairstyle, which my Daddy always did. He used to create lots of ponytails with my hair using different color pins and the other girls thought it was cool. After my mother and I shared some unforgettable memories, my mother started crying. I was scared—I knew something wasn't right.

My mother started talking and I felt like a child in need of a blanket for comfort. She told me that eleven years ago, she thought she was in love, but the person she was in love with was not my father. At least, not the man I always called Daddy. I told her that I didn't want to hear anymore—I didn't want to hear the truth. She kept talking anyway. She told me that when she was pregnant, the man she had married and loved for four years, my real father, had left her because he wanted freedom. He was six years younger than she was and wanted no responsibility; he was not ready to be a father. His family was happy about my being born, but even my biological grandmother couldn't convince her son that he was ready to be a dad. It was worthless. My father only thought of hanging out with his friends and going out with other girls.

My mother went on with her story. She explained that she moved out of their house and back to her mother's and eventually met her new husband, the person I always thought was my father—my Daddy. She told me about all the love, help, and support he gave her, how he helped her move into a new apartment, and how he was always there to make sure everything was all right.

When I was born, my biological father was there in the hospital with his family. Even though my mom asked him to stay, he left. My mother was scared and turned to her family for help. Eventually, she moved in with the man I call Daddy after my father moved out of the country. My mother finished her story with this, and at that moment I found myself confused. My birthday had ended up very differently from what I had expected.

Six months later, I spoke to my biological father on the phone. His voice was deep and hard and he sounded like he was holding something back. I didn't know what to do, so I hung up. I couldn't help it. I hated my mother for bringing me into this world and lying to me. My mother has always said, "A father is not the one who created you but the one who raised you," but how could I believe a person who kept the truth from me? Soon, when anyone asked me about my dad, all I replied was, "I don't have one."

As days, months, and years passed by, I hated John, my biological father, and my life even more. My mother said not to hate him; he just didn't know what he was missing. My mother had always been there for me through good times and bad, but I felt so distant from her, as if a huge wall separated her from me. I loved her so much but at the same time I blamed her for all of the confusion in my life.

Now, I'm thirteen and I've learned that it wasn't my mother's fault or my fault. All my hurt and anger are finally starting to heal. I learned that things happen for a reason, although I'm still not really sure what that reason is just yet. I know I will find out in time. The person I was so angry with, my stepfather, was just trying to protect me and I was too mad to look past that fact. I still ask my mother why she told me, why she decided I needed to know the truth. She said I was bound to know. I guess I just have to trust her.

My father who raised me, my Daddy, will always be my number one, even though my birth certificate says otherwise. I sometimes am amazed by how one little thing can change the balance in your life. But then again, I know that my Daddy will always be my Daddy.

~Sharendalle Murga

Chapter 10

Teens Talk Middle School

The People Who Are There For Us

*Dare to reach out your hand into the darkness,
to pull another hand into the light.*

~Norman B. Rice

In Mr. Burgen's Office

Stand up for what is right even if you are standing alone.
~Author Unknown

I'm the kid who sees a counselor
During school hours,
Every eye lifting as I speed out of the room,
On my way to Mr. Burgen's office.
Mr. Burgen, with breath like Swiss cheese.

I spill forth my hurt and longings
To that heavy man who listens without interrupting,
Murmuring gentle expressions like,
"It's okay," and "I understand."
Somehow, he does.

This year, I failed math on all three of my report cards.
This year, my sister won the Justin Wynn Scholarship for Gifted and
      Talented children.
This year, Jackie Lipka told every kid in the school I was a loser.
This year, Mr. Burgen was my only friend.

Nearing the end of it,
I heft battered books from my locker as two teachers breeze by.
"Burgen asked me out!" one squeals.

"No!" the other laughs. "He's so pathetic. Did you hear him lisp
      through the faculty meeting?"

I crash my books to the floor and stand glaring as they turn to
      notice me.
"Mr. Burgen is nice to me," I say.
One of them, red-faced and shaky, steps over to help me pick up
      my books.
"We didn't mean anything..." she stammers.
The other one rolls her eyes and looks away.

I take my books and watch them scatter.
It dawns on me then that I am not the only one,
Making my way through these thorns and sharp briars.
Mr. Burgen is in middle school too.

~Juliet C. Bond

89

A Port in the Storm

You may not realize it when it happens,
but a kick in the teeth may be the best thing in the world for you.
~Walt Disney

" I hate this school. And I hate your stupid rules," I muttered.

"We have rules for a reason, Miss," the principal said.

He scribbled on some papers. I read it upside down—ONE WEEK SUSPENSION. That wasn't going to look so great on my record, but what did I care? This was my third school in three years—a middle school with the stupidest rules I'd ever heard of. Who knew leaving school grounds in the middle of the day would be such a big deal?

I was hungry and there was a Burger King right around the corner. "I'll only be a minute," I reasoned. When I pushed open the side door and dashed out, something in my head told me I was making a mistake, but I didn't care. I probably wouldn't be here long anyway.

I wished we'd never moved back to Wisconsin. We went to Arizona a year and a half ago and I'd made friends. Then one night, Dad sat all of us kids down at the kitchen table. "We're moving back," he told us. "You girls will go first, then your mom and I will follow with your brother."

Now I was two months into the new school year. I couldn't figure out what assignment we were working on or what the homework was, and I was sick of living with my aunt whose house smelled like Lysol.

Then Mom and Dad got back and crammed us all into a small apartment.

"You're grounded," Dad said when he found out about the suspension. "For a week."

"You're kidding," I said. "What am I gonna do?"

"Help your mother unpack."

"Yeah, right. Like that's what I want to do."

"Don't sass back. This move has been hard on all of us," Dad replied.

"It's been a lot harder on me!" I shouted and ran up to the bedroom I shared with my two sisters. I threw myself on my bed and sobbed.

By Monday morning I was bored. "Mom, can't I go to the mall?"

"Your dad and I discussed it. I'm taking you to your grandmother's house. She said you're welcome to spend your days with her."

"You're kidding, right? Grandma is, like, so old. What am I going to do there?"

"She'll think of something," Mom said.

There was no arguing about it. Later that morning, she drove me to my grandmother's. On the long ride, I had time to think. I'd fight any suggestions Grandma had. Why should I be nice to someone so old? She wasn't anything like me. She couldn't possibly understand what I was going through.

"Hi, Barbie," Grandma said when she opened the door. "Come in. I've got lots of fun things planned."

"I think I'll just watch TV if that's okay with you," I said.

"That's not okay with me. We're going to do things together."

"Whatever," I replied.

Mom left. She'd be back that night to pick me up.

"There's laundry to fold. Why don't you help me?" Grandma said.

"Nah. You do it. I'm tired."

"Tired? A young girl like you? Grab the towels from the dryer and bring them here."

I walked into the laundry room and opened the dryer. Filling my arms with warm, fluffy towels, I inhaled the aroma of fresh laundry soap. "Here ya go," I said as I plopped them on the couch.

"Sit here and help me," she said.

What could I do? I was stuck there for the whole day. After the towels were folded, Grandma said it was time to clean up the dishes. Then she got stuff from the fridge for lunch. We made sandwiches of lunchmeat and cheese, and she poured me a big, tall glass of milk.

"A growing girl like you needs a healthy dose of milk and some cookies for dessert."

Now that's what I was talking about. We rarely had any sweets in our house lately. "These are good, Grandma."

"Oh, you like them? Maybe we'll make some this week."

I guessed that would be okay. Why not? Anything to pass the time.

Later that afternoon, we played Go Fish. Before I knew it the clock's hands said 5:00 and Mom was at the door.

"Bye, Barbie. See you tomorrow," Grandma called out sweetly as I got in the car.

"How was your day?" Mom asked.

"Fine." I still wasn't sure how I felt about being with my old grandmother, but I wasn't going to tell my mom we had any fun, either.

The next day we played Yahtzee and Clue. And Grandma let me help her chop liver into tiny pieces after she cooked it for her Chihuahua, Princess. "Grandma, why don't you just feed her the hard dry stuff? Why do you go to all this trouble?"

"Because she's special. And I like to treat her nicely," Grandma replied.

The third day, Grandma had all the stuff out to make cookies. It was fun to watch them bake in the oven and decorate them with sugar. She even let me eat some warm ones.

"So what's going on with school?" she asked between bites.

"Nothin'," I replied.

"It's not nothing when you get suspended."

"School is stupid. No one understands. I'm all alone again and don't fit in." I grabbed another cookie and took a long drink of milk.

"You're not alone, Sweetheart. Your mom and dad are trying their best."

"They're not the ones who have to walk into a new school. I have no idea what's going on in class and everyone stares at me. I feel so different. And I don't have any friends."

"I know all about being different. And not having friends, too. Your grandpa died when you were little. All my friends had husbands and they didn't want me around. It hurt."

"What did you do?"

"I crocheted blankets for all of you grandkids; I joined the church down the road and helped out with the potluck dinners. Everybody loved my cooking."

I stuffed another cookie into my mouth. She was right about that. And I didn't realize she had been alone for all those years.

"Life is what you make of it, Barbie. You can be mad at the world because of the way things are, or you can turn yourself around and decide to make the best of it."

"Like you did?" I said.

Grandma smiled. "Want to play Checkers?"

"Sure, but can I have one more cookie, please?"

"You bet. You can have all you want." She paused. "Remember, your mom and dad love you, even if life is hard sometimes."

I took my plate to the sink and thought about how hard Dad worked so he could give Mom and us kids the best that he could. Maybe if I didn't walk around school with my head hanging down I'd make friends. Maybe if I smiled at others they'd smile back.

I knew changes wouldn't happen overnight. But I had a feeling I could come to Grandma and she'd help me.

"Mom and Dad are trying their best, huh?" I asked.

"Yup, just like you are. Now grab the checkerboard. We have a game to play."

~B.J. Taylor

90

Making My Music

*Music expresses that which cannot be said
and on which it is impossible to be silent.*
~Victor Hugo

Throughout my life, I have had many teachers. They come in many forms—parents, friends, brothers, sisters, teachers, and the kind that has had the most effect on my life—piano teachers.

I had been playing classical piano for five years when I walked up the steps of the porch of a yellow house with peeling paint. I had acquired an interest in jazz and needed a new teacher with different knowledge to introduce me to jazz piano. I knocked on the door and waited. This pause would become familiar to me, as I often had to knock twice before I heard any movement from inside the house. The man who opened the door was short, with curly dark hair streaked with gray.

He spoke carefully, never wasting words. "Hello, my name is Michael. I assume you are Charlie?" After my affirmative response, he showed me into his house.

The first thing I noticed about his piano was its shine. It was like a dark mirror, so clear that you could easily watch your hands dance along the keys. Michael would sit next to me in a folding chair and we would discuss, play, and write about my discoveries in jazz. He was friendly and easy to get along with, and he always challenged me to think and learn about the new world I had entered.

I remember our last lesson together well. I was tired on that particular day, and ready to go home. We were working on improvising. He told me to sing a passage, then find it on the keyboard and play it. I was having a hard time with this because I'm shy and I almost never sing, so we stopped. I asked why we were learning this way.

"Because otherwise," Michael said, "you won't be expressing yourself. You will just be randomly playing notes on a piano. The song won't be you anymore, it will just be sound." Then he bid me farewell and I left. I never saw him again.

I stepped onto the same porch two weeks later and began the familiar wait at the door, but this time, I had a companion. A tall, dismal gray tank stood next to me. Reading the side, I learned that the tank held oxygen. It was empty. The door opened revealing an older man who peered at me curiously.

"I have a lesson here, with Michael," I told the man, who continued to look at me carefully. At the mention of Michael's name, the man's face melted into sadness. "Michael won't be giving any lessons today. Would you like to talk to his wife, Carol?" the man asked quietly.

"Yes, please," I answered, with dread filling me as I waited for her. She came to the porch and told me news that was both startling and confusing.

"I am so sorry you came all the way here," Carol said. "I called your home, but I guess you never got the message. Michael is very sick and unable to leave his bed," she told me, but by the tone of her voice, he seemed to be suffering from more than a cold.

"How sick is he?" I responded, eyeing the oxygen tank suspiciously.

"Very sick," Carol said with her voice faltering. Tears came to her eyes. I quickly expressed my sorrow and left the porch, alarmed.

On the following Monday, my worry for Michael had faded in the rush of schoolwork. Once I got home, my mother told me the horrible news that Michael had passed away over the weekend. I sat in our armchair and let the shock pass through me.

I thought back to our last lesson and the importance of what he taught me. I still remember leaving and thinking of how important his last statement was. He had told me the true way to make music, is to make music with meaning—otherwise, you're only making sound. To this day, every time I sit down at the piano, I think of how I have to express myself through my music. I will always remember Michael for the last lesson he gave me—the lesson of how to truly make music.

~Charles Hoffert

A Lasting Kindness

The greatest gift God can give a person is another person.
~Franz Werfel

Once there was a ten-year-old girl whose family life was in sudden chaos because her little sister died without warning. As the family adjusted to the grief and their new reality, the young girl found comfort in the routine of school. Her teachers were sensitive, and warned the other students to be nice.

One teacher, Mrs. Cohen, gave her extra doses of attention. She often discreetly called the girl over to her desk to ask her questions about her home life, actively searching for ways she could help her. It was in this way that Mrs. Cohen discovered that the girl was in charge of walking her sister and brother home from school—a ten-minute walk in a safe neighborhood. Still, Mrs. Cohen was alarmed. She felt the girl was too young. The very next day, she called the girl to her desk and told her that she had found someone who was willing and eager to pick up the girl and her siblings every day after school and drive her home for the rest of the year—another seven months or so.

Once school was over for the day, Mrs. Cohen walked the girl to what would become their meeting area. There waited a lady, quite a bit older than Mrs. Cohen, who seemed nice and really pleased to help out the kids, despite the fact that she had never met them. Mrs. Cohen introduced her as Gita and soon their routine was born.

It's not always easy being on the receiving end of kindness, especially for young kids going through rough times. The girl was antagonistic, often even rude. But Gita was patient and understanding. She proceeded to wait at their meeting spot, rain or shine, for the rest of the year and drove the kids home from school every day. She always asked them about their day and weekly brought them to her house for treats of popcorn, chocolate cake, and hot chocolate.

The days slowly became weeks, which soon melted into months and pretty soon, the year was over. The girl turned eleven. During the summer, Gita remained in close contact with the kids and their family.

The next year, the girl was a grade older and no longer in Mrs. Cohen's class. One day, somehow, the family discovered something interesting about their friend Gita—she was Mrs. Cohen's mother.

When Mrs. Cohen was asked about it, she explained: She had purposely not told the family this fact because she had been so worried that the girl would feel awkward about having a relationship with her teacher's mother! (As soon as the girl found out, she started frantically reeling back in her head, horrified at the thought of how many times she had complained to Gita about her teachers!)

Even though she was young, the girl felt warmed by the realization of just how much her teacher had cared for her. Mrs. Cohen had not only given the girl a wonderful gift—her own mother!—but she had wrapped her gift with genuine sensitivity and thoughtfulness.

The years passed and that gift is still enjoyed today. Gita remains a fixture in the lives of this girl and her family. She has been present at school productions, graduations, and most of the girl's other life milestones. Essentially, Gita became like another cherished grandmother. Gita was involved in the girl's journey through dating, marriage, childbearing, and rearing.

It has been almost twenty years since then, and I am the little girl that Gita took care of. It is with true delight and love that Gita and I still carry on a correspondence today, despite living on different continents.

I am forever grateful to my teacher Mrs. Cohen for bringing Gita into our lives. Who would have thought that a simple arrangement could have evolved into something so enriching?

~Rochel Burstyn

92

Middle School All Over Again

Act as if what you do makes a difference. It does.
~William James

When I started teaching seventh grade social studies, I didn't know that I'd be transported back to my own thirteenth year. It happened after my student, Mary, came to school with cuts and bruises on her body. I'd kept a close eye on her ever since seeing her around town. Barefoot and without a curfew, she'd ride her skateboard or bike and hang out at the 7-Eleven.

Because of Mary's apparent lack of parental supervision, I made a special effort to connect with her, which was easy because of her sunny and winning personality. When she came to school looking like she'd been in a fight, it seemed only natural that I'd ask her what happened. She shared that her brother's friends were beating her up when they were high on drugs. I tried to comfort her even though I felt sick inside, not only because of the abuse she endured, but because at that age my stepfather had also left marks on my body.

In my junior high years, when I had to change for P.E., I dressed with my back to the wall to hide my welt marks. Randomly, he would beat me for wearing nail polish, forgetting my homework, or some other perceived infraction. If he had been drinking, he became a lunatic. Now as a wife and mother of three teenagers, I hadn't thought about my stepfather in years. But seeing Mary's bruises ripped off a scab from a wound that I didn't even know was there.

After Mary told me her story, I called the principal. He told me I had to write a Child Protective Services (CPS) report, which I did, but I asked that my name be kept out of it. Although the situation wasn't about me, I felt anxious about sharing the information Mary had told me.

During all the years of my abuse, the unspoken rule in my house remained: keep your mouth shut. My mom was also abusive when she was drunk or high. As much as it disgusted me, I would do anything to prove my love to my mother. I craved her approval and thought that if I acted perfectly, our house would be like *The Brady Bunch*. But it never worked. Her words and actions made me crazy, but I craved the carefree life of a normal kid, so I kept my mouth shut. Confused, I burned with rage, but I also knew that no one would ever take my word against hers. I was stuck—she was too good at making everyone else look wrong. And I knew if I called out for help and no one rescued me, that would be worse than never asking for help at all.

A couple of weeks passed, and I thought that Mary's family would think that a neighbor called CPS. Surely someone else noticed her condition. On one Friday, however, Mary stormed into my class when I was teaching seventh period and said, "I have to talk to you, NOW!" I was bewildered but I saw the urgency in her eyes and stepped outside the door while my class worked on their journals. "You told! How could you tell? It had to be you because I didn't tell anyone else. How could you do this to me? Now my brother will be taken from me forever. I love him. He needs me. I take care of him. I trusted you and this is how you repay me." As she accused me, I could hear my mom's voice in her words.

My head started swirling and I thought I'd throw up. I tried to answer Mary as an adult, but I felt like the thirteen-year-old who had spilled my family's dark secret. I tried to find the words to comfort Mary, but she didn't give me time to answer. "The marks are from my skateboard." She said and then bolted out the door leaving me to face my students. Feeling paralyzed, I bit the inside of my cheeks to keep from crying. Somehow I made it through seventh period and sprinted for my car, sobbing all the way home.

When I arrived, my husband met me with the phone. "An irate parent wants you to call; here's the number." I returned Mary's parents' call explaining over and over, "If I think a student is in physical trouble, I am required by law to call CPS."

They were unaffected by my argument. "She is always getting hurt. She says that you initiated the conversation and for some reason made these stories up. Do you know what you've done to our family?" they accused.

Finally, the dad grew weary of my repeated explanations and said, "Just don't talk to the principal about us anymore. Let us manage our own family." As I hung up the phone, the tears started and wouldn't stop.

When I arrived at school the next day, I saw Mary. She wouldn't make eye contact with me. As a professional, I treated her just like my other students, but my heart twisted every time I thought about it. I felt insecure and inadequate—raw on the inside. After Mary's class left, on my desk was a note—unsigned. But I knew it was from Mary:

> Mrs. Ryan, you need to learn to be a teacher and not a parent. What we need is for you to do your job as a teacher and leave the parenting to the parents.

It sounds odd, but I was glad that she wrote the note—it had to make her feel better. Before the incident, we'd connected in a special way, but I knew our relationship would never be the same. In the next couple of weeks, she came to school with a broken arm, broken fingers, and a black eye. I didn't say a word. It was almost as if she wanted to prove that the injuries were from her skateboard. Abruptly they stopped, and I never saw another mark on her body. I still saw her around town looking homeless, and I acted friendly. But I never made it personal, and we never spoke of the incident again.

When I think of Mary, my hope is that my actions allowed her life to improve. I know mine did. They forced me to face the ghosts of my childhood. And by trying to help Mary, I helped myself. I tackled one of my fears and alerted authorities to what I thought was a dangerous situation.

The fact that I was blamed only made me dig deeper into my own painful past. Thankfully, I wasn't a middle school student; I was a middle school teacher. I didn't have to be afraid of the truth. The truth sets you free, and the truth is, what happened to me was wrong, but I wasn't wrong to try and help Mary. Maybe one day, she'll understand. Maybe one day, she'll even use the experience to help another abuse victim. Mary is one seventh grade social studies student I'll never forget. I just hope she remembers I cared.

~Suzy Ryan

93

Mother's Little Helper

Love is more than a noun—it is a verb;
it is more than a feeling—
it is caring, sharing, helping, sacrificing.
~William Arthur Ward

The first day of seventh grade was a maze of locker combinations and up and down staircases, five minute passages through crowded hallways from English to Math classes, and girls with cuter outfits than mine. It also involved a packed lunch—my first and last. Webster Elementary School allowed me to go home for lunch but Sheridan Junior High was seven blocks from home and promoted a hot lunch program, so that those with thirty-five cents could buy a tray full of meatballs, mashed potatoes, green beans, and milk in cartons, all served up by women in hairnets.

My mom must have had a burst of maternal energy, sending her last child off to the junior high world, so she packed me a tuna salad sandwich on white bread wrapped in waxed paper, complete with mitered corners. Her intention was right and I knew nothing of packed lunches so I slumped off to school, sure of social failure, and carrying a brown paper lunch bag as my last connection to a home where I didn't need to look like an American Girl model.

I survived the morning, found my way from room 105 (Modern Math) to room 302 (American History, taught by a teacher who put on films about WWII and promptly fell asleep with her head upon her cluttered desk) and room 20 for a science class that was horrifying, with periodic tables on the wall and promises of "interesting experiments" in the year ahead.

I went to my locker at lunchtime and finessed the combination lock, only to be greeted by the bouquet of tuna fish left too long in September temperatures. The bag was a speckled mess of grease stains and my locker-mate would surely live forever with that smell in the yellow cotton sweater she had hung so sweetly on the hook.

If I wasn't unsure enough, now I stood with this stinking brown bag that might have held a day-old cadaver, judging from the smell. I looked about for a giant garbage can and hoped for a break in the hallway traffic so I could dispose of this evidence of my uncoolness and my mother's stupidity. When the break came, I dashed to the girls' room to wash the stink from my hands, and went hungry. I would not carry a lunch again. I was glad it was not my mom's natural style to get up and pack these embarrassments and planned to just steal change from her purse forevermore.

Second day lunch found me wiser. I had a gleaming quarter. I bypassed the hairnet ladies and went into the freezer for an ice cream sandwich. The cashier, somebody's busybody mom no doubt, asked if I had a lunch to eat before this dessert. I nodded to the table where Dianne, whom I had just met in English class, was seated with her brown bag and said, "Yes, I left it on the table over there." I was allowed change and passage to be seated.

Being watched, I went to sit next to Dianne. She made room on the bench and asked where my lunch was. "Right here." I said as I unwrapped the ice cream sandwich. A natural caregiver, she cut her bologna on Wonder Bread in half and slipped one diagonal piece to me without any comment. It looked familiar and inviting.

Soon enough, she was bringing two of those daily and I sat beside her and accepted her mother's kind gift. I'll never know if she went home and reported that she sat by a poor hungry waif or knew I was too lazy to tend to lunches on my own. For the entire seventh grade I ate bologna on Wonder Bread for lunch, provided by Dianne's mom, Alvina. I used the stolen change from mom's tips for ice cream treats for Dianne and me.

Eventually, Dianne brought me home with her, to the source of that white bread largesse. Assaulted by heat and the scent of cinnamon upon entering the back door, we found we were in Alvina's kitchen.

"Come in and sit down! You have to eat some rolls. I sure don't need them. I'm getting so heavy! I'm so glad Dianne finally brought you home, but I look a mess." She ran her hands through her beauty shop hair. In years to come, I would see her anxiety grow in the forty-eight hours preceding her standing salon appointment and eventually, Dianne and I took to setting her hair for her on brush rollers with harsh plastic pins that left dents in her scalp when we fixed them in place especially well.

"I bet your mother isn't heavy. Don't I look too heavy?" She would ask this regularly over the years. This question was punctuated by a stomach lifted, an inward breath, and her work-weary hands pressed to her stomach's center. A sideways view was then offered and no response expected. As the soft folds regained their position she reinforced them with a warm caramel bun, sticky, sweet and billowing with calories and love.

From then on, Alvina fed me love and acceptance through bologna sandwiches, lard-fried hamburgers, and eggs fried in bacon grease after sleepovers. All the while, she would apologize for everything she couldn't forgive about herself. Her apologies were wasted on me, though. I thought she was flawless.

Today, I have her recipe, written in her own hand and style, misspelled with no discernible order, and composed entirely in run-on sentences just as she spoke. The recipe begins with "melt some ole in a pan" and becomes less specific after that. I've tried to follow it, to create the smell and taste and sugary mess of her cinnamon buns, but it's no use. In my oven, her directions like "scald milk until hot" and "add flour until the dough is just right" only yields—well—bread.

Dianne and I grew apart after our lives took different paths, but Alvina became a patient of mine when I became a nurse later on. She always showed up to our clinic visits dressed up with her hair set. One morning, I came to work and the doctor I worked with called me to his office and closed the door. "I got called last night," he said. "Alvina died."

There are things we carry from those junior high halls. Modern math, history, first loves, and the last vestiges of innocence. We're lucky if, somewhere along the line while we're discovering bad skin, too-big feet, and too-ugly clothes, we find a surrogate parent or a special teacher to shelter us and guide us.

~Beadrin Youngdahl

94

The Diving Lesson

People never forget that helping hand especially when times are tough.
~Catherine Pulsifer

Back in grade school, we had Phys Ed class once a week. That averaged out to about thirty-six times a year if you take into account winter holidays, spring breaks, and the occasional day off. A person can stand anything if he only has to do it thirty-six times a year. Back when I was younger, I actually enjoyed Phys Ed. We had a ton of kids in our class and we rarely had to do anything hard like climb a rope and try to touch the ceiling or walk on the balance beam. Our teacher was okay too in elementary school. She was kind of goofy and fun, and I didn't mind Phys Ed in those days.

Then I got to middle school, where we had Phys Ed every day. Every single day. To make things even worse, I was scheduled to have it first thing in the morning. This wasn't bad when the school year started and we were doing soccer outside but when September turned into October and we were still going outside for flag football, I started hating Phys Ed.

The teacher I had didn't help with my dislike for Phys Ed. Ms. Jefferson was shorter than most of the kids and although she looked nice, seventh grade was the year I learned that the old saying, "Looks can be deceiving," was absolutely true. Ms. Jefferson was meaner than a coffee fiend on day seven of caffeine withdrawal. Ms. Jefferson didn't care if you were sick or your stomach hurt or if you'd been hit between the eyes with a football. She expected everyone to participate and if you didn't, you were forced to write a research paper on whatever unit we were doing. By November, I felt as if I were going to throw up every single morning.

Little did I know that things were going to get a whole lot worse before they got better. After the school finally decided that it was cold enough to let us have Phys Ed indoors, we started the swimming unit. Swimming. For an entire six weeks. First thing in the morning. Is it any surprise that half the class came down with sore throats the very first day the swimming unit started?

Not that Ms. Jefferson cared. She made us all get into the pool, swollen tonsils or not, and had us swim laps. After we swam about two hundred laps, she informed us that we'd be working on the crawl, the backstroke, treading water, and diving. I wanted to drown myself right then and there because of those four water-related things, the only one I could do was tread water. Barely.

It wasn't that I didn't know how to swim; I just hated putting my head under the water. I hated how my ears felt when the water rushed into them and I couldn't stand feeling water go up my nose. I'd taken swimming lessons back when I was really little, and as hard as I tried not to get that panicky feeling whenever I had to go all the way under the water, it never worked.

I made it through learning how to do the crawl and the backstroke and I got to be a master at treading water. Finally, the last week of swimming arrived and we all had to get up on the diving board.

Nervously, I waited for my turn to come while I watched everyone else leap off. Some of the other kids were pretty good divers but a lot were really, really bad. I knew I was going to be the absolute worst. My stomach started knotting up as it got closer and closer to being my turn, and I kept swiveling my head between checking out what time it was and watching whoever was on the diving board. "Maybe I won't have to go today," I thought. "Maybe class will be over before it's my turn."

"Hank, you're up!" Ms. Jefferson's voice brought me back to reality. "Hurry, you're the last one and then it's time to hit the showers."

Slowly, I climbed up onto the diving board, the knots in my stomach growing tighter as the board wobbled beneath my bare feet. The aqua-colored water looked to be about half a mile away, and it took every bit of control I had not to turn around and run back off that board. But I knew I couldn't do that. Not only would I look stupid, but Ms. Jefferson would undoubtedly make me get back up and start all over again.

I was halfway down the board when I glanced over at Ms. Jefferson, holding her clipboard and staring up at me. I couldn't believe it—she actually looked like she felt sorry for me, as if she knew what I was going through. "Hold on a second," she said, looking down at her watch. "Class, time has run out today. You're all dismissed."

My legs turned into raspberry Jell-O. Shakily, I turned around and started back toward the ladder that would take me down from the board and back to safety. Ms. Jefferson stopped me. "You're scared to death, aren't you?" She spoke softly so none of the other kids could hear her. They were all heading toward the locker room anyway.

Reluctantly, I nodded.

"Don't you know how to dive?" she asked.

"Not really."

Ms. Jefferson chewed on her bottom lip for a second or two. "What class do you have next?"

"Study hall."

"Perfect," She said. "Get back up on the board."

"What?"

"I'm going to teach you how to dive, Hank. Believe it or not, I know how you feel. I couldn't dive until I got into college. But if you just do what I tell you to do, you'll be fine."

Getting back up on the diving board the second time was slightly easier. It was also easier without the rest of the class standing around watching me. But diving was still hard. Ms. Jefferson worked with me for half an hour and while I can't say I was an expert when we were through, at least I didn't feel like I was going to throw up into the pool.

"It just takes practice," she told me after we finished. "You can do practically anything if you practice long enough."

Nodding, I picked up my towel and started toward the locker room. Halfway there, I turned around. "Thank you, Ms. Jefferson," I said. "You really helped me."

And then, for the first time since school started in September, Ms. Jefferson smiled. "You're welcome, Hank." Suddenly she didn't seem like the worst teacher ever. Maybe I still didn't like her, or like putting my head under water very much, but I no longer hated her. Walking the rest of the way to the locker room, I realized that I didn't hate Phys Ed anymore either. Even if it was every single day.

~Hank Musolf

Teens Talk Middle School

Doing What's Right

Never look down on anybody unless you're helping him up.

~Jesse Jackson

95

The Decision

Don't try to be different. Just be good. To be good is different enough.
~Arthur Freed

My cousin had the best birthday parties. I attended them every year, marveling at the pretty decorations and brightly wrapped gifts, and always the beautiful cake. Because my cousin's birthday falls in early December, it was like a double whammy of festivity in our extended family, what with Christmas being just a few short weeks away. But the year I was in seventh grade, my cousin's party and our family's upcoming Christmas gathering were the last things on my mind. I was struggling to find myself, though of course I didn't know it. I just knew I wanted to grow up, and while I wouldn't have admitted it, I didn't have the first clue how.

For some reason that year, my mom insisted on taking my two younger sisters and me for a picture with Santa Claus at our local mall on the same afternoon as my cousin's party later that night. Christmas in those days wasn't quite so full of dazzle as it is now, and at our house it was much more of a religious tradition than a commercial one, so this picture-at-the-mall thing was different for us. Plus I was obviously way too old for it. In first or second grade, sure — but seventh? I wasn't a kid anymore, after all, and I didn't see why this silly picture was even part of our plan. My sisters, who were ten and eight years old, were happy about it, but I was a total Grinch about it.

I made sure my mom knew my feelings too, but she told me that taking the picture was something my youngest sister had especially requested. My baby sister could always tug at my heartstrings, and after much muttering and eye-rolling, I resigned myself to the picture, thinking, well, if it makes her happy... Santa, here we come.

My mom picked us up from school that day and we drove to the mall in the half-light of late afternoon. The actual picture taking with the man himself was pretty uneventful, thankfully. No huge embarrassments, like seeing one of my friends there, or—gulp—the boy I liked. No, the great embarrassment came afterward, at my cousin's party.

By the time we got home from the mall, Polaroid in hand, it was almost entirely dark out, and there were Christmas lights coming on here and there around our neighborhood. We hadn't yet put up our Christmas tree, but the excitement of the holidays bubbled in the air all around us. We entered our house to the smell of my dad's chili, and my sisters and I rushed to change out of our parochial school uniforms. After dinner, we piled in our car and left, watching the sparkling Christmas lights go by as my dad drove. When we arrived at my aunt and uncle's, it was truly cold outside, and our breath steamed out in puffs of white as we trudged to their front door.

The party was in full swing as we went in, even more crowded than usual because my aunt had invited relatives from my uncle's side of the family as well as some of my cousin's friends. I was older than all of them, and as such, I had a certain image to uphold. Seventh grade was no small deal, and I wanted to be sure they all knew it. So that was why I freaked when I discovered that my mom had brought... the picture. What's more, she was telling everyone about it, to my extreme mortification.

Before she could do further damage, I nudged her—let's go back to the bedroom—and she followed me down the hall. "Mom," I said, "please! I don't want anyone seeing that picture. It's embarrassing, okay? Please stop talking about it!"

She gave me that all-innocent look mothers have down to perfection. "Why?" she asked. "It's so cute, and it means so much to your sister. I thought you'd want to show it around."

Um, no.

Here I was, a big-cheese seventh grader, and I'd taken a picture with Santa Claus! Heck, I'd even smiled!

When my mom saw I wasn't budging, she sighed, giving me that all-disappointed look, another perfected expression. "Well, whatever," she told me. "We don't have to show it if you don't want to, but I brought it just in case. I'll let you make the decision."

I'm sure my mom didn't realize it then, but entrusting me with that decision was probably one of her best calls. I didn't think so at the time, though. No, I dithered and debated all through the blowing out of candles; I simmered and stewed during the unwrapping of gifts.

My sisters, on the other hand, were little paragons of bliss. Content smiles on their cherub faces. Looks of awe in their wide eyes. My youngest sister had curled up in my grandmother's lap, her blond head nestled against Gram's shoulder, my middle sister was being a complete Chatty Cathy, keeping my grandfather entertained. A sudden pang of jealousy flew through me. My whole day had been ruined by that picture, while my sisters didn't seem the least bit affected. Should I show the dumb thing or not? What if my cousin and her friends laughed at me? What if they no longer looked up to me, or worse, stopped thinking I was cool?

It was the glow in my baby sister's eyes that finally did me in. She had sat on Santa's lap that afternoon so happily, so full of expectation. She was so clearly proud of that picture, and now it all rested with me.

I can still recall the exact moment I decided to walk back to the bedroom, to find my mom's purse, to put my hand inside and retrieve the picture from the pocket where she had so carefully tucked it. I recall striding back into the living room, feeling a flash of embarrassment burn across my skin. I recall too how the embarrassment amazingly subsided the more I showed the picture, the more I shrugged off everyone's teasing and got over myself. Most of all, I recall the smile on my mom's lips, the joy on both my sisters' faces.

That picture is long gone, but there are many times I wish I still had it. For it symbolizes to me one of the first steps I took toward growing up. That night, I put someone else's feelings over mine. That night, I started learning that sometimes you have to risk people's laughter or criticism to make your stand, and that being a grown-up doesn't mean "being cool" as much as it means "being me." Maybe learning to make good decisions is the real meaning of being a big-cheese seventh grader, even though sometimes decisions are hard. And sometimes the right decision isn't always the one you want to make or even the one that's most comfortable, it's just the one that's right. Sometimes it's just the one that's kind.

~Theresa Sanders

96

Brains and Brawn

Do the right thing.
It will gratify some people and astonish the rest.
~Mark Twain

t was strange to us how we kids from the orphanage were always the last to be picked when it came to any type of a game at school—baseball, football, and even dodge ball. It didn't seem to make a difference if we were tall or short, thin or fat, fast or slow. The fact that we came from the orphanage appeared to be all that mattered to those who did the choosing.

I am not sure what came over me the day the teacher picked me to be one of the captains of the dodge ball team. I was rather shocked—even the teacher treated us as though we were different from the other kids. This time, I decided, my team was going to win. I knew who was the fastest and who had the best aim. This was the day I was going to become the winner. As we gathered in a group on the schoolground, the teacher flipped a coin to see who would be the first to pick.

"Heads," yelled Mrs. Cherry, the teacher.

I smiled, since I was the one who had picked heads. I am not sure what came over me at that moment. Winning the game didn't seem so important to me now. I looked around the large group of boys and my eyes stopped at Jeffrey. He was slow and weighed a whopping ninety-eight pounds.

"JEFFREY!" I yelled as I pointed at him.

He looked up in total shock as he began to move his massive body toward me.

"You picked me?" he asked.

I reached over and patted him on the back.

My next pick was Leonard. He was a small boy who wore black, thick-rimmed glasses and never combed his hair. He was the quiet type and was not liked by very many of the popular kids. He was, without a doubt, the brain of the class. The remainder of my picks were kids I knew from the orphanage or kids who were always the last to be picked — kids who never got to play.

"He picked a bunch of losers. We're gonna win without even trying," said the captain of the other team.

"We're gonna lose," said Jeffrey as our team huddled in a tight circle.

"Of course, we're gonna lose," I told them.

"Then why did you pick me?" asked Jeffrey.

"And why did you pick me? I can't see without my glasses," said Leonard.

As the game started, I made sure Jeffrey stood behind the ones of us who were faster. That way, he could get out of the way of the ball before it reached him. I made sure that my team didn't stay in the center of the circle. We moved around the circle, rather than across the circle. That seemed to give us a big advantage.

The ball was thrown five or six times before Robert was hit, and another five or six times before the ball hit Wayne. One at a time, my team members were hit and fell out. They hit us with the ball as hard as they could, slamming the ball against our backs when we could not get out of the way. Their team laughed and mocked us the entire time. Soon it was down to just Jeffrey and me.

"I can't believe it's just you and me," said Jeffrey panting as hard as he could.

"Just stay behind me," I said.

"Get that fat Jeffrey kid," yelled one of their team members.

They threw the ball ten more times without hitting either one of us. The harder they threw, the more they missed and the madder they seemed to get.

"Okay, that's enough. You're getting too rough," yelled Mrs. Cherry.

I will never forget the look on Jeffrey's face when the game ended. He could hardly believe that he had made it that far. When Jeffrey and I went to the bathroom to wash up, he had tears in his eyes.

"You made me feel good by picking me first," he said, as he stood crying over the sink.

I learned a very good lesson that day. We were just a bunch of kids who were not popular at all. Earlier that morning, Mrs. Cherry had talked to us about "brains" and "brawn." She told us that if we were to succeed in life, we had to learn to use all of our skills, and that we had to work together as a team. I just wanted to see if the teacher really knew what she was talking about.

~Roger Dean Kiser

Growing a Spine

A lot of people are afraid to tell the truth, to say no.
That's where toughness comes into play.
Toughness is not being a bully. It's having backbone.
~Robert Kiyosaki

I don't remember important things from middle school: student council elections, school dances, most of algebra... but I'll always remember the little things, like a single bench in the gym locker room, because that's where I started the slow process of growing a spine.

It was seventh grade, and it was supposed to be the turning point of my middle school career.

Sixth grade had been awful. I hadn't wanted to go to optional sixth grade at a middle school at all—I'd wanted to stay in sixth grade at my elementary school with my best friend in the universe, Jesse. But Mom insisted, and so I went forth to the middle school along with the more "mature" students from my elementary, girls who cared more about nail polish and gossip than reading and pretend. In elementary school, Jesse and I had scorned those girls as being shallow and unoriginal. In sixth grade I found myself trying to fit in with those same girls.

I gossiped and schemed my way into a small group. There were four of us: Tina, Ashley, Katie, and me. Tina was the ringleader, our Queen of Hearts. We spent most of our time trying to get on her good side, and neurotically worrying that she was talking about us behind our backs. And we were right to stress. Not unlike the Queen of Hearts, Tina's whims were subject to change, and she chose a different group member to ostracize every month. (Only instead of "Off with her head!" it was more like "Off of our exclusive lunch table!")

You might ask, "Why would you want to stay friends with someone like that?" I often asked myself the same question. What it came down to was fear. I was a spineless little wuss who avoided confrontation whenever possible and had relied on Jesse for protection throughout my entire childhood. The group offered me the same protection—a place to sit at lunch, someone to walk with between classes. Being friends with Tina was better than being confronted by her. Plus, I told myself, it would only last a year. In seventh grade, Jesse would come to my school, and everything would go back to normal.

And that day had finally arrived. I sought Jesse out and knowledgably led her to our homeroom.

While we waited for our new class assignments, Jesse introduced me to her friend Alice, an unsure-looking, fast-talking girl who she'd met in sixth grade. I greeted her enthusiastically, telling her, "Maybe you'll be in the same class as Jesse and me." Jesse was the smartest girl I knew, and I had no doubt that she'd get into the accelerated class with me. If Alice was smart too, we'd almost be enough to have a group of our own!

Papers were passed out that held our schedules and class assignments. "7X," I recited my class name proudly.

"7X," Alice read.

"7Y," said Jesse, crestfallen.

I swear, for a moment my heart stopped beating. "That can't be right," I said. "Look in the upper right hand corner. It should say 7X."

She shook her head, and I grabbed the paper from her. Sure enough, she was in a different class with a different schedule. I would be stuck in Cliqueland without an ally for two more years.

We ranted angrily for the rest of the class—Jesse and I for obvious reasons, Alice because she would not know anyone in the accelerated class. "Don't worry," said Jesse confidently. "Val's my best friend. She'll take care of you."

At that point, I probably gulped.

You see, our first class was Art, a room with huge double desks. In our group, we had an arrangement. Whenever the class had to pick partners, I was always with Katie, leaving Tina free to sit with the marginally-cooler Ashley. So I found myself hovering in the back of the Art room, staring at two empty chairs. Would I abandon Katie and risk Tina's possessive wrath or would I sit with Alice, who I didn't even know?

I took a deep breath and sat beside Alice.

I power-walked into the hallway when that first class ended, but Tina caught up with me anyway. "So are you, like, dumping Katie now?" she asked.

"Of course not!" I said. "I can be friends with both of them."

That was easier said than done.

Alice threw off the number of girls in our class from eight to an uneven nine, and so the partner issue came up over and over. When history projects were assigned, Katie moved her desk expectantly toward mine. "Maybe we can ask Mr. P if we could have a third person," I said.

"He said only two people," said Katie, with an air of "there's nothing we can do." So, being my typical spineless self, we left Alice alone.

After a few weeks of trying to bounce between Alice and the group, Tina decided that it was time to be more forceful. "Why are you hanging out with Alice, anyway?" she demanded, as we walked to gym class. "She doesn't even like you. She's just using you because she has no friends."

I walked on to the locker room, to the gym bench where our group always changed clothes, fear clenching up my stomach, my heart pounding. Nothing would ever change. I asked myself why I even bothered to help someone like Alice, who I hadn't really bonded with. We probably, I rationalized, had nothing in common.

Then Alice dumped her gym bag on our bench and Tina said, "There isn't really room for you."

I stood silently, watching Alice pull her gym bag off the bench and leave, the words "She'll protect you" repeating insistently in my head. I listened to Tina laugh, watched Katie smirk, and it hit me—it didn't matter if Alice and I never got close. The girls in my group were not the type of people I wanted to be.

I wish I could tell you that I confronted Tina then and there, that I called her all kinds of deliciously vicious names and declared my alliance to Alice, once and for all. But I don't think people go from being completely spineless to speaking their mind in a matter of minutes. A transition like that takes time. But I can tell you that I never chose the group over Alice again.

The funny part is: once Tina saw that I wouldn't back down, she abruptly decided Alice was cool. We were a group of five for the two months before Tina moved (oh happy day!) to Pennsylvania.

A few weeks after the gym bench incident, Alice called me with a homework question. We somehow got onto the topic of books, and realized we loved all the same authors. We talked for hours.

Ten years later, we're still friends.

~Valerie Howlett

Liar, Liar

There is no pillow so soft as a clear conscience.
~French Proverb

The first time I met the guy at the swimming pool, I didn't know he would change my life. He oozed muscles and dripped handsome all over the lifeguard stand. When my sister, Ouida, and I entered, she stopped to pay, but I just walked in as if I weren't twelve years old. The lifeguard raised one eyebrow and grinned at me.

"Are you sure you're only eleven?" he asked.

I nodded sheepishly, afraid he would guess the truth—that I was just too poor to pay. Visiting our older sister, Ruth, for the summer, we spent our days at the pool and our evenings at church youth activities. Every time I passed the cute lifeguard, I had to act eleven, while my sixteen-year-old sister flirted non-stop.

The problem was further complicated at church. To be in the youth department, I had to be thirteen. It seemed only fair to me that if I smudged the truth to go swimming, I should at least smudge the truth to go to church.

We had lots of fun all summer until the church youth retreat. I left the cabin, heading for the dining room, when I saw him.

"Oh, no!" I cried and pointed at him as if he were death itself. "The lifeguard from the city pool." Heat flooded my face. "What's he doing here?"

"Wonderful!" Ouida squealed.

"He'll know I lied," I whispered in humiliation.

"He won't even remember you, Twerp."

"I can't go in there." I turned and went behind a row of trees.

"You'll miss supper," Ouida said as she rushed into the dining hall.

I hid in the trees and hoped he would leave soon.

"Peggy," Ouida called through the trees. "He's staying the entire weekend. He's one of the youth leaders. You'll have to see him sooner or later."

"No, I can't." Tears burned my eyes. Shame felt like a lump of fat in my throat. Darkness crept across camp as singing and laughter floated through the night air, but I felt as if I couldn't join in. Liars didn't belong in the church youth group and I was a liar.

"Peggy." The deep voice calling through the trees shook me as if it were the voice of God. "Peggy," the Lifeguard called louder.

"Yes," I whispered.

"Hey, sweetheart," he sat down on the log beside me. "Why are you hiding from me?"

"I lied."

"Yea, I know." He tugged on my ponytail. "I forgive you."

"How can you forgive me? I'm nothing but a liar."

"The Bible says that if we confess our sin, He is faithful and will forgive us and clean us of all unrighteousness."

"I confess! I really do," I cried. "I won't ever go swimming again unless I can pay."

"Then it's forgotten. If God forgives you, then I do too." He squeezed my shoulder.

"But... there's more. I'm really too young to be in the youth group. I'm twelve. I lied."

"I wish everyone was as eager to get into church as you are." He stood up and took my hand. "Let's go in and tell the pastor. He has a very big heart. I bet he'll forgive you too."

He did.

~Peggy Purser Freeman

Opening My Eyes

Live as if you were to die tomorrow.
Learn as if you were to live forever.
~Mahatma Gandhi

My mom homeschools me. No—travelschool is a better word for it. She likes to go on lengthy trips with my two younger brothers and me, sometimes for up to four months at a time. My brothers and I hop from school to airport to hotel. We've been around the world and back again, from Australia to France to China.

It's really cool, because we can just say "Okay, why don't we go to New York City this weekend!" and off we go. It's much better to have your mom teach just you and your brothers than having to worry about bullies and mean teachers. However, we have to work really hard at our homework to keep up with everybody else. Even though we're not in school, we write in a journal every day and study as hard as we can. We are taught the entire regular school curriculum as we travel (math, reading, writing, spelling, etc.) but that's not all we learn, either.

When I go to countries all around the world, from Thailand to Brazil, it always amazes me how poor people are. In these places, there are people who have no electricity or running water. Clothed in rags, their worldly possessions only include a tiny hut and perhaps a pig, although they can always afford a smile and a friendly wave. You can see their teeth as they smile—you know they probably have never heard the word "dentist." It makes me feel guilty that they have to work hard every day to survive, while I think taking out the trash is Herculean labor.

Still, everyone from the poorest pig farmer to the wealthiest merchant was always willing to lend a hand. There is an old Spanish saying—"The rich help the rich and the poor help those poorer then themselves." If a fruit seller runs out of fruit, you can bet that another fruit seller will lend him some. I remember once when we hitched a ride with a friend in his jam-packed truck. There must have been seven people in the car, with all of their luggage. Then we spotted three women hitchhiking. I thought there was no way that they could fit in the vehicle. Our friend, however, told them to get in the back of the truck, where they fit easily. I felt ashamed because I knew if I had been driving the truck, they would have been on that road a lot longer.

I discovered that just because you're not rich doesn't mean you can't have fun. When you don't have toys, a stick can be a sword, a cornhusk can become a doll, or a tree a jungle gym. Who needs a Nintendo when there are streams to splash in, rocks to scale and brothers to wrestle with? What those children experience is like nothing that can come from a remote control or video game. I remember playing on the edge of a lake in Bariloche, Argentina with some other kids, picking up rocks to try to find the ones with the most mica and trying to skip stones in the water. The strangest thing was that they didn't speak a word of English and I didn't speak any Spanish. Before that day, I couldn't imagine playing with another kid who I couldn't talk to.

However, the most incredible thing is how content everyone is. Waving at a complete stranger may seem strange where we live, but around the world it's no big deal. Smiles are passed around more quickly than can be returned, and street sellers will often chat so loudly to each other, you have to tap one on their shoulder to get their attention. I remember one frenzied night in Bangkok, when we were in a tuk-tuk (a cross between a bike and a rickshaw) and our driver was yelling good-naturedly to some of his friends on tuk-tuks across the street. Occasionally, they would toss packs of cigarettes to each other. At the time, I was almost scared to death and furious at our driver, but now I realize that those men drove their tuk-tuks day and night; they deserved to be able to have a little fun.

I'm usually not very big on morals. I find them too gushy and mushy, like "Every cloud has a silver lining." I think anyone who says that sounds like a weather forecaster, not an optimist. However, this one I think is really good: You don't have to be rich or famous, or pretty (even though sometimes it might feel that way) to be happy. Traveling has sort of made me grow up, in a weird way. It hasn't made me bigger or stronger, but more aware. It's allowed me to open my eyes to the rest of the world. So next time I catch myself complaining about eating my Brussels sprouts, I remind myself to be grateful for what I have and keep my mouth shut.

~Chloe Rosenberg

Lending a Hand

The greatest healing therapy is friendship and love.
~Hubert H. Humphrey

"Hey... Get up... Get loud... We're pumping up the party now!" was the sound of Martha and Samantha singing along to their iPods.

Martha was the prettiest girl in the whole school, and she always greeted everyone with a smile and cheered you up if you were sad. She was a great friend.

We had just started sixth grade. She lived down the street from me and also obsessed over the Jonas Brothers.

Samantha was one of Martha's best friends. They sang together on the bus all of the time. They were always thinking up different ways to have fun—they were both always so happy. Martha especially had fun all the time. I looked up to her. I was never as optimistic as her, and I probably never will be.

One day, Martha and Samantha were in the car on the way to pick up Martha's brother from Boy Scout camp. It was rainy and another car was coming in the opposite direction. That car was going ten miles over the speed limit and it hydroplaned, hitting Martha's Jeep head on and flipping Martha, her dad, and Samantha into a ditch. The other driver was killed instantly.

Martha and Samantha had been in the back seat watching Jaws. The side airbags had popped out and hit Martha in the head, breaking her neck. Samantha broke her leg and ruptured her spleen. Martha's dad broke both of his legs. Martha died.

When I found out, I cried for what seemed like three days. Not Martha... Not Martha! I don't know why it happened. It shouldn't have happened. Not Martha.

Then I started to get angry. Why couldn't they have left a few seconds later? Why couldn't the other driver have gone a little bit slower? Why did Martha have to sit on that side? Why her? Why not me? I felt like someone needed to be blamed.

People put posters on her locker and pictures of her all over the walls of our school. They tied white bows to trees. We made a memorial for Martha and I wrote letters to her family. We released balloons with notes to her on them, but I still cried. Nothing helped. I felt like I needed to do something, but I wasn't sure what.

I went to Martha's visitation. At visitations, you are supposed to give the family words of wisdom and kindness, to help get them through the tough times. I stood in line to talk to Martha's mom. When I reached the front with my friends, her mom pulled me into a hug. "I want you to be able to move on with your lives," she said to me, "and don't let this affect you. I know it's hard, but I need you to get through this time and appreciate the fact that you are still here."

I stood, unsure of what to say. Her daughter had died, but she was the one helping me get over it. "I'm so sorry about your loss..." I tried to say.

Martha's mom held me at shoulder length. "I know what you are thinking—that I'm supposed to be crying and you're supposed to help me. But I know that Martha is looking at us right now and wanting us to get over it quickly. She wants us to be happy and successful. I am doing what Martha would have wanted."

I was instantly inspired. I started going around and helping people cry, helping them think of the good times they had with Martha. I helped in every way that I could think of. I knew this was what I was supposed to be doing.

The next day, I went to Martha's funeral. My writing teacher came up to the podium and told us she would be reading from Martha's

English journal. It was an entry from August. Our teacher had asked us to write our opinions on the saying, "People create their own punishments."

Here is what Martha wrote:

> *I believe that sometimes, people do create their own punishments. For instance, someone who tries to rob a bank. They know they will get in trouble and they do it anyway. But sometimes, completely innocent people end up in fatal situations that nobody can ever prevent, and it isn't anyone's fault.*

I don't believe that it was a coincidence that Martha wrote that. I believe that the journal entry was Martha's way of talking to us and helping us feel better.

Since that day, I have learned to appreciate life and make the best of everything. I have gotten better at talking about Martha, but I still miss her.

~Bethany Beago

No One's Words
But My Own

Righteousness is easy in retrospect.
~Arthur Schlesinger Jr.

The classroom was packed with those of us who wanted to work on the school newspaper. I hadn't written much before, other than the little newspapers I used to make up when I was home sick from grammar school. Still, working on the paper sounded like fun. I liked the idea of being a reporter, interviewing my friends, and covering middle school events.

To be considered, we had to turn in a sample of our writing. I had written a piece about the joys of summer. I showed the article to my father, a brilliant lawyer and poet. He read it, frown lines appearing between his brows.

"It's okay," my father said, taking out a pencil. "But how about if we change this sentence to..." And that was that. He rewrote the whole piece—not with me, for I never said a thing to stop him—but for me.

No surprise—his version was wonderful. He had a gift for language that I had yet to discover in myself. I remember the last line was something like "Once we see the convertible tops coming down, can summer be far behind?" I wished I could write like that. It was so much better than my original piece, that against my better judgment, I turned in his version instead of mine.

"Welcome to the Dundee School News," my teacher said to me. But before I could be excited about the making the paper, he added: "Based on that terrific article you wrote about summer, I'm making you Second Page Editor."

My lunch nearly leaped out of my stomach. Now I was expected to write a personal opinion column every week for the second page. I was no more equipped to write at that level than I was to be a rock star. I couldn't confess the truth to the teacher who ran the paper, and I couldn't ask my father to write a weekly column for me.

That semester working on the paper was nothing short of painful. My teacher was clearly disappointed.

"Can't you write something more like that first piece you wrote?" he said, each time I turned in my column.

I couldn't, because at that age, I was no match for a writer of my father's ability and experience. Week after week, I struggled with my writing. My stomach was a pretzel; my nails, gnawed to the bone; my confidence non-existent. My columns never measured up to the one that got me the job.

Eventually, to my total humiliation, I was replaced as the Second Page Editor. Alone in my room, I railed against my father for taking over the assignment, instead of simply trying to help. But in my heart I knew the fault was mine for allowing him to do it. I wasn't sure I'd ever write again.

I did go on to become a successful writer. On my own, I became an advertising copywriter with a national agency, and eventually found my true creative love—writing for children. Looking back, I realize that the pain and humiliation of that school experience had a positive side. It taught me to trust myself and not try to be anyone else. I would have been a fine reporter for that school paper. That's where I belonged. I wasn't ready to be an editor.

Every day, I struggle to use my own words, find my own style, be my own best self. And you know what? It feels great.

~Myra Sanderman

Meet Our Contributors!

Emily Adams received her Bachelor of Music in Clarinet Performance from Bishop's University in 2007, and her Artist Diploma in Performance from the University of Western Ontario in 2008. Besides playing and teaching the clarinet, Emily's interests include painting, working out, practicing yoga, and writing poetry.

Arin Anderson is a freshman in the '08-'09 school year. She likes writing and listening to music. She also likes to shop and hang out with friends. She hopes to be a famous writer some day.

Carol Band is a mother of three whose humorous columns on parenting appear monthly in parenting publications nationwide.

Bethany Beago currently attends middle school as a thirteen year-old seventh grader. She lives with her mom, dad, sister, and her many pets. She enjoys English, reading and art. Please e-mail her at: bethanyncs@austin.rr.com.

Ms. **Jackson Beard** is an eighth grader. Jackson is an avid reader who also enjoys long distance running, African dance, and cooking. She is also passionate about global politics and environmental issues.

JoAnne Bennett's greatest achievement has been raising three wonderful daughters alongside her husband of thirty-three years. One of JoAnne's passions is making a difference in young peoples' lives. She feels blessed to be able to continue sharing a number of her stories with the world. Her e-mail is storiesbyjb@yahoo.com.

Amy Bernstein received her Bachelor of Arts in English from Nazareth College in 2005. She lives, works and writes in Boston, MA. Amy enjoys traveling and spending time with friends. Amy grew up at a summer camp in upstate NY, where part of her story is set. Please e-mail her at aberns24@yahoo.com.

Chase Bernstein graduated from Boston University with a degree in Journalism in 2008. This is only the first of many great stories to come. Please e-mail her at chasebern@gmail.com.

Nicholas Berson is a middle school student. The school subjects he likes the most are science, history, and English. His favorite activities include playing video games, reading, traveling, and hanging out with friends. He plans to become a writer of fictional books and scripts.

Harris Bloom is a writer, stand-up comedian and an accountant. Guess which one he would like to quit? He's been published in books such as *The Ultimate Dog Lover, Underground Voices* and *Surreal Magazine*. He's also been published online at mcsweeneys.net, ypr.org and reallysmalltalk.com. You can find him at harrisbloom.com.

Ginger Boda has contributed to various online publications. She is also published in *Chicken Soup for the Bride's Soul*, and the Christmas Edition of the *God's Way* series. Ginger resides in California with her husband of thirty-one years and has three grown children and two grandchildren. E-mail her at Rhymerbabe@aol.com.

Juliet C. Bond is a Licensed Clinical Social Worker and children's book author from Evanston, IL. She teaches at both Columbia College and Northeastern University in Chicago. She is forever inspired by the transformative power of an extraordinary story. Please visit her website at julietcbond.tripod.com.

Pamela Bostwick's publishings include *Chicken Soup for Soul: Children with Special Needs*. Although she is legally blind and hearing impaired, she enjoys a fulfilling life. She loves her country home, the beach, playing guitar and is a volunteer counselor. She has seven children and nine grandchildren. She happily remarried 7/7/07. E-mail: pamloves7@verizon.net.

Rochel Burstyn is an Australian currently living in Michigan. She enjoys her wonderful husband, her lovely children, ice cream, and trips to Australia with her kids. She hopes to one day become the president of some really marvelous organization, but right now she is a stay-at-home mom. She can be reached at yackrack@yeshivanet.com.

Andrea Canale is a junior in high school maintaining high honor roll for the past three years. She also writes for the school newspaper. She is a percussionist in the school concert and jazz band. She volunteers in her community and hopes to pursue a career in the medical field.

Nacie Carson graduated magna cum laude from the College of the Holy Cross in 2007 with an honors degree in history. She is a member of Phi Beta Kappa and loves her work as a freelance writer. She is currently working on her first novel. Please e-mail her at: nacie.carson@gmail.com.

Megan Carty is currently attending a high school of the arts in an extensive drama program. She lives with her mom, dad, two sisters, three cats, and puppy. Her hobbies include figure skating, track, baking, and scrapbooking. Megan would like to pursue a career in acting or directing.

Jennifer Chase is currently a full-time student at Salem State College earning her Bachelors Degree in English and Creative Writing. She volunteers for MASSPIRG, directing the Hunger and Homelessness campaign at her school. Jennifer is an aspiring writer and activist. Contact: jchase87@me.com.

Ariel Chu is an eighth grader who has enjoyed writing ever since elementary school. Writing about her middle school year has helped her overcome friendship issues and the challenges of seventh grade. She believes teens should see their problems through different perspectives and can do that best through words.

Kevin Chu received his Bachelor of Arts in Journalism and East Asian Studies from New York University in 2008. In his free time Kevin enjoys reading crime fiction and playing video games. Please feel free to e-mail him at kdc243@gmail.com.

Jennifer Lynn Clay, eighteen, has been published almost eighty times in national and international magazines and in several world-wide-syndicated books including *Chicken Soup for the Soul: A Tribute to Moms, Chicken Soup for the Preteen Soul 2, Chicken Soup for the Girl's Soul, House Blessings*, and *Forever in Love*. She was a State Finalist for Power of the Pen in 2004.

Maddy Curtis attends high school with her brother Jonny — class of 2011. She loves acting and singing and plans a career in theater. She is the ninth of twelve children.

Emily Cutler lives in Alabama with her family and two dogs. She enjoys writing poetry, short stories, and has written a novel. Besides writing, her hobbies are reading, art, traveling, and swimming.

Massachusetts native **Shana Donohue** graduated from UMass Amherst in 1999, and lives in South Boston. She is a Boston Public School teacher, is pursuing a master's degree in Math Education from the Harvard Extension School, and is a part-time tutor. Shana also writes and produces screenplays and music videos.

Ali Edelson is in seventh grade. She loves to read, write, sing, and draw. It has always been Ali's dream to become a published author. She plans to become an architect when she grows up.

Lena James Edwards is a writer/executive. She enjoys spending time with her family, traveling and learning how to garden. Her interests include (but are not limited to) reading, writing, yoga, household organization, metaphysics, philanthropy, new media and politics. She hopes to learn surfing in the near future. Visit www.toolsforthespirit.com for more.

Melissa Face received her Bachelor of Arts from Coastal Carolina University and her master of human resources from Webster University. She works as an English teacher at a private school and writes on a freelance basis. She has written for newspapers, magazines, and journals and has also done copywriting work. Please e-mail her at: writermsface@yahoo.com.

Andrea Feczko is an on-air personality, reporter, blogger, and writer extraordinaire. When not traveling around the world seeking adventure, she's in New York City. She received her B.S. magna cum laude in Journalism and Communications from New York University in 2007. For more information please visit: www.AndreaFeczko.com.

Victoria Fedden is finishing her MFA in Creative Writing at Florida Atlantic University. She lives in Ft. Lauderdale, Florida with her husband and cat where she enjoys cooking, gardening and swimming in the sea. She plans to teach Creative Writing and to write more memoirs, fiction and poetry.

Carole Fowkes is a Registered Nurse who also has a Bachelor of Arts in Communication. She is currently a Clinical Instructor in North Texas. In addition to her nonfiction works, Carole enjoys writing fantasies and science fiction. Please e-mail her at cgfowkes@yahoo.com.

Peggy Purser Freeman, author of *The Coldest Day in Texas, Swept Back to a Texas Future* and numerous articles including: *Chicken Soup for the Bride's Soul* and public affairs shows for Radio Disney/Dallas, is currently editor for *Granbury Showcase Magazine* and teaches writing with games and fun activities. www.peggypurserfreeman.com.

AC Gaughen is twenty-three years old and a graduate of the University of St. Andrews in Scotland, where she fell madly in love with the UK, and Scotland in particular. Check out her blog at blog.finalword.org, and please contact her at acgaughen@gmail.com.

Nancy Gilliam is an accomplished performing artist, author, educator and mother. She has contributed three stories to *Chicken Soup for the African American Soul*, for which she also served as Special Projects Manager. Visit her at www.myspace.com/nagils_space.

Conrado Gomez is a Clinical Assistant Professor at Arizona State University's Polytechnic campus in Mesa, AZ. He came to the United States from a small town in Mexico. He writes stories of growing up in a small Mexican village and his vicissitudes in moving to a large school and city.

Tina Haapala looks back on her middle school days as a time of learning and growing. Her wish for teens is that they understand the importance of being true to themselves during times of struggle. Tina enjoys reading, concerts, yoga, and belly dance. She can be contacted at tinahaapala@gmail.com.

Samantha Harper is a junior in high school where she participates in theater, cross-country, and writing. Her public speaking skills have led her to place 4th in the Wisconsin State Forensics Tournament sophomore year. She hopes to write her first novel this summer and someday open her own publishing company.

Juliana Harris is an actress, singer, and writer whose work has appeared in *The Kansas City Star, The Mid-America Poetry Review* and *The New York Times*, among many other publications. She moved to

Connecticut last spring where she works in a bookshop during the day and sings in the evenings.

Miriam Hill is co-author of *Fabulous Florida* and a frequent contributor to *Chicken Soup for the Soul* books. She's been published in *The Christian Science Monitor, Grit, St. Petersburg Times, Sacramento Bee* and *Poynter Online*. Miriam's manuscript received Honorable Mention for Inspirational Writing in a Writer's Digest Writing Competition.

Renee Hixson had barely survived middle school before she stumbled into the jaws of high school. Not a pretty story. Still, she had the presence of mind to document her struggles on stained napkins, toilet paper and bathroom walls. This nail-biting blurry-eyed author may be reached at rhixson@telus.net.

Charlie Hoffert attends middle/high school in Vermont. He enjoys math, running, soccer, and playing the piano. Charlie would like to pursue a career in the renewable energy field.

Roswitha Houghton received her RN in Nursing from Mercer Hospital in New Jersey, her BA in Economics from George Mason University in Virginia and her Masters of Fine Arts in Writing for Children and Young Adults from Vermont College. Her work as a nurse, an economist and muralist have all lead to her current efforts at writing and illustrating children's books. You can view her work at www.rosehoughton.com.

Claire Howlett is a sixth grade student who has always loved to create stories. Her writing experience includes first place fiction in the Stamford Literary Competition for two years. She also enjoys karate, acting and playing the piano, which she has been doing for seven years.

Kathleen Ingraham lives in Lawrence, Kansas. She has loved writing since first grade and has spent many years dreaming up stories. She hopes to someday travel the world but feels at this time there really is "no place like home."

Josy Hicks Jablons is an eighth grader who lives with her two parents, younger sister and three dogs. She is very passionate about music, especially singing. She loves science, math, performing in operas, traveling to other countries, and working with young children.

Kelsey Johnson is an eighth grade student. She enjoys school, soccer, football, music, writing and spending time with her friends.

Pat Stockett Johnston is a published writer. She enjoys growing chrysanthemums for show, reading best-sellers, and the writing process. Her latest book is *Should I Kiss or Shake Hands?: Surviving in Another Culture*. She's glad her middle school years are behind her. Contact Pat via e-mail at writerpat@charter.net.

Rachel Joyce attended middle school in Colorado. She loves to write and follow politics with her family. Rachel plans to combine these two passions and become a political journalist. She lives with her mother, father, sister and dog Ginger.

Anna Kendall received her Master of Arts in Writing in 2007. She works as a freelance writer and editor in Chicago. Anna enjoys writing about her school experiences (and she hopes that other people will be able to identify with—and laugh at—some of her embarrassing school moments).

Erica Lyn Kinne is currently working toward her major in Psychology at the University of Central Florida. She enjoys playing piano, camping, yoga, reading, and of course, writing. Erica has written a few Young Adult novels and she plans to get them published in the future. Erica can be e-mailed at: remember@writing.com.

Author **Roger Dean Kiser's** stories take you into the heart of a child abandoned by his family and abused by the system responsible for his care. Today, Kiser lives in Brunswick, Georgia with his wife Judy, where he continues to write and publish most of his work on his website at www.geocities.com/trampolineone.

Mary Kolesnikova is working on her MFA in creative writing at the University of San Francisco, where she lives with her boyfriend and two cats. She is the author of the forthcoming young adult novel, *Coven*, and you can find her online at www.marykolesnikova.com.

Britt Leigh grew up in Florida. She now lives in Boston, growing up in different ways. She is earning her Master of Fine Arts in Writing for Children at Simmons College. Her stories, real and imagined, focus on faith, friends, family and fancy. Please e-mail her at beeleigh312@yahoo.com.

Justin Lynema attends middle school and will be heading into high school next year. He enjoys playing video games and hanging out with friends and family. He mainly writes for school assignments, but is excited to be published.

Nancy Maggio hails from California where she received her teaching credentials in music. Still singing and giving vocal lessons, she works full time while enjoying writing, designing jewelry and volunteering in various ministries at her church. Nancy writes poetry inspired by sermons and non-fiction stories from life changing experiences.

Julia McDaniel, fourteen, spends her free time working on her school's literary magazine and helping to create and manage Orb28, an online community for girls. When she is not working on a novel, she often horseback rides, goes to drive-in movies, and calls her best friend and pen pal, Emily.

Hale McSharry, twelve, lives with his family and grandparents. He is currently in middle school. Hale is an accomplished violist.

Hale volunteers at the American Red Cross and his school's Young Volunteers Club. He likes to ski, play water polo, swim, sing, act, and read.

Marshawna Moore received her Masters Degree in Education from the University of Notre Dame in 2001. She is the owner of Moore Professional Childcare, LLC in Chicago, Illinois. Marshawna enjoys traveling, reading, and working with at-risk youth. Please e-mail her at info@mpchildcare.com.

Sharendalle Murga attends an arts middle school where she enjoys writing poems and short stories. She has been Figure Ice Skating for the past six years and participates in different dance schools. Recently she won gold, silver and bronze medals in ballroom dancing competitions. She hopes to be a published writer, an ice skater and a professional dancer.

Hank Musolf was born in Wisconsin and now lives in Minnesota. He plays the cello in his high school orchestra and is also on the Speech Team. Hank likes many activities but he still doesn't like diving all that much.

Brittany Newell is an avid writer as well as a classical singer, horseback rider, and filmmaker. When she was ten, she had a story published in literary magazine *Stone Soup*—now, with one in *Chicken Soup for the Soul*, there seems to be some sort of theme....

Cindy Ovard enjoys writing and teaching. She teaches at Palomar College in San Diego. She plans on writing an anthology on the memories of childhood in small town USA in the 1960s and 1970s. You can e-mail her at cindyovard@hotmail.com.

Mark Parisi's "off the mark" comic, syndicated since 1987, is distributed by United Media. Mark's humor also graces greeting cards, T-shirts, calendars, magazines, newsletters and books. Check out:

offthemark.com. Lynn is his wife/business partner. Their daughter, Jen, contributes with inspiration (as do three cats).

Adam Patla has recently graduated and is going to be a freshman in high school this fall. He has been writing since he was six years old. He enjoys writing poetry and fiction and hopes to be a best-selling author someday.

Bobby Pellegrino earned degrees in Journalism and International Relations from Boston University in 2008. He has worked for publications in Boston and London and enjoys writing, traveling and all things awesome. Bobby loves seeing his name in print and hopes to break into the magazine industry. Reach him at rpelleg81@gmail.com.

Ava Pennington is a freelance writer, speaker, and Bible teacher, with an MBA from St. John's University and a Bible Studies Certificate from Moody Bible Institute. She has published magazine articles and contributed stories to nine *Chicken Soup for the Soul* books. For more information, visit www.avawrites.com.

Jennifer Perkin is now in tenth grade and enjoys drama club, reading and writing stories. Please contact her at perkinjennifer@yahoo.com.

P.A. Perry-Armes began writing in 2003 after a thirty-year hiatus. She enjoys a variety of crafts and writing, both inspirational and Southern-related short stories. She lives with her husband Steve and six furry, four-legged children. Please e-mail her at pattiperry74@hotmail.com.

Mariel Reed is currently a student at Georgetown University in Washington, D.C. There, she is studying International Politics and Mandarin Chinese. She will be spending six months in China—hopefully, the first of many more adventures. She plans to travel and live all over the world.

Nicole Roberts is an eighth grade student who enjoys spending time with her friends and family. She enjoys reading, writing short stories, playing softball, and swimming. She plans to attend college and pursue a career in law enforcement.

Chloe Rosenberg lives in Connecticut with her wonderful parents, two brothers, three cats and two dogs. When she is not traveling, she is usually reading, cooking or chasing her brothers for dunking her kitten in the toilet. She hopes to become either a travel guidebook writer, lawyer or acclaimed pastry chef.

Carol S. Rothchild received her master's degree in writing from The Johns Hopkins University. She is currently the Editorial Director of *SIX78th*, the junior high lifestyle magazine. She has previously published in the *Chicken Soup for the Soul* series, and is passionate about writing for young adults. Carol can be reached at carsusnh1@comcast.net.

Sara Rowe has a BA in English Writing and History and is studying for her MA in Children's Literature in London. She is a freelance writer who enjoys reading, traveling and spending time with her wacky friends and family. She plans to write novels for teens. Contact her at: s.rowe54@yahoo.com.

Suzy Ryan lives and works in Carlsbad, California. She is currently writing a novel about a teacher's middle school experiences. Suzy enjoys running, swimming, biking, tennis, and reading with her husband and three teenage children. Please e-mail her at: Kensuzyr@aol.com.

Myra Sanderman never lost her love of writing for children, even though she spent many years as an advertising copywriter. Now she publishes in *Highlights for Children* and *Spider Magazine*, among others, and is working on several children's books. She lives in Chicago with her family. E-mail her at Rojo42@aol.com.

Theresa Sanders has four grown children, her greatest joy and accomplishment. She graduated with honors from the University of

Maryland, worked for years as a technical writer, and has been published in trade journals. She lives with her husband near St. Louis, and is thrilled to be included in *Chicken Soup for the Soul*.

Spencer Scarvey is a 2008 graduate of the North Carolina School of Science and Mathematics and now attends the University of Georgia. She sometimes enjoys writing, but plans to major in science. In her free time, she enjoys eating her sister's baking and working out to compensate.

Quinn Scarvey, sixteen, lives in Salisbury, NC. Diagnosed with a brain tumor in 2002, she wrote this essay in 2003 for the Andre Sobel River of Life Foundation. Quinn feels great these days and recently completed a half marathon. She loves photography and walking her dog, Edy.

Laura L. Smith is the author of the teen novel, *Skinny*, and the children's book *Cantaloupe Trees*. She lives in Oxford, Ohio with her husband and four children.

StarAsia Smith is an honor roll student. She is an ice skater, singer, dancer and future poet. E-mail her at starinasia@aol.com.

Helen Stein lives in the Great Lakes state of Michigan. She has four children and five grandchildren. For eighteen years, she edited and wrote safety articles for a motor carrier. She spends time with family, assists her parents, digs in the dirt of her perennial garden, and plays tennis.

Cynda Strong is a high school English teacher in Springfield, Illinois, and the author of *Where Do Angels Sleep?*, her first children's picture book. Cynda loves teaching others how to write. She and her husband Michael enjoy traveling, their grandbabies, and their lhasa apso, Honey.

Annmarie Tait lives in Conshohocken, PA with her husband Joe and

Sammy the "Wonder Yorkie." In addition to writing stories about life in a large Irish Catholic family, Annmarie also enjoys singing and recording American and Irish folk songs which reflect her heritage. E-mail address: irishbloom@aol.com.

B.J. Taylor often thinks about those difficult years growing up, but realizes that the hard times made her stronger. She is now an award-winning author whose work has appeared in *Guideposts*, many *Chicken Soup for the Soul* books, and numerous magazines and newspapers. B.J. has a wonderful husband, four children and two adorable grandsons.

Becky Tidberg and her husband Paul have been working with troubled youth for more than five years and have parented over 100 children through group homes, foster care, and their own children. She is a free-lance writer and speaker to teen, women and parenting ministries. To learn more, check out BeckyTidberg.com.

Don Verkow received his undergrad and grad degrees from Western Michigan University. He is Assistant Principal at Paramount Charter Academy in Kalamazoo, Michigan. Don enjoys traveling, reading, writing and studying Abraham Lincoln. He has been married to Katie for thirty-three years. Please e-mail him at: kadon@ameritech.net.

Wendy Walker is the author of *Four Wives*, released in 2008 and widely acclaimed. *The Queen of Suburbia* will be released in 2009. Wendy is also editing *Chicken Soup for the Soul: Power Moms*. Look for *Power Moms* for Mother's Day!

Carmelle Wasch is a twelve-year-old seventh grader. Her inspiration to write this story was the deep loss of her best friend, Sarah. Carmelle enjoys reading, sports, singing and her puggle Moxie. Her dream job is to become a news reporter some day.

Chelsea Watson has edited and submitted pieces to her school's literary magazine. In her free time she plays soccer, tennis and track. Chelsea also plays piano and sings in the town's select choir. She enjoys going to New York City, painting, musical theater, nature, movies, the beach and hanging out with her friends.

Carol Wong is a fourteen-year-old freshman attending high school. In her spare time, she enjoys writing, drawing, and reading books. She is currently working on her first novel and hopes to get it published before finishing high school.

Jennifer Youngblood is the co-author of *Livin' in High Cotton* and of the bestselling novel, *Stoney Creek, Alabama*. She and her mom, Sandra Poole, write together. They're currently working on their third and fourth novels. A native of Alabama, Jennifer currently lives in Hawaii with her husband and children.

Beadrin (Pixie) Youngdahl is a registered nurse, wife, mother, grandmother, knitter, quilter, reader, writer of fiction, essay and poetry and recently a chicken farmer. She is a life long Minnesotan which means she has all those long cold months to pursue all those passions. Reach her at Beadrin@aol.com.

Meet the Authors

Chicken Soup for the Soul

Who Is
Jack Canfield?

Jack Canfield is the co-creator and editor of the *Chicken Soup for the Soul* series, which *Time* magazine has called "the publishing phenomenon of the decade." Jack is also the co-author of eight other bestselling books including *The Success Principles™: How to Get from Where You Are to Where You Want to Be, Dare to Win, The Aladdin Factor, You've Got to Read This Book,* and *The Power of Focus: How to Hit Your Business and Personal and Financial Targets with Absolute Certainty.*

Jack is the CEO of the Canfield Training Group in Santa Barbara, California, and founder of the Foundation for Self-Esteem in Culver City, California. He has conducted intensive personal and professional development seminars on the principles of success for over a million people in twenty-three countries. Jack is a dynamic keynote speaker and he has spoken to hundreds of thousands of others at more than 1,000 corporations, universities, professional conferences and conventions, and has been seen by millions more on national television shows such as *The Today Show, Fox and Friends, Inside Edition, Hard Copy,* CNN's *Talk Back Live, 20/20, Eye to Eye,* and the *NBC Nightly News* and the *CBS Evening News.*

Jack is the recipient of many awards and honors, including three honorary doctorates and a Guinness World Records Certificate for having seven books from the *Chicken Soup for the Soul* series appearing on the *New York Times* bestseller list on May 24, 1998.

You can reach Jack at:

Jack Canfield
The Canfield Companies
P. O. Box 30880 • Santa Barbara, CA 93130
phone: 805-563-2935 • fax: 805-563-2945
www.jackcanfield.com

Mark Victor Hansen?

Mark Victor Hansen is the co-founder of Chicken Soup for the Soul, along with Jack Canfield. He is also a sought-after keynote speaker, bestselling author, and marketing maven. For more than thirty years, Mark's powerful messages of possibility, opportunity, and action have created powerful change in thousands of organizations and millions of individuals worldwide.

Mark's credentials include a lifetime of entrepreneurial success. He is a prolific writer with many bestselling books, such as *The One Minute Millionaire*, *Cracking the Millionaire Code*, *How to Make the Rest of Your Life the Best of Your Life*, *The Power of Focus*, *The Aladdin Factor*, and *Dare to Win*, in addition to the *Chicken Soup for the Soul* series. Mark has had a profound influence in the field of human potential through his library of audios, videos, and articles in the areas of big thinking, sales achievement, wealth building, publishing success, and personal and professional development. Mark is also the founder of the MEGA Seminar Series.

He has appeared on *Oprah*, CNN, and *The Today Show*. He has been quoted in *Time*, *US News & World Report*, *USA Today*, *The New York Times*, and *Entrepreneur* and has given countless radio interviews, assuring our planet's people that "You can easily create the life you deserve."

Mark is the recipient of numerous awards that honor his entrepreneurial spirit, philanthropic heart, and business acumen. He is a lifetime member of the Horatio Alger Association of Distinguished Americans, an organization that honored Mark with the prestigious Horatio Alger Award for his extraordinary life achievements.

You can reach Mark at:

Mark Victor Hansen & Associates, Inc.
P. O. Box 7665 • Newport Beach, CA 92658
phone: 949-764-2640 • fax: 949-722-6912
www.markvictorhansen.com

Who Is
Madeline Clapps?

Madeline Clapps is an editor for Chicken Soup for the Soul, as well as a co-author of *Chicken Soup for the Soul: Teens Talk High School*. She is incredibly thankful for the opportunities that have been given to her at Chicken Soup for the Soul, and for everything Amy, Bill, and Bob have done for her.

Madeline is currently a student at New York University, where she is on the Dean's List, majoring in Journalism and Vocal Performance with a concentration in Music Theatre. Her passions are writing and singing, but she has also found that editing and book production can be added to that ever-growing list. You can read her stories in other Chicken Soup for the Soul books, including *Chicken Soup for the Soul; Teens Talk Getting In... to College* and the upcoming *Chicken Soup for the Soul: Campus Chronicles*.

Madeline has a very supportive family, and she owes so much to her parents and grandparents. Keep an eye out for Madeline on the stage, in books, and in periodicals in the future, because she has a long list of big goals to achieve.

You can reach her through the Chicken Soup webmaster at:

webmaster@chickensoupforthesoul.com

Who Is
Valerie Howlett?

Valerie Howlett had the amazing opportunity to edit teen books for Chicken Soup for the Soul after joining the company for a chance internship and then falling back in love with the books she read as a teenager.

She is a graduate of Hampshire College, where she studied theater education, children's literature and creative writing. Her youth outreach work includes designing and implementing drama courses for homeschoolers and summer camps, mentoring at a teen educational summer program, and performing in a nonprofit theater company that traveled to schools and community centers throughout the Northern Midwest.

Valerie recently completed *Odd Dream*, a collection of short stories for children based on Brothers Grimm fairy tales. She currently works for Bloomsbury Publishing in the children's division. She lives in New York.

Acknowledgments

Chicken Soup for the Soul

Thank You!

We owe huge thanks to all of our contributors. We know that you pour your hearts and souls into the stories and poems that you share with us, and ultimately with each other. We appreciate your willingness to open up your lives to other Chicken Soup readers.

We can only publish a small percentage of the stories that are submitted, but we read every single one and even the ones that do not appear in the book have an influence on us and on the final manuscript.

We also want to thank our Publisher and mentor, Amy Newmark, who edited every story and helped us shape this manuscript, D'ette Corona, our Assistant Publisher, who is the heart and soul of the Chicken Soup for the Soul publishing operation, and Barbara LoMonaco, our Webmaster and Chicken Soup for the Soul Editor, for invaluable assistance in maintaining our story database and proofreading this manuscript. We would also like to thank Chicken Soup for the Soul editor Kristiana Glavin for assistance with the final manuscript and proofreading, and Leigh Holmes, who keeps our Connecticut office running smoothly.

We owe a very special thanks to our Creative Director and book producer, Brian Taylor at Pneuma Books, for his brilliant vision for our covers and interiors. Finally, none of this would be possible without the business and creative leadership of our CEO, Bill Rouhana, and our president, Bob Jacobs.

More Chicken Soup

Being a preteen is harder than it looks. School is more challenging, bodies are changing, boys and girls notice each other, relationships with parents are different, and new issues arise with friends. This book, with 101 stories from Chicken Soup's library, supports and inspires preteens and reminds them they are not alone. Stories written by preteens just like them cover friends, family, love, school, sports, challenges, embarrassing moments, and overcoming obstacles.

978-1-935096-00-9

Check out our great books for

The teenage years are difficult. Old friends drift away, new friends come with new issues, teens fall in and out of love, and relationships with family members change. This book reminds teenagers that they are not alone, as they read the 101 best stories from Chicken Soup's library written, by other teens just like themselves, about the problems and issues they face every day — stories about friends, family, love, loss, and many lessons learned.

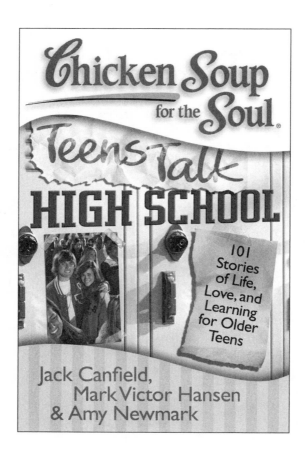

This book focuses on issues specific to high school age kids, ages fourteen to eighteen. Teens in high school have mainly moved past worrying about puberty and cliques, so stories in this book cover topics of interest to older teens such as sports and clubs, religion and faith, driving, curfews, growing up, self-image and self-acceptance, dating and sex, family relationships, friends, divorce, illness, death, pregnancy, drinking, failure, and preparing for life after high school. High school students will find comfort and inspiration in the words of this book, referring to it through all four years of their high school experience, like a portable support group.

978-1-935096-25-2

*C*heck out our great books for

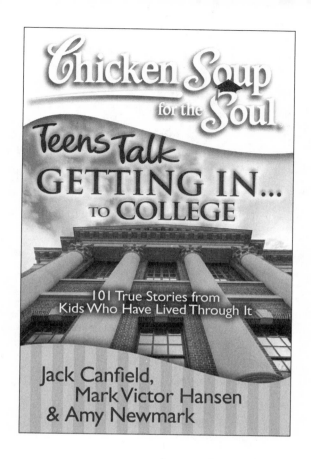

These days, colleges are deluged with applications, and the application process has become something traumatic that students and parents experience together. This book isn't about how to get into college — it's about providing emotional support. The stories in this book are written by kids who have been there and want to pass on their words of support to the kids about to go through the whole ordeal. Story topics include parental and peer pressure, the stress of grades and standardized tests, applications and interviews, recruiting, disappointments, and successes. Parents and students alike will find Getting In... to College a great source of inspiration.

978-1-935096-27-6

Teens!

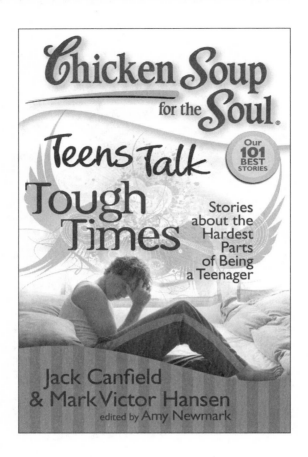

Being a teenager is difficult even under idyllic circumstances. But when bad things happen, the challenges of being a teenager can be overwhelming, leading to self-destructive behavior, eating disorders, substance abuse, and other challenges. In addition, many teens are faced with illness, car accidents, loss of loved ones, divorces, or other upheavals. This book includes 101 of our best stories about the toughest teenage times — and how to overcome them.

978-1-935096-03-0

Check out our great books for

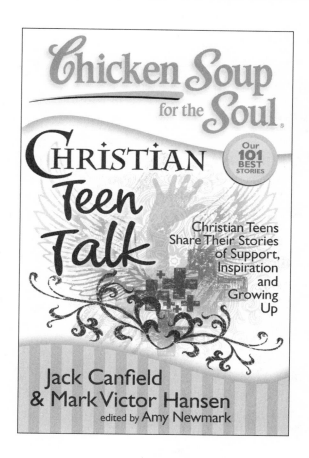

Chicken Soup for the Soul

CHRISTIAN Teen Talk

Our 101 BEST STORIES

Christian Teens Share Their Stories of Support, Inspiration and Growing Up

Jack Canfield
& Mark Victor Hansen
edited by Amy Newmark

Devout Christian teens care about their connection and relationship with God, but they are also experiencing all the ups and downs of teenage life. This book provides support to teens who care about their faith but are trying to navigate their teenage years. This book includes 101 heartfelt, true stories about love, compassion, loss, forgiveness, friends, school, and faith. It also covers tough issues such as self-destructive behavior, substance abuse, teen pregnancy, and divorce.

978-1-935096-12-2

Teens!

The Wisdom of Dads

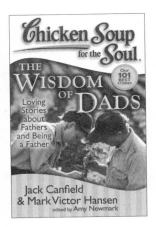

Children view their fathers with awe from the day they are born. Fathers are big and strong and seem to know everything, except for a few teenage years when fathers are perceived to know nothing! This book represents a new theme for Chicken Soup — 101 stories selected from 35 past books, all stories focusing on the wisdom of dads. Stories are written by sons and daughters about their fathers, and by fathers relating stories about their children.

Moms & Sons

There is a special bond between mothers and their sons and it never goes away. This new book contains the 101 best stories and poems from Chicken Soup's library honoring that lifelong relationship between mothers and their male offspring. These heartfelt and loving stories written by mothers, grandmothers, and sons, about each other, span generations and show how the mother-son bond transcends time.

Loving Our Dogs

We are all crazy about our dogs and can't read enough about them, whether they're misbehaving and giving us big, innocent looks, or loyally standing by us in times of need. This new book from Chicken Soup for the Soul contains the 101 best dog stories from the company's extensive library. Readers will revel in the heartwarming, amusing, inspirational, and occasionally tearful stories about our best friends and faithful companions — our dogs.

Books for Boys!

Moms Know Best

"Mom will know where it is…what to say…how to fix it." This Chicken Soup book focuses on the pervasive wisdom of mothers everywhere, and includes the best 101 stories from Chicken Soup's library on our perceptive, understanding, and insightful mothers. These stories celebrate the special bond between mothers and children, our mothers' unerring wisdom about everything from the mundane to the life-changing, and the hard work that goes into being a mother every day.

Like Mother, Like Daughter

Fathers, brothers, and friends sometimes shake their head in wonder as girls "turn into their mothers." This new collection from Chicken Soup represents the best 101 stories from Chicken Soup's library on the special bond between mothers and daughters, and the magical, mysterious similarities between them. Mothers and daughters of all ages will laugh, cry, and find inspiration in these stories that remind them how much they appreciate each other.

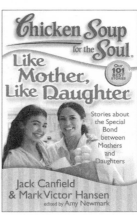

Dads & Daughters

Whether she is ten years old or fifty – she will always be his little girl. And daughters take care of their dads too, whether it is a tea party for two at age five or loving care fifty years later. This wide-ranging exploration of the relationship between fathers and daughters from forty past Chicken Soup books. Stories was written by fathers about their daughters and by daughters about their fathers, celebrating the special bond between fathers and daughters.

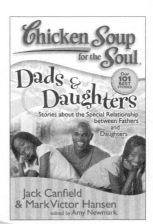

Books for Girls!

Everyone loves Christmas and the holiday season. We reunite scattered family members, watch the wonder in a child's eyes, and feel the joy of giving gifts. The rituals of the holiday season give a rhythm to the years and create a foundation for our lives, as we gather with family, with our communities at church, at school, and even at the mall, to share the special spirit of the season, brightening those long winter days.   978-1-935096-15-3

Check out our
favorites for

Parenting is the hardest and most rewarding job in the world. This upbeat and compelling new book includes the best selections on parenting from Chicken Soup's rich history, with 101 stories carefully selected to appeal to both mothers and fathers. This is a great book for couples to share, whether they are embarking on a new adventure as parents or reflecting on their lifetime experience, with stories written by parents about children and by children about their parents.

978-1-935096-20-7

Mom or Dad

Chicken Soup for the Soul

Share with Us

We would like to know how these stories affected you and which ones were your favorites. Please e-mail us and let us know.

We also would like to share your stories with future readers. You may be able to help another reader, and become a published author at the same time. Please send us your own stories and poems for our future books. Some of our past contributors have launched writing and speaking careers from the publication of their stories in our books!

Your stories have the best chance of being used if you submit them through our web site, at:

www.chickensoup.com

If you do not have access to the Internet, you may submit your stories by mail or by facsimile. Please do not send us any book manuscripts, unless through a literary agent, as these will be automatically discarded.

Chicken Soup for the Soul
P.O. Box 700
Cos Cob, CT 06807-0700
Fax 203-861-7194